The Law of Flats

The Law of Flats

Third Edition

Trevor M Aldridge
QC(Hon), MA(Cantab), Solicitor

© Longman Group UK Ltd 1989
This edition © Longman Group Ltd 1994

ISBN 075200 0713

Published by
Longman Law, Tax and Finance
Longman Group UK Ltd
21–27 Lamb's Conduit Street,
London WC1N 3NJ

Associated offices:
Australia, Hong Kong, Malaysia, Singapore, USA

A CIP catalogue record for this book is available
from the British Library.

Set in Times and Univers by
Kerrypress Ltd, Luton and
printed by Bell & Bain

Contents

Part 2: Disposal of Flats

Part 3: Security of Tenure

Part 4: Precedents

Preface to Third Edition

Major developments in the law relating to flats were introduced by the Leasehold Reform, Housing and Urban Development Act 1993. Tenants under long leases now have two new rights. First, some or all of the tenants of flats in a block can cooperate to exercise a right of a collective enfranchisement. That allows them to put up a nominee to buy the freehold of the block on their behalf. Secondly, as an alternative, a tenant under a long lease may buy a 90-year extension.

Both these rights offer ways to address the problems faced by tenants of flats whose leases are running out. In addition, enfranchisement allows the tenants, collectively, to take over the management of their block. The qualifying conditions for these new rights are not straightforward, but they are explained, along with the procedure which has to be followed, in new chapters.

Collective enfranchisement in particular may prove complicated to organise. For this reason, tenants will be well advised to enter into a formal preliminary agreement amongst themselves. This is a type of agreement which has seldom been needed until now, and of course none has been tailored to fit the demands of the 1993 Act. However, this book now offers the answer. A form of agreement for tenants who want to take advantage of the new opportunity has been added to the precedents in the last section.

Since the last edition was prepared in 1988, there have also been many minor developments in this area of the law, both through reported cases and statutory amendments. I have tried to incorporate all of these, to bring the text up-to-date to 1 March 1994. It has also been possible to take advantage of this opportunity to revise and modernise the precedents.

TREVOR M ALDRIDGE

1 May 1994

Table of Cases

Table of Statutes

Table of Statutory Instruments

Part 1

General Considerations

Chapter 1

Preliminary

1.1 Definitions

The word 'flat', in common use, describes a dwelling which forms part only of a building, but it is applied in a wide variety of circumstances. A flat is usually, but not always, self contained and on a single floor. There is generally more than one flat in a building. That may be a purpose built block of identical or similar flats, or it may be the result of the conversion of a large house or a building formerly put to some other use. For convenience in this book, the word 'block' describes any building containing a number of flats, even if formed by a conversion. Sometimes there is only one flat in a building, and the rest of it is used for something else. Examples of this are: a flat over a neighbourhood shop, a caretaker's flat in an office block or a factory, or the residential part of a mews house where it is occupied separately from the garage below.

In the general discussions in this book, 'flat' is used in this very wide sense. Often, the construction and layout of the flat makes no difference to the rules of law that apply. Whether behaviour constitutes a nuisance, or when an easement is required for services, does not depend on a flat being originally built as such. When rules apply only to flats complying with a particular definition, this is stated.

1.1.1 Judicial definitions

There have been a few judicial attempts to define a flat. They were probably influenced by their context, and demonstrate how difficult a comprehensive definition is.

'A flat is, in ordinary language, as defined in the Oxford Dictionary, "a suite of rooms on one floor, forming a complete residence". The term is itself derived from an old English word meaning "floor"' (*Boyle v Fitzsimons* [1926] IR 378, 383 per Hanna J). Actually, the dictionary gives its origin as the Scots word 'flet'.

'The natural meaning of the word "flat" is, I think, a separate self contained dwelling' (*Murgatroyd v Tresarden* (1946) 63 TLR 62, 63 per Somervell LJ).

1.1.2 Legislative definitions

There are four current statutory definitions of 'flat'.

> (2) A dwellinghouse is a house if, and only if, it (or so much of it as does not consist of land . . .) is a structure reasonably so called; so that—
>> (*a*) where a building is divided horizontally, the flats or other units into which it is divided are not houses;
>> (*b*) where a building is divided vertically, the units into which it is divided may be houses;
>> (*c*) where a building is not structurally detached it is not a house if a material part of it lies above or below the remainder of the structure.
>
> (3) A dwellinghouse which is not a house is a flat (Housing Act 1985, s 183).

> 'Flat' means a separate set of premises, whether or not on the same floor, which—
>> (*a*) forms part of a building; and
>> (*b*) is divided horizontally from some other part of that building; and
>> (*c*) is constructed or adapted for use for the purposes of a dwelling (Landlord and Tenant Act 1987, s 60(1)).

The third definition is only a slight variant on the second, it requires at least two flats in the building.

> 4 . . . 'flat' means a dwellinghouse which—
>> (*a*) forms part only of a building; and
>> (*b*) is separated horizontally from another dwellinghouse which forms part of the same building (Rent Act 1977, Sched 2).

The fourth and most recent definition makes it clear, as earlier definitions may have intended, that only part, although a material part, of the flat need be above or below some other part of the block.

> 'Flat' means a separate set of premises (whether or not on the same floor)—
>> (*a*) which forms part of a building, and
>> (*b*) which is constructed or adapted for use for the purposes of a dwelling, and
>> (*c*) either the whole or a material part of which lies above or below some other part of the building (Leasehold Reform, Housing and Urban Development Act 1993, s 101(1)).

1.1.3 Maisonette

There seems to be two common meanings of the word 'maisonette'. First, it means a self contained dwelling forming part of a building with accommodation on two floors. To all intents and purposes, this is a two-floor flat. The Americans call it a 'duplex'. In the application of legal rules, there seems to be no distinction between a maisonette in this sense and a flat. For this reason, the word is not used in this way in this book. It can be assumed that 'flat' bears an extended meaning which includes these maisonettes.

The word 'maisonette' is also used in connection with a type of building which is common in North and West London, and is found elsewhere. Externally, it looks like a single house, but the ground and first floors are built to be independently occupied. They do not interconnect, and each has a separate front door at ground level. Each floor is referred to as a 'maisonette'. This is probably a later use of the word. In *Ilford Park Estates Ltd v Jacobs* [1903] 2 Ch 522—which decided that such a building comprised two 'houses' and thus contravened a covenant not to build more than one house on the site—the term was not used at all. On the other hand, it was held that a building of that type, expressly referred to as containing two maisonettes, could reasonably be called 'a house' for the purpose of individual leasehold enfranchisement (*Malpas v St Ermin's Property Ltd* (1992) 64 P&CR 436).

Most of the principles that apply to flats apply equally to maisonettes in this sense. However, practical differences arise when an owner wants to make arrangements for a pair of maisonettes to be managed on their own. These will be dealt with when they arise, and the word 'maisonette' in this book refers to this type of accommodation.

1.2 Reform

The 'owners' of flats, who are normally tenants under long leases, have over the years expressed two fundamental discontents which reformers have addressed. First, they would prefer to exercise the management control that a freeholder has over his own property. Secondly, a lease is inherently a wasting asset, which becomes unmarketable even before it finally expires because prospective buyers and mortgagees look for an asset which they will be able to sell later.

The reason why long leases of flats are generally granted, rather than the flats being sold freehold, is that there is no other satisfactory way to ensure that the burden of positive covenants runs with the land whose owners are intended to comply. This is a problem which cannot be ignored when dealing with flats. The owner and occupier of each flat has to be concerned that the other flats in the block are properly maintained and that all contribute to the joint expenses. Obligations to repair and to pay a service charge are typical positive covenants.

1.2.1 Leasehold Reform, Housing and Urban Development Act 1993

The 1993 Act, introducing collective enfranchisement and purchased new leases, addresses both the major concerns of leaseholders. It can be seen as the first step in overcoming the disadvantages in owning flats.

Collective enfranchisement is a mechanism by which freehold owner-ship of a block of flats, and with it responsibility for management, is transferred from a third party to the leaseholders of the flats collectively. It extends the currently understood meaning of 'enfranchisement', because the individual leases continue to exist and are not converted into freeholds. Necessarily, the lessees of the flats must cooperate to acquire the freehold.

The problem of the wasting asset is addressed in two alternative ways. If there is collective enfranchisement, the new freeholders, who are also the lessees, can of course without difficulty grant themselves longer leases. In some cases the lessees will not choose, or will not be able to choose, to enfranchise. Each will then be able to take an individual initiative and purchase a new lease, extending the existing term by 90 years.

1.2.2 Commonhold

The proposals for the introduction of a condominium system (*Commonhold–Freehold Flats and Freehold Ownership of Other Interdependent Buildings*, Cm 179, 1987) will, when enacted, provide for true and satisfactory freehold ownership of individual flats.

Statutory provisions would cure the difficulties about the enforcement of positive covenants, offer the advantages of standard documentation, regulate management and provide predetermined arrangements for winding up a scheme. There should be some simplification of conveyanc-ing. The wasting asset problem would be definitively cured, because the flats would be freehold so there would never be the need for a lease to be renewed or extended.

On the other hand, a block of flats will always require to be managed. Most need communal services and have common parts, and it is generally sensible to arrange for structural repairs and exterior decoration to be undertaken at collective expense. Arrangements will need to be agreed between freeholders, just as they are between leaseholders.

This further reform will require legislation to implement it. Clearly, some time must elapse before the law is changed, and it will inevitably be years before commonhold flats are commonplace.

Chapter 2

Extent of Flat

2.1 Definition of extent

How precise the definition of the extent of a flat must be depends upon the use to which the information is to be put. A disposition of a flat, whether a freehold conveyance or a lease, will not be valid unless the property is sufficiently identified. Established conveyancing practice is to define which rooms on what floor are included, but not, merely to ensure the validity of the document, to settle such minutiae as how much of the exterior wall is disposed of. All the same, a description which is not detailed must still be accurate, otherwise it may be necessary to rectify the deed. A degree of precision can be important to determine the extent of a party's repairing responsibilities and to ascertain whether the flat owner can use the outside of a wall for fixing a window box or television aerial.

The description of the parcels in the conveyance or lease of a flat is the primary source of information about its precise boundaries. If that is not enough, the presumptions dealt with in the succeeding sections of this Chapter may help.

Flats are commonly described as being on a particular floor of the building, and indeed are often registered at the Land Registry in that way. While the building exists, this causes no difficulty. In the event of accidental destruction, it presupposes reconstruction to the same dimensions, so that each flat owner's property occupies the same space as it did previously. To build in any other way would be a trespass, or would involve mutual conveyances or assignments to adjust the boundaries. A precise reproduction of the old building may be neither possible nor desirable, but there is no reported case of any resulting difficulties.

2.2 Vertical boundaries

If nothing is said about the ownership of the external walls of a flat—the boundary walls not adjoining any other property—they are included in it. In fact the flat extends slightly beyond the outside face of the

7

walls, to include sufficient air space to allow the flat owner to use the outside wall, eg to fix a balanced flue to it, or a window box (*Hope Bros Ltd v Cowan* [1913] 2 Ch 312). The inclusion of that additional air space presumably depends on the grantor of the flat owning adjoining property. If the block were built along the boundary of the property belonging to the developer, there is no reason for the adjoining owner to be forced to accept protrusions from the flats, overlapping his property.

This presumption about the external walls is not displaced by a lease that makes the landlord responsible for repairing them (*Sturge v Hackett* [1962] 1 WLR 1257). Repairing liability does not automatically indicate ownership. The reverse may also apply: excluding the walls will not necessarily preclude a duty to repair. One flat let on a short lease was expressly defined to exclude the outside walls. The question then arose whether the landlord's statutory implied repairing covenant, which applies to 'the exterior of the dwellinghouse' (Landlord and Tenant Act 1985, s 11(1)(*a*)) included the exterior walls which were not demised. The Court of Appeal held that it did, because, whatever the lease said, those walls remained the exterior of the flat (*Campden Hill Towers Ltd v Gardner* [1977] QB 823).

There seems little to be gained from excluding external walls from flats, unless that is a means of defining repairing responsibilities. If the landlord is to be responsible for the repair of common parts, exterior walls, roof, foundations, etc, it may be convenient for him to covenant to repair all parts of the building other than the flat—defined to exclude the outside walls—and other flats demised on similar terms. Even so, the flat owner will normally be responsible for decorations and minor repairs, so that it is appropriate to save the decorative internal finishes from the exclusion. The prospect of this complication demonstrates that it is best separately to define the boundaries of a flat on the one hand, and on the other the liability for repairing different parts of it.

The internal boundary walls of a flat divide it either from another flat or from the common parts. If the position of the flat's boundary on those sides is not defined by the documents of title, there is no presumption precisely pinpointing it. All that can be said is that some part of those walls is included, but not the whole of them (*Phelps v City of London Corporation* [1916] 2 Ch 255, 263).

When the internal boundary walls are load bearing, it may be convenient for the purposes of defining repairing responsibilities to exclude them from the flat in the same way as external walls. In other cases, the convenient course is to state that the flat includes the wall to half its depth, or to declare it to be a party wall. A party wall which would be subject to a tenancy in common were that permitted at law, is severed vertically (Law of Property Act 1925, s 38). Statute does not even then define the precise position of the boundary. It is presumed to be in the middle, if only because 'equality is equity'. Anyone interested in a party wall can apply to the court for a declaration as to his rights.

In a block of flats that is attached to another building in separate ownership, some of the flats will have a boundary wall dividing them from that other building. In principle, the whole of those walls, other than any belonging to the adjoining freeholder, should be included in the flat. The extent depends on the freehold title, and they may well be party walls.

2.3 Horizontal boundaries

If the precise boundary of a flat upwards and downwards is not defined, there are no presumptions that really help. Certainly, at least part of the floor of a flat is included in it (*Phelps v City of London Corporation* [1916] 2 Ch 255, 264), but there is no rule as to just how much. Upwards, a flat may extend to half way through the joists supporting the floor above, or even to their upper surface (*Sturge v Hackett* [1962] 1 WLR 1257, 1266). The decision may turn on the surrounding circumstances. The void between a false ceiling and the original ceiling above was held to be included in a demise largely because the landlord had no access to it (*Graystone Property Investments Ltd v Margulies* (1984) 47 P&CR 472).

The position is not even certain in relation to a top flat. It may extend to include the roof, but even where the limit of the flat is not expressly defined, the document in question may be construed on the basis that the roof is excluded (*Cockburn v Smith* [1924] 2 KB 119). Although on the basis of that decision it is sometimes accepted that the roof is excluded when not mentioned, it should be noted that the landlord's statutory repairing duty, in the case of a short lease, may still apply (*Douglas-Scott v Scargie* [1984] 1 WLR 716).

If the roof is included in the demise of the flat, and no express provision is made, such airspace above as the freeholder owns is included in the demise (*Davies v Yadegar* [1989] 1 EGLR 71). Accordingly, an improvement made by the tenant can extend into that airspace (*Haines v Florensa* (1989) 59 P&CR 200).

An express description of a flat usually includes the floorboards and the ceiling, together with one half in depth of the joists to which they are attached. The form of construction of the block must be considered, because if there are solid concrete floors a reference to joists will not be appropriate. In that case, the inclusion of one half in depth of floors and ceilings will generally suffice. In every case, special consideration must be given to the bottom and top flats, where it may be necessary to include, respectively, the whole of the substructure with the foundations and the whole of the roof.

Floors and ceilings are sometimes declared to be party structures. Without more, this is not satisfactory. Section 38 of the Law of Property Act 1925 refers to 'a party wall or structure', but it goes on to say 'that structure shall be and remain severed vertically'. Although the view has been expressed that the section applies to floors and ceilings and that 'vertically' can be construed as 'horizontally', it is suggested that it strains the interpretation of the statute too far to turn it through ninety degrees.

2.4 Plans

Often the easiest and most accurate way to define the boundaries of a flat, particularly one formed as a result of a conversion, is by reference to a plan. One of an appropriate scale should be chosen.

> . . . if the draftsman of the conveyance chooses to identify the property solely by reference to a plan, it is of the utmost importance that he should make use of the plan which is on a scale sufficiently large to make it possible to represent the property and its boundaries in precise detail, giving dimensions and any other features which may be necessary to put beyond doubt the subject matter of the conveyance (*Kingston v Phillips* (1976) unreported, per Buckley LJ).

In one case, the use of an Ordnance map on a scale of 1:2,500 was described as 'worse than useless' (*Scarfe v Adams* [1981] 1 All ER 843, 845 per Cumming-Bruce LJ).

One difficulty to guard against is a conflict between any verbal description and the plan. Mistakes are commonest where a large scale plan allows boundaries to be clearly marked as including or excluding the walls, or running through them, and the colouring on the plan is at variance with a precise definition in words. In one case where the parcels clearly included the roof but the plan excluded the roof space, a flat was held to include that roof space partly because of the mention of the roof and partly because of the surrounding circumstances relating to access (*Hatfield v Moss* [1988] 2 EGLR 58).

Where there is a conflict, it is a question of construction of the document whether the verbal description or the plan prevails, but unless the words direct, there will normally only be a reference to a plan if the parcels are ambiguous. A flat stated to be 'more particularly described' on the plan extends to the boundaries shown on the plan (*Eastwood v Ashton* [1915] AC 900). The plan also predominates if it is introduced by the words 'more particularly delineated in' (*Wallington v Townsend* [1939] Ch 588). A plan stated to be 'for identification only' is intended to show the location of a property, not its extent (*Moreton C Cullimore (Gravels) Ltd v Routledge* (1977) 121 SJ 202), and it will rarely be appropriate to describe a flat in that way. Such a plan can, however, be used to elucidate a verbal description that is not otherwise clear (*Wiggington & Milner Ltd v Winster Engineering Ltd* [1978] 1 WLR 1462).

2.5 Land Registry practice

Unless it is possible to define a flat verbally with sufficient accuracy for Land Registry purposes, an applicant for registration of a flat must supply a plan of the surface area over which the flat lies (Land Registration Rules 1925, r 54). This must be accompanied by any further description that is necessary, and the Registrar has a discretion to decide what is required. In practice, although sometimes a purely verbal description may suffice, the Registrar will normally insist on a plan, believing it to be in the best interests of the parties that he should do so.

The Land Registry has adopted a standard set of colourings for filed plans. There is no compulsion on an applicant for registration to use them, but to do so may prevent confusion. They are:

Red edging: the extent of the registered land.

Green edging: land removed from the title.

Green tinting: islands of land within the red edging removed from the title.

Brown tinting or hatching: land over which the registered land enjoys a right of way.

Blue tinting or hatching: part of the registered land subject to a right of way.

Where more different colourings are required, it is suggested that there be used in the following order: pink, blue, yellow and mauve tinting; blue, yellow and mauve edging; hatching, but not in black or green; numbering or lettering small self-contained areas.

Chapter 3

Ancillary Rights

3.1 Nature of rights

It is in the nature of a flat, as part only of a building, that its satisfactory enjoyment demands the use of ancillary rights over other property. Ideally, the rights should be expressly granted so that their extent is clear, and their adequacy can be established. Similarly, the ownership of the flat will need to be subject to rights in favour of others, which should also be spelled out. The grant or reservation of these rights will create easements.

It is important to ensure that rights which are essential for the use of the property are granted as easements which will bind the owners for the time being of the servient tenement. In one case, a right created by deed to use an access route for fire escape purposes was held, on the construction of the document, to be no more than a personal licence (*IDC Group Ltd v Clark* (1992) 65 P&CR 179).

Where the easement is for a service that the tenant is to pay for, the fact that he does not pay does not automatically justify the landlord in discontinuing the service (*Hersey v White* (1893) 9 TLR 335: a flat was let with all rights, easements and appurtenances, which included a gas supply. When the tenant did not pay for gas, the landlord's remedy was to sue for the cost, not to cut off the gas.)

The easements and other rights considered here are those which have particular relevance to flats. Rights relating to repairs are considered in the Chapter on that subject. Particulars of other easements of general application, eg rights of light and air, should be sought in more general books.

Flat owners often enjoy, as a matter of contract, other services which are not easements because they are in the nature of personal services rather than for the benefit of the property. These are also considered here, as a flat owner will rightly regard them as essential to the satisfactory occupation of the flat.

3.2 Implied easements

Where a lease or conveyance of an existing flat is granted, the fact that statute implies the grant of legal easements to exercise rights already in use is of considerable importance. It means that gaps in the rights expressly granted to the flat owner—either by oversight or because the draftsman did not know they were needed—are filled automatically. Indeed, rights previously exercised under revocable licence can be converted into a legal easement (*Goldberg v Edwards* [1950] Ch 247).

Section 62 of the Law of Property Act 1925 provides that a conveyance—which includes a lease (s 205(1)(ii)), but not an oral lease (*Rye v Rye* [1962] AC 496) nor an agreement for lease longer than three years (*Borman v Griffith* [1930] 1 Ch 493)—is deemed to include and convey all 'liberties, privileges, easements, rights, and advantages whatsoever, appertaining or reputed to appertain' to the flat at that date or then enjoyed with it. This has been held to cover such diverse matters as a right of way (*International Tea Stores Co v Hobbs* [1903] 2 Ch 165), a right to water supply (*Westwood v Heywood* [1921] 2 Ch 130) and the right to store coal in a shed (*Wright v Macadam* [1949] 2 KB 744). It has been suggested that it might even extend to allowing a tenant to repair a roof not demised to him (*Sedgwick Forbes Bland Payne Group Ltd v Regional Properties Ltd* (1981) 257 EG 64, 70), but there is doubt about this because of the decision that there cannot be an easement of protection against the weather (*Phipps v Pears* [1965] 1 QB 76).

The statute does not go so far as to imply an easement to supply personal services, eg porterage (*Regis Property Co Ltd v Redman* [1956] 2 QB 612). 'The obligation in question involves the performance of services, and is essentially a matter of personal contract as distinct from a right, easement or privilege capable of being granted by lease or conveyance so as to pass under the general words implied by s 62' (p 627, per Jenkins LJ).

Easements for the benefit of a flat owner may also be implied on the ground that they were continuous and apparent at the date of the grant (*Wheeldon v Burrows* (1879) 12 ChD 31). Also, he has the benefit of easements of necessity (eg, the right to use the lift and integral rubbish chutes in a tower block: *Liverpool City Council v Irwin* [1977] AC 239). An easement of necessity can arise where the flat has not previously been occupied.

3.3 Support

The support that one flat affords to another within a block is clearly essential for its stability. However, there is no automatic easement for the support of one building by another (*Peyton v London Corporation* (1829) 9 B&C 725). In a block of flats, rights of support will normally be regulated by express repairing covenants or the express grant of easements. If they are not, there will often be implied easements by the operation of s 62 of the Law of Property Act 1925.

Where there is a mere right of support, as opposed to the benefit of a covenant to repair, the flat owner's rights are limited. He is entitled to ensure that the adjoining owner—whether it be another flat owner, the landlord or other owner of the common parts, or the owner of adjoining property—does not actively remove support. The neighbour does not have to do repairs. If he does not, and his inactivity jeopardises the stability of the flat, the flat owner is entitled to enter to do necessary repairs by way of self help.

Sir Wilfred Greene MR comprehensively summarised the position (*Bond v Nottingham Corporation* [1940] Ch 429, 438–9):

> The owner of the servient tenement is under no obligation to repair that part of his building which provides support for his neighbour. He can let it fall into decay. If it does so, and support is removed, the owner of the dominant tenement is not bound to sit by and watch the gradual deterioration of the support constituted by his neighbour's building. He is entitled to enter and take the necessary steps to ensure that the support continues by effecting repairs, and so forth, to the part of the building which gives the support. But what the owner of the servient tenement is not allowed to do is, by an act of his own, to remove the support without providing an equivalent.

That last qualification—that the neighbour is not entitled to take steps to remove support—is important. An owner who does is liable for the consequences, such as dry rot resulting from exposure to the elements (*Bradburn v Lindsay* [1983] 2 All ER 408).

3.4 Privacy

'Our law does not recognise any easement of prospect or privacy' (*Browne v Flower* [1911] 1 Ch 219, 225 per Parker J). In that case, a flat owner found himself without a remedy when an outside staircase was built, to give access to another part of the building, and passed between the bedroom windows of his flat. Although that involved a considerable invasion of his privacy, it infringed no enforceable right.

A flat owner who wishes to protect his privacy must resort to indirect means. Those on the ground floor may seek to have the land outside their windows included in the demise, so that they can forbid entry to it. Otherwise, if an intrusion similar to the construction of the outside staircase is feared, it would be possible to have a covenant from the landlord against exercising or granting any rights of entry or way within a defined area outside the walls of the flat, presumably with exceptions for cleaning, decoration and repairs.

3.5 Access

Rights of access to a flat should be considered in two parts: access to the building from the highway, and access within the building to the flat itself.

Where the curtilage of the building is not demised to the flat owner, he needs a right of way between the building and the road. A right of way over a drive will arise as an easement of necessity (*Cory v Davies* [1923] 2 Ch 95). If a vehicular right of way is granted, that gives the flat owner the right also to stop for loading and unloading (*McIlraith v Grady* [1968] 1 QB 468), but it does not extend to parking. A tenant of a flat who has an express right of way over a forecourt can insist on being able to use that particular route. He is not obliged to accept an alternative (*Oswald v Watkins* (1972) 224 EG 239).

Flat owners clearly have a right of way into the block to get to their flats. The needs of security to prevent unauthorised entrants must be balanced against interference with this easement. In one case, tenants protested against the fitting of an automatic dead lock to the front door. It inconvenienced visitors and sometimes delayed mail when the postman could not get access. Flat owners could still personally exercise their easements because they were given keys. No order was made in an action by the flat owners, on the landlord giving an undertaking that a porter would take in mail (*Dawes v Adela Estates Ltd* (1970) 216 EG 1405).

Inside the building the same principle applies: in the absence of express rights of access to the flat, there is an easement of necessity. The right to use a lift is a right in the nature of an easement. It can arise as an easement of necessity in a tower block where, although there is a staircase, the only reasonable means of access is by lift (*Liverpool City Council v Irwin* [1977] AC 239). A landlord who lets a flat 'together with the use of the lift' has an obligation to provide a working lift, subject to reasonable allowance for breakdowns and repairs. He is liable in damages for breach of covenant if he fails to repair or replace an unserviceable lift (*De Meza v Ve-Ri-Best Manufacturing Co Ltd* (1952) 160 EG 364). In an appropriate case the obligation can be enforced by an interlocutory mandatory injunction, notwithstanding a pending action to forfeit the lease (*Peninsular Maritime Ltd v Padseal Ltd* (1981) 259 EG 860). Where a landlord provides a lift for passenger use only, the tenant can restrain him from allowing it to be used for goods (*Alexander v Mansions Proprietary Ltd* (1900) 16 TLR 431).

The landlord's responsibility for injury to those using the common parts for access rests on negligence. A tenant who is injured using an unlighted staircase cannot automatically recover damages for breach of the landlord's common duty of care (Occupiers' Liability Act 1957, s 2). A landlord who takes reasonable steps to light the stairs, eg by installing lights controlled by a time clock which is slightly but not unreasonably inaccurate in ensuring that the lights are on during the hours of darkness, escapes liability (*Irving v London County Council* (1965) 109 SJ 157). Whether the landlord's common law duty, as occupier, to keep the stairs reasonably safe extends beyond physical repairs to adequate lighting is a question that has been left open (*Huggett v Miers* [1908] 2 KB 278).

3.6 Storage and parking

Easements for storage and parking—and parking can be regarded as a specialised form of storage—are anomalous. In principle, there should not be an easement which confers on the dominant owner the exclusive right to use the land in question. The essence of an easement is non-exclusive use. On this ground, a claim to park an unlimited number of vehicles on a designated strip of land was rejected (*Copeland v Greenhalf* [1952] Ch 488). It amounted to a takeover of the land.

However, an easement to store coal in a shed has been accepted (*Wright v Macadam* [1949] 2 KB 744, which was not cited in *Copeland v Greenhalf*). Presumably, that decision would justify the grant of an easement to use a luggage storeroom or put a dustbin in a designated area. Nevertheless it is better, if the flat owner is going to have the use of such ancillary accommodation however small it is, to include that property in the demise or the conveyance, to prevent any question of the validity of the easement.

Whether there can technically be an easement to park cars is still not finally decided (the question was left open in *London and Blenheim Estates Ltd v Ladbroke Retail Parks Ltd* [1993] 4 All ER 157). Nevertheless, it is not uncommon for landlords to purport to grant such rights, commonly in the form of a right to park on a large area, frequently shared with others. Tenants of flats whose leases expressly granted them rights to use private forecourts and roadways were held to be entitled to park there without payment (*Papworth v Linthaven Ltd* [1988] EGCS 54).

3.7 Pipes and wires

Easements are required for the pipes and wires carrying services to the flat through other property, for water, drainage, electricity, gas, telephones, etc. Such an easement automatically carries with it the right to maintain the pipe or wire, and any necessary right of entry for that purpose (*Pwllbach Colliery Co Ltd v Woodman* [1915] AC 634). Developers often reserve the right to lay further pipes and wires in the future but, without more, this is not enough to deal with innovations (*Trailfinders Ltd v Razuki* [1988] 2 EGLR 46). For new services, an express reservation of sufficient breadth will be needed. The period for which the right is reserved must be limited to the perpetuity period (*Dunn v Blackdown Properties Ltd* [1961] Ch 433). It is now normal to take advantage of the fixed 80 year period for this purpose, instead of using one calculated from the death of a life or lives in being (Perpetuities and Accumulations Act 1964, s 1).

3.8 Waste disposal

Blocks of flats generally have communal or centralised waste disposal arrangements, as refuse will not be collected from each flat, even if it is convenient to store it there. In some blocks, there are built in chutes from the flats to the storage area. The right to use these chutes can constitute a legal easement (*Liverpool City Council v Irwin* [1977] AC 239). On the other hand, the arrangements may be that a porter collects the refuse. In that case, the arrangement will rest on a purely contractual basis.

Commonly, an area outside the flats is allocated as a communal dustbin area, which forms part of the common parts not owned by an individual flat owner. The right to use that area is capable of existing as an easement (cf *Wright v Macadam* [1949] 2 KB 744). Whether or not a landlord is liable to provide dustbins or other suitable receptacles must depend on the wording of the lease. A right to use the area for the deposit of rubbish can hardly of itself imply such a duty. Linked to a tenant's covenant not to deposit rubbish otherwise than in the receptacle provided, it would probably impose one despite the absence of an express landlord's covenant.

3.9 Porterage

The provision of service to the occupier of a flat cannot constitute an easement. Nevertheless, a landlord may have an obligation to provide service, and to do so in a particular appropriate form.

Whether specific performance, or an injunction to similar effect, is available in respect of a duty to provide porter service will depend on the form of the obligation. If it is vague and general, this will not be an appropriate remedy, because that would require supervision by the court (*Ryan v Mutual Tontine Westminster Chambers Association* [1893] 1 Ch 116). However, if the landlord's obligation is in precise terms, an order can be made (*Posner v Scott-Lewis* [1987] Ch 25). There may be less direct ways to prevent a landlord from resiling. Damages can be awarded for breach of contract (*Alexander v Mansions Proprietary Ltd* (1900) 16 TLR 431).

In one case, the leaseholder of a flat in a luxury block sold on long lease was able to insist on the employment of a resident porter, for whom the services of a visiting contract cleaner were held to be no substitute. Even though the lease contained no express covenant to provide a resident porter—merely a covenant to employ persons necessary for the proper management of the block—the court made a declaration that the landlord had that duty and it granted an injunction to prevent the sale of the porter's flat (*Hupfield v Bourne* (1974) 28 P&CR 77). However, tenants in another block where there had been resident porters were held to be entitled to porterage services, but not necessarily provided by someone resident (*Russell v Laimond Properties Ltd* (1984) 269 EG 947).

Even if the landlord's covenant is limited to using his best endeavours to provide such services as taking in and delivering letters, parcels and messages and removing refuse, he cannot do nothing towards providing the services, which amounts to deliberately withholding them (*Mills v Senlay* (1972) 224 EG 2020).

3.10 Fixtures and fittings

The letting of a flat 'with the use of the fixtures and fittings' imposes an obligation on the landlord to continue to provide facilities needed to enable the tenant to enjoy the fixtures and fittings. Where, eg, a refrigerator in a flat depends on motive power from a central apparatus maintained by the landlord, he has a duty to continue to supply the power so that the refrigerator is usable (*Penn v Gatenex Co Ltd* [1958] 2 QB 210). This principle could apply to the provision of television signals received from a communal aerial.

How far such an obligation can be implied in the absence of an express reference to fixtures and fittings has not been decided. As the fixtures and fittings will necessarily be let with the flat, and presumably will have been inspected by the tenant in advance, it seems likely that a duty on the landlord to continue necessary facilities would be implied.

This duty is not to be confused with the obligation to repair any fixture or fitting inside the flat. This will normally be expressly and separately dealt with.

3.11 Other amenities

Some flat owners are given the right to use other land, for various purposes, in circumstances that amount to an easement.

Particularly for flats that are not purpose built, there may be the right to share the use of specified rooms. This sharing can amount to an easement, even if it is on the basis of successive rather than simultaneous use, eg, sharing a lavatory (*Miller v Emcer Products Ltd* [1956] Ch 304).

Outside, easements may be to complement the use of the flat, eg to hang washing on a line (*Drewell v Towler* (1832) 3 B & Ad 735). This is similar to the right to use a pipe or wire, but also involves a right of entry for hanging and removing the laundry. Or, the easement may be for extra amenity facilities, such as the use of a garden (*Re Ellenborough Park* [1956] Ch 131). Doubts whether an easement could exist to wander over a wide area have now been allayed.

3.12 Excluding liability

Landlords and managing agents of flats may incur substantial liabilities to the tenants. Where agents were held negligent in their recruitment of porters and their security system, they were responsible when a porter stole a tenant's jewellery (*Nahhas v Pier House (Cheyne Walk) Management Ltd* (1984) 270 EG 328).

Understandably, landlords are anxious to limit or exclude their liability for injury and damage in connection with the ancillary rights granted with a flat, particularly where the matters are outside their effective control. Examples are: injuries to people using the common parts of a block of flats; the acts of their employees; and the malfunctioning of apparatus such as boilers and lifts. There are limits on the extent to which any clause in a lease of a flat can achieve this. The landlord's liability to third parties, such as the tenant's visitors, cannot be affected because the lease is a contract to which they are not a party. The landlord may be able to achieve this objective by taking an indemnity from the tenant. A direct limit on liability would involve posting notices for visitors to see.

There are also statutory limits on the restrictions that the landlord can impose by lease. His statutory repairing responsibility, on granting a tenancy of less than seven years, can only be reduced or eliminated by a term approved by court order (Landlord and Tenant Act 1985, s 12(2). In other cases, the Unfair Contract Terms Act 1977 may reduce the effect of a lease provision, or render it completely ineffective.

The Act only affects the letting of a flat by a landlord in the course of a business (s 1(3)). Further it does not apply to a contract 'so far as it relates to the creation . . . of an interest in land' (Sched 1, para 1(b)). Clearly, that is the primary purpose of a lease, but the terms of most leases create connected obligations. It has been held that 'all the covenants that are integral to the lease which creates the interest in land "relate to" the creation of that interest in land' (*Electricity Supply Nominees Ltd v IAF Group plc* [1993] 3 All ER 372, 376, per Adrian Hamilton QC), and are therefore excluded from the Act. Covenants to pay rent and to do repairs are within that category (ibid).

It is suggested that necessary access must come within the exception, so that the Act does not prejudice exclusions of liability for injury or damage in connection with the stairs or lift. On the other hand, cleaning services, porterage and rubbish removal might all be sufficiently far from the basic purpose of the lease to be affected by the Act.

When the 1977 Act does apply, it is concerned with liability for negligence, whether tortious or by contract (s 1(1)). Liability for death or personal injury cannot be excluded. For loss or damage, liability can only be restricted by a term which satisfies a reasonableness test. This means that the lease term must be a fair and reasonable one to include having regard to the circumstances known to or in the contemplation of the parties when the contract was made, or which they ought reasonably to have known (ss 2, 11(1)).

Chapter 4

Services: Management and Payment

4.1 Management arrangements

Satisfactory arrangements for the provision of services used in common
by the flat owners demand some central management for the block.
The responsibility for paying for the services is frequently intended to
fall on the flat owners who share the benefit, and for that reason the
decision about which method to adopt involves considering the
enforceability of covenants by and against future flat owners.

There are three ways in which central management can be provided:
first, by the landlord or developer; secondly, by a third party; and thirdly,
by flat owners cooperatively. These will be considered separately.

The principal tests to be applied to management arrangements, to
see whether they are satisfactory, are considerations for the flat owners.
Whoever is responsible for providing services is only concerned that
any service charge can be collected. The problem for them is one of
enforcement against successors to the original contracting party of
covenants to make payments. From the flat owner's point of view, the
questions go beyond the basic ones of whether there is a covenant to
provide all necessary services and whether that covenant can be enforced
notwithstanding transfers of the interests involved. He must also be
assured that the body covenanting to provide the services is likely to
have the resources to fulfil its commitments. (Lack of money is no excuse
for not carrying out lift repairs: *Francis v Cowcliff Ltd* (1976) 33 P&CR
368; but in practice it may still stop them getting done.) Linked to that
are the consequences of another flat owner's default. If twenty flat owners
each covenant to contribute five per cent of the cost of services, but
one goes bankrupt so that it is only possible to collect ninety-five per
cent of any expenditure, will the practical consequence be the withdrawal
of some or all of the services?

4.1.1 Landlord or developer

In the case of flats let for short periods, the landlord will normally
be responsible for providing services. He may charge a rent that is inclusive

of services or he may collect a service charge, either of a fixed sum or one that fluctuates according to the cost of the services. This presents no problems. The landlord should covenant to provide the services, with any qualifications for interruptions beyond his control that he thinks proper, and the tenant should covenant to pay whatever contribution is required.

Exactly the same procedure can be adopted when granting long leases, and it is the simplest method of arranging for management.

A landlord must consult a recognised tenants' association about employing managing agents if the association serves notice requesting him to do so (Landlord and Tenant Act 1985, s 30B). If there is then no agent, he must consult if he proposes to employ one, giving notice of the name, and the duties to be delegated. If an agent is already employed, he must give notice specifying the delegated duties. Unless the association's notice is withdrawn, the landlord must consult about any new appointment, and at least once every five years give notice of any change in the agent's duties. Each of the notices must give a period for making observations. On a change of landlord, any notice given by the association lapses, but can be renewed.

An owner or developer of a block of flats who intends to dispose of them by freehold sales can also remain responsible for their management, but this is less satisfactory. The way to arrange it is for the owner of the block to reserve an estate rentcharge when conveying each individual flat, the total of which will pay for the services. But if the rentcharge is to be capable of being validly created and is to escape the statutory right of redemption, it cannot be for any more than an amount that is 'reasonable in relation to that covenant' to provide services (Rentcharges Act 1977, s 2(5)). It cannot therefore provide the developer with any profit which would be a financial incentive to ensure that he attends diligently to the management. In contrast, even though a lease cannot require the tenant to pay more than is reasonable by way of service charge, a landlord can receive a ground rent in addition to the service charge, which gives him a financial stake in the satisfactory running of the block.

4.1.2 Third party

The developer of a block of flats may want the management to be in the hands of a third party, in the sense of a party who has no property interest in the block, such as a management company. Anyone who is responsible for management may decide to employ agents to do the work involved: that does not change the responsible party's legal duties. It is not that type of delegation that is in question here. Some organisations concentrate all their management functions, covering many different properties, in a single company to achieve economies of scale, and to simplify accounting and their own taxation position. Where flats are built and let on long lease, it may be that the reversion carrying the entitlement to the ground rents is more saleable as an investment if it is not encumbered with the practical responsibilities of management.

On freehold sales, it rarely seems to be appropriate to make a third party responsible for the management, although estate rentcharges could be vested in one.

The management company can, and no doubt should, be made a party to the lease of each flat. Nevertheless, once the tenant assigns the lease to a new flat owner, the problems of the enforceability of the covenants arise. In this case as well, the tenants will not be sure that the management company will be able to make up any deficit arising from the default of another tenant.

The best way to tackle the problem is to make the landlord effectively a guarantor for the management company. The landlord covenants with the tenant to carry out the work and provide the services, but only if and to the extent that the management company does not do so. This is better than the landlord covenanting with the tenant that it will make up to the management company any deficit caused by another tenant's default. (But it should be noted that there would not, in the absence of an express obligation, be any duty on the landlord to contribute to the management company's expenses: *Alton House Holdings Ltd v Calflane (Management) Ltd* [1987] 2 EGLR 52). The enforcement of such a covenant can involve difficult questions as to the measure of damage suffered by the tenant, and it may not be a covenant that touches and concerns the land.

A similar effect is achieved by the landlord accepting responsibility for providing services and having the right to collect the service charge, but revocably delegating both that duty and that right to a third party, eg a tenants' association. For the time being, the landlord divests himself of day to day concern with the services. Yet the tenants retain their right of recourse against the landlord, because it is with the landlord that they have their contract. If the arrangements break down, the landlord revokes the delegation. This necessarily means that there is no half way position between continuing with the delegated arrangements or ending them.

Landlords may object that to stand surety for the management company defeats their object in separating the obligation to provide services from the reversion. If that consideration is paramount, it is better that they arrange matters so that the landlord demises the whole block to the management company at a ground rent, and the management company in turn grants the leases of the individual flats at ground rents that together total what it will have to pay under the head lease. If a tenant defaulted in such a case, the management company, as immediate landlord, would have the effective remedies of distress (if the service charge is reserved as rent) and forfeiture with which to ensure that it received the money needed to pay for the services.

Buyers of freehold flats cannot have the effective guarantee of the provision of services from the developer that he can give if he remains landlord. The fall back covenant of a landlord to do work and provide services will bind his successor in title, and there will always be an owner of the reversion. But once a developer has disposed of his freehold interest in the block, his covenant will be a mere personal obligation. Its enforceability will depend on the flat owner being able to trace the developer, and on the developer's continuing solvency.

4.1.3 Flat owners

Where the owner of a block of flats wants completely to dispose of his interest in it, the flat owners must necessarily be responsible for providing the communal services that they need. This is best done by setting up a limited company of which the members are the flat owners, so that it is effectively a tenants' cooperative. A developer may prefer to have the service charges collected by a tenants' cooperative even though he retains an interest in the property, in order to receive the ground rents, because that arrangement prevents his having the statutory duty to give tenants information about their service charges.

A flat owners' company can be involved in a number of ways. On the sale of freehold flats, rentcharges created to pay for the provision of services can be vested in the company. Similarly, a developer granting long leases will sometimes arrange to transfer the reversion to a tenants' company once he has disposed of all the flats. Or, he may grant a head lease of the whole block to the company. In either of these cases, the tenants collectively become landlords of each individual tenant.

Again, a third party charged with management may be a tenants' company. This can help the problem of the enforcement of covenants. The memorandum and articles of association can put on the members— ie, the tenants, albeit in a different capacity—an obligation to contribute, or make good any deficit. Provided that successive flat owners take transfers of the shares, the company can enforce payment qua member if not qua tenant.

The position if one tenant defaults is improved, but not greatly. The other tenants, who have a financial and practical interest in the matter, are the ones who can initiate enforcement action. This will probably therefore be done more efficiently. But if the defaulter is bankrupt, there will still be a shortfall on the money required. An obligation can be placed on the company members to contribute to this, but this is merely the solvent tenants paying more than their fair shares.

4.2 Information about service charges

Tenants of flats, along with tenants of other dwellings, in many cases have a statutory right under the Landlord and Tenant Act 1985, as amended by the Landlord and Tenant Act 1987, to information about the composition of their service charges. This does not apply to the owner of a freehold flat. All tenants, including statutory tenants, qualify, with two exceptions. First, the tenant of a flat for which a fair rent is registered only has rights to information if the registration is of an amount variable with the cost of services, under s 71(4) of the Rent Act 1977. Second, tenants of certain public authorities are only covered if their leases are for more than twenty-one years. The authorities in question are: local authorities, new town development corporations, the Commission for the New Towns and the Development Board for Rural Wales (Landlord and Tenant Act 1985, ss 26, 27).

If the tenant is represented by a recognised tenants' association, its secretary can exercise the right to require information if the tenant consents (Landlord and Tenant Act 1985, s 21(2)). The tenant has to consent, because the landlord need only supply the information once, either to the tenant or to the association. This is to avoid an unnecessary burden on the landlord. The need for the association to seek the tenant's consent gives the tenant priority over the association in claiming the right to information.

4.2.1 Definition

In the interpretation of these provisions, a wide meaning is given to 'service charge'. It is a payment, in addition to rent, for services, repairs, maintenance or insurance, or the landlord's costs of management. All or part of it varies or may vary according to the relevant costs, ie costs or estimated costs including overheads which the landlord or a superior landlord has incurred or will incur in connection with items for which the service charge is payable (Landlord and Tenant Act 1985, s 18). The requirement of variation means that the Act applies both to charges which are calculated fully to reimburse the landlord, and to those consisting of a fixed sum plus a percentage of any excess over a certain figure. The latter comes within the Act even before the figure rises above the level when the percentage begins to apply.

4.2.2 Information to be supplied

The information to which the tenant is entitled is a written summary of the costs incurred in the relevant period, which are relevant to the service charges payable or demanded in that or any other period. That 'relevant period' is the last twelve month period for which accounts have been made up before the tenant put in his request, or, if there are no such accounts, the twelve months ending on the request date (Landlord and Tenant Act 1985, s 21(1)).

What the summary has to show is how the costs are or will be reflected in service charge demands. Normally, the summary must be certified by a qualified accountant. The only exception is where there are no more than four flats in a building and the costs relate exclusively to that building. The accountant must certify that it is in his opinion a fair summary, complying with the requirement that it shows how the costs are reflected, and that it is sufficiently supported by accounts, receipts and other documents produced to him (Landlord and Tenant Act 1985, s 21(5), (6)). The tenant, or with his consent the secretary of the recognised tenants' association, may demand facilities for inspecting and copying those vouchers. He must give written notice to the landlord within six months of obtaining the summary. That entitles him to inspection and copying facilities for a period of two months starting within a month after he makes his request. Inspection facilities must be provided free, although they may feature as part of the landlord's management expenses, but the landlord may make a reasonable charge for copying facilities (s 22).

An accountant is a qualified accountant for the purpose of certifying a summary of service charge costs if he is a member of one of the following professional bodies: the Institute of Chartered Accountants in England and Wales, the Institute of Chartered Accountants of Scotland, the Association of Certified Accounts, the Institute of Chartered Accountants in Ireland, any other body of accountants established in the United Kingdom and recognised by the Secretary of State for company audits, and—where the landlord is a local authority, new town development corporation, the Commission for the New Towns or the Development Board for Rural Wales—the Chartered Institute of Public Finance and Accountancy. There are exceptions. A body corporate, other than a Scottish firm, does not qualify. Nor, except in the case of one of the public authorities just named, can the accountant be an officer, employee or partner of the landlord or of a member of the same group of companies as the landlord, nor a partner nor employee of an excluded person. The landlord's managing agent, and his employees and partners are also outside the qualified class (Landlord and Tenant Act 1985, s 28).

4.2.3 Procedure and default

A tenant who wants information about his service charge makes a written request to his landlord. That request can be served on the landlord's agent named in the tenant's rent book or similar document, or the person who receives rent on the landlord's behalf. The recipient must forward the request to the landlord as soon as may be (Landlord and Tenant Act 1985, s 21(1), (3)).

If it was a superior landlord who incurred some or all of the relevant costs, and the landlord does not have the information, he in turn makes a request to his immediate landlord. That process is repeated if necessary up a chain of landlords. The time for supplying the information is extended as is reasonable in the circumstances. Where the tenant, or the secretary of the recognised tenants' association, asks for facilities to inspect or copy vouchers in respect of costs incurred by the superior landlord, the landlord must tell him the position and give him the superior landlord's name and address. It is for the superior landlord to provide the necessary facilities (Landlord and Tenant Act 1985, s 23).

An assignment of the lease does not make any difference to any request for information or vouchers that the tenant had made. The landlord does not, however, have to provide a summary or facilities more than once for the same flat in respect of the same period (Landlord and Tenant Act 1985, s 24).

Failure to satisfy these requirements can be an offence. A landlord or a superior landlord who fails to perform any of these statutory duties without reasonable excuse is liable on summary conviction to a fine of up to £2,500 (Landlord and Tenant Act 1985, s 25).

4.3 Management audit

Another way for tenants to obtain service charge information is to call for a management audit. This is a statutory right, exercisable by two-thirds of the tenants of flats let on long leases by a single landlord, to appoint a qualified accountant or a qualified surveyor to carry out an audit (Leasehold Reform, Housing and Urban Development Act 1993, ss 76–84).

The object of the audit is to determine how far the landlord's management obligations are being discharged in an efficient and effective manner, and how far the tenants' service charges are being so applied. The auditor has statutory rights to inspect the necessary documents.

4.4 Tenants' association

A body which is effectively a tenants' cooperative or association may have a legal estate in a block of flats, and be given the responsibility for maintenance. In other cases, an association may be formed as a watchdog for the tenants, whether long leaseholders or tenants on short term tenancies.

For a form of rules for an unincorporated tenants' association, see Precedent E:2, p 251.

4.4.1 Formation

Unless the tenants decide to form a corporate body, to ensure permanence and obtain the benefit of limited liability, there is no need for a tenants' association to be incorporated. There are nevertheless advantages in establishing it with agreed rules to regulate its proceedings.

Among matters to be considered in formulating the rules are:
(1)   What are the association's objects to be? It may be seen merely

as a means to keep up standards and maintain property values. Or, it may represent the tenants collectively both in dealings with the landlord, and in other matters of common interest eg, in negotiating and contesting planning proposals. Again, it could have an active role in providing supplementary services, beyond the scope of the leases;

(2) Who is to be eligible for membership? If all the flats are owner-occupied, this causes no problem. As soon as there are sublettings, the question arises whether an occupier may join, and if so whether in addition to, or instead of, the flat owner who sublet;

(3) How are its activities to be financed? The main, and perhaps only, source of money is likely to be subscriptions. If the association provides services for tenants, problems can arise if some decline to join. An association of this type will not be able to insist on contributions from non-members, even if they have the benefit of the communal services.

4.4.2 Recognised tenants' association

A recognised tenants' association has a role to play both in the statutory process of obtaining information about the service charge that a tenant must pay—in which case the secretary of the association can obtain the information instead of the tenant—and in the control of expenditure on major works, in which case copies of notices and estimates must be sent to the secretary.

An association must satisfy two requirements to qualify as a recognised tenants' association (Landlord and Tenant Act 1985, s 29). First, it must be an association of qualifying tenants—ie tenants whose leases contain obligations to contribute by way of service charge to the same costs— with or without other tenants.

Secondly, an association must be recognised. This can come about in either of two ways. The landlord can give written notice of recognition to the secretary of the association. There is no procedure to oblige the landlord to accord recognition. If he does, he can withdraw it by giving the association's secretary at least six months' notice in writing. Alternatively, one of the Lord Chancellor's appointees to the local rent assessment panel can give a certificate conferring recognition. That certificate can be cancelled at any time by one of the people qualified to grant it. The Secretary of State has power to make regulations laying down matters to be taken into account in giving or cancelling a certificate. No regulations have yet been made.

4.5 Amount of service charge

The amount that the tenant of a flat must pay as a service charge is restricted in a number of ways: by contract and by statute. The statutory provisions do not apply to what the owner of a freehold flat must pay, the contractual limits can.

4.5.1 Contract

Any provision for payment of a service charge should state what items are to be paid for. There is no liability in respect of any item that is omitted, but when an item is covered, the lease wording may extend to capital expenditure incurred for that purpose (*Sun Alliance & London Assurance Co Ltd v British Railways Board* [1989] 2 EGLR 237: eg window cleaning expenses for a substantial commercial building covered the cost of a fully automatic cradle system).

Even where an item of service is clearly within the scope of the service charge, it is still open to question whether the landlord, or whoever does the work, can charge the tenant with the whole of what he spends, or whether there has been unwarranted extravagance. Normally, the party doing the work has a complete discretion. Certainly, there is no duty to restrict the cost by opting for cheap 'first aid', instead of a more expensive solution which should eliminate the problem (*Manor House Drive Ltd v Shahbazian* (1965) 195 EG 283).

On the letting of a flat, albeit in circumstances concerning the issue of a landlord's managing agents' certificate of which the Court of Appeal did not approve, this freedom was questioned.

> Is there an implication that the costs claimed are to be 'fair and reasonable'? . . . I am of the opinion that such an implication must be made here. It cannot be supposed that the [landlords] were entitled to be as extravagant as they chose in the standards of repair, the appointment of porters, etc . . . . In my opinion, the parties cannot have intended that the landlords should have an unfettered discretion to adopt the highest conceivable standard and to charge the tenant with it (*Finchbourne Ltd v Rodrigues* [1976] 3 All ER 581, 587 per Cairns LJ).

4.5.2 Statute

The service charge payable by the tenant of a flat is limited by statute. Costs incurred on the services or works are to be taken into account in calculating the service charge only to the extent that they were reasonably incurred, and only if the standard of the works and services was reasonable (Landlord and Tenant Act 1985, s 19(1)).

It is suggested that the test that the costs must be reasonably incurred actually involves three separate tests. The answer must be Yes to all the following questions. Was the item something on which it was reasonable at that time to spend any money at all? Was it a reasonable allocation of resources, to spend the amount in question on that particular item, considering the other claims on the available funds? Was the price charged reasonable value for the work actually done or the service actually rendered?

The temptation is only to ask the final question, judging whether or not the price was exorbitant. An extreme example illustrates the importance of the other questions. Say a block of flats had decorative statuary in the entrance hall and stained glass windows on the staircase. At a particular time, an objective judgment might be that it was not reasonable to spend anything at all to repair the statues. Again, if the stained glass windows were broken, it might be reasonable only to spend a limited sum on staircase windows, which would dictate replacement with plain rather than stained glass. These, then, are questions to ask before deciding whether the work actually done was fair value for money.

In the case of a service charge which includes costs yet to be incurred, the amount of the charge is to be no greater than is reasonable. Any necessary adjustment is to be made when the costs have been incurred (Landlord and Tenant Act 1985, s 19(2)). The provision as to later adjustments leaves a number of pertinent questions unanswered. It does expressly say that the adjustment is to be 'by repayment, reduction of subsequent charges or otherwise'. Does that allow a tenant to insist on repayment, rather than a credit carried forward? What happens if the lease comes to an end? Can there be adjustments if the work done is not up to standard?

There are further restrictions on service charges relating to works on the building or other premises—but not to services provided—judged by their cost (Landlord and Tenant Act 1985, s 20). A special preliminary procedure must be followed if the costs incurred in total, not merely attributable to a single flat, exceed the prescribed amount. This is £50 multiplied by the number of flats in the building, with a minimum of £1,000. If any flat in the building is let on different terms—eg a rack rent inclusive of services, or occupied as a porter's flat rent free—it is excluded from the calculation.

The procedure required in the case of these works differs depending on whether there is a recognised tenants' association. If there is none, it is:

(1) Two estimates are obtained for carrying out the work, of which at least one is from someone wholly unconnected with the landlord;

(2) Each of the tenants is given a notice describing the works, accompanied by copies of the estimates. The notice must invite observations on the works and estimates. It gives a name and address in the United Kingdom of a person to whom observations may be sent, by a stated date at least one month ahead. As an alternative to giving each tenant notice, the notice and copy estimates may be displayed where they are likely to come to the attention of all the tenants;

(3) The landlord 'has regard' to the observations. The start of the

work is delayed until after the date given in the notice, unless
it is urgent.

Where the tenants are represented by a recognised tenants' association,
the procedure is:

(1) The landlord gives the association secretary a notice with a detailed
     specification of the works, giving a reasonable period for the
     association to propose the names of one or more persons from
     whom it considers that the landlord should obtain estimates;

(2) At least two estimates are obtained, one from someone wholly
     unconnected with the landlord, and a copy of each is given to
     the association secretary;

(3) Each of the tenants is given a notice briefly describing the works,
     summarising the estimates, stating that the tenant has the right
     to inspect and take copies of the detailed specification and
     estimates, inviting observations, and giving an address in the
     United Kingdom of a person to whom they may be sent by a
     stated date at least a month later.

The sanction for not complying with the preliminary procedure where
works are proposed is severe. Any excess in the cost, above the prescribed
amount, is not to be taken into account in calculating the service charge.
The court does however, have discretion to dispense with all or any
of the requirements when satisfied that the landlord acted reasonably.

Apart from cases of oversight or ignorance of the statutory requirements, examples of cases where strict compliance may be waived are:
repairs are needed to specialised equipment, such as a lift, and only
the original manufacturer will maintain its products, so that to obtain
a competitive estimate is impracticable; previously hidden and unfore-
seeable faults are revealed in the course of repair work, forcing the cost
up above the prescribed amount.

4.5.3 Right to buy

There are two restrictions on a service charge provision inserted in a
lease granted on the exercise by a secure tenant of his statutory right
to buy. Both relate to a requirement that the tenant contribute towards
the cost of carrying out external and structural repairs, and repairs to
property over which the tenant has rights, where the work is made the
landlord's responsibility. A covenant to contribute is void to the extent
that (Housing Act 1980, Sched 2, paras 15–17):

(1) The part of the cost that the tenant must bear is not reasonable;
     and

(2) It relates to the cost of making good structural defects of which
     the landlord was aware earlier than ten years after the lease was
     granted, but the existence of which he did not notify to the tenant
     before it was granted.

4.6 Management charge

The inclusion of a profit element, or management charge, in a service charge is often a bone of contention. It is generally perfectly proper, and probably does not need to be expressly mentioned in the list of items for which the lease authorises the landlord to charge. To do so will, however, be useful in order to avoid arguments. The charges of a management company formed for the purpose by a resident landlord, which was found not to be a sham, have been allowed (*Skilleter v Charles* [1992] 1 EGLR 73).

In the case of flats for which statute limits the service charge, the charge is defined to include 'the landlord's costs of management' (Landlord and Tenant Act 1985, s 18(1)). In context it might seem that the phrase should be limited to costs incurred by the landlord to a third party. There is no logic in including management fees a landlord pays to outside agents, while disallowing the cost of management that the landlord undertakes himself. It is suggested that both are equally recoverable. No specific figure or percentage is laid down as being permissible. These costs come within the general requirement that they are reasonably incurred.

Charges for management can also be included in a fair rent for a regulated tenancy. '. . . there is plenty of authority for the proposition that management costs, and indeed in appropriate circumstances management profit, may be properly admitted' (*Metropolitan Properties Co (FGC) Ltd v Lannon* [1968] 1 WLR 815, 836 per Widgery J). The management charge included in a fair rent can be a lump sum, or a percentage of the cost of the services. Ten per cent was suggested in one case without being expressly approved or disapproved (*Metropolitan Properties Co Ltd v Noble* [1968] 1 WLR 838).

However, it will not be possible to include all costs in a service charge. Costs incurred by a maintenance trustee, which held a fund contributed by tenants, in suing to enforce tenants' repairing obligations did so as the landlord's agent. The expense of the litigation could not be charged to the fund (*Holding and Management Ltd v Property Holding and Investment Trust plc* [1988] 2 All ER 702).

4.6.1 Interest

The landlord or the management company responsible for providing the services may incur expenses before being able to collect service charges, and the question then arises whether any interest paid to borrow money can be added to the service charge. Normally, if the covenant to pay service charges makes no mention of interest, none can be passed on to the tenant (*Frobisher (Second Investments) Ltd v Killoran Trust Co Ltd* [1980] 1 WLR 425). On the construction of one covenant, it did not come within 'sums spent on general administration and manage-

ment' (*Boldmark Ltd v Cohen* [1986] 1 EGLR 47). However, interest
is an item which can properly be mentioned expressly as a constituent
of the service charge.

4.6.2 Legal costs

Costs incurred by the landlord, or management company, in providing
services and enforcing the service charge are another expense which may
be expressly included within the service charge. This is perfectly proper.
Normally, a lease will make clear that the service charge only includes
costs which are not recoverable from defaulting tenants, and that imposes
a duty on the landlord to try to recover them from defaulters (*Skilleter
v Charles* [1992] 1 EGLR 73).

There is, however, scope for abuse. For example, a landlord who
unjustifiably seeks to enforce payment of a service charge may be ordered
to pay the costs of his unsuccessful action. It could be less than fair
if the successful defendant then found himself paying those costs in the
guise of an addition to the service charge. For this reason, statute gives
tenants the chance to apply for an order that particular costs be excluded
from a service charge (Landlord and Tenant Act 1985, s 20C).

4.7 Reserve fund

The arrangements for funding maintenance and repairs to a block of
flats may include building up a reserve fund, from contributions built
into the annual service charge paid by flat owners. The object is to
ensure that money is available for major items of expenditure, without
undue fluctuation in the service charge from one year to the next. Items
that could be a call on such a fund are exterior decoration, and
replacement of boilers and lifts.

4.7.1 Held in trust

A reserve fund must be held in trust for the contributing tenants, ie
those whose leases require them to contribute to the same costs (Landlord
and Tenant Act 1987, s 42). This applies to all service charges, but is
of most importance in relation to reserve funds.

The landlord, or whoever holds the fund, must hold all charges paid
and investments representing them, with accrued interest, in one or more
funds. The trusts are:
   (1) To defray the costs for which the relevant service charge was
       payable. These objects of the trust will be defined by the lease;
   (2) Subject to that, for the contributing tenants for the time being
       in the proportions that they are liable to pay relevant service
       charges, while there are such tenants;

(3) After the termination of the lease when there are no longer contributing tenants, for the landlord.

The trusts in paragraphs (1) and (2) may be varied by the express terms of the lease, whenever it was granted. Otherwise these statutory terms override any lease terms.

Some managing agents who administer reserve funds in connection with several separate blocks of flats have expressed concern that they will be expected to maintain an individual bank account for each. Although the Act requires each be held 'as a single fund', or as more than one, separate bank accounts can hardly be the intended meaning. The 'fund' referred to includes not only the money held, but also investments.

4.7.2 Other safeguards

A number of other safeguards should be considered.

First, tenants will wish to ensure that when an item covered by the fund has to be attended to, the landlord does draw money from the fund rather than continuing to retain the reserve and simply increasing the current year's service charge demand. If prices were constant, this would be simple enough to arrange. However, when the cost of items chargeable to the fund escalates more than expected, the landlord may be loath to denude the fund, because the balance, after paying for the item needed, may be less than an adequate reserve for the others it is intended to cover. That could lead to a situation when scarcely anything was ever drawn from the fund. As a compromise, the lease might contain an obligation on the landlord to pay at least half of the cost of any relevant item from the fund. If what was left was low, the tenants would have to pay higher contributions in later years.

Secondly, a tenant who assigns his lease will hope to recover from the purchaser the amount of the contributions that he has made to the fund, and from which his successor will benefit. The extent to which this is appropriate is a matter of bargain between them, but unless there is a duty on the landlord to supply a figure of the current balance of the fund at any time, the parties will not have the facts upon which to base their negotiation.

Thirdly, just as the landlord should contribute to the cost of services, repairs and maintenance in respect of any flat which is unlet, so he should make appropriate payments to a reserve fund in those circumstances. There is a difference. The landlord's share of the cost of current work may simply be contributed by means of his doing the work and only being able to collect part of the expense. He would have to make cash contributions to the reserve fund.

Fourthly, the existence of the fund should not be allowed to prejudice any insurance claim. As a policy is a contract of indemnity, an insurer might argue, on a total demolition, that the loss the parties suffered is reduced by the amount of a fund already set aside for specified repairs and replacements. That contention can probably be successfully countered by providing that the fund reverts to the tenants unconditionally upon the happening of any event that gives rise to a claim.

4.8 Certificate of amount

It is common in leases to make provision for the amount of the service charge to be certified by a third party. The advantage of this is to fix the sum due with certainty and to identify the date on which it is payable. It also gives the person who is liable to pay some reassurance that the sum demanded is correct. It is customary to draft these provisions in such a manner that the certificate is conclusive and incontestable. It seems that courts are now likely to accept that the parties have delegated the power to decide a question of law, such as whether a particular item falls within the service charge, even though it is decided erroneously (*Nikko Hotels (UK) Ltd v MEPC plc* [1991] 2 EGLR 103). The point may not, however, be finally decided.

There may nevertheless be a number of grounds on which the certificate may be challenged. First, calculation errors can also be challenged in court (*Dean v Prince* [1954] Ch 409, 427 per Denning LJ). Secondly, where the statutory controls on service charges payable in respect of flats apply, the only type of third party determination that is valid is by arbitration, subject to the Arbitration Act 1950. Any other method, short of going to court, of determining the amount payable for services or work, its reasonableness or the standard of what was provided, is void (Landlord and Tenant Act 1985, s 19(3)).

It may also be possible to challenge a certificate on the ground that the person giving it lacks the necessary independence. One lease provided for certification by 'the lessors' managing agents', and the certificate was given by a firm of which the sole proprietor was the beneficial owner of the landlord's interest in the property, although that was vested in a company (*Finchbourne Ltd v Rodrigues* [1976] 3 All ER 581). Cairns LJ said that the words of the lease, referring to the lessors' managing agents, required that the certificate be given by someone other than the landlord. If the firm of agents was merely another name for the landlord, 'then there has been no valid certificate' (p 586). Browne LJ said, 'The intention clearly was that the tenant should be entitled to rely on the expertise of such a third person' (p 587). In another case it was suggested that the landlord's managing agents were not sufficiently independent to give a certificate as 'the landlord's surveyor' (*Concorde Graphics Ltd v Andromeda Investments SA* (1982) 265 EG 386).

This leads to severe doubt as to whether a full-time employee of the landlord can validly give a certificate. A surveyor on the landlord's staff could well be described as the 'landlord's surveyor'—a phrase commonly found in leases—but he probably does not have the necessary independence. His acts as employee are effectively the acts of his employer. Where the statutory restrictions do not apply, there is nothing against the lease stating that the landlord himself will certify the amount of the service charge. If that is the intention, it should be made unambiguously clear. In such a case, the landlord could have his employee give the certificate on his behalf.

4.9 Regulated tenancies

In most cases, when the rent for a regulated tenancy is registered, the registered amount will include anything the tenant has to pay for the provision of services by the landlord (Rent Act 1977, s 71(1)).

A landlord who applies to register a fair rent must specify what sum is included in the proposed rent for services, and give details of his expenditure in providing them (Rent Act 1977, s 67(2)(*b*); Housing Act 1980, s 59(2)). The rent officer sends a copy of the expenditure details to the tenant (Rent Act 1977, Sched 11, para 3(2)(*b*); Regulated Tenancies (Procedure) Regulations 1980, Sched 1, para 1).

Among the services the cost of which has been included in a registered fair rent are: central heating, wages, insurance, staircase lighting, notional rent for housekeeper's flat, porters' expenses, uniforms, window cleaning, and fire extinguishing. The actual cost of an item to the landlord can be reduced for the purpose of calculating what the tenant should pay, if it seems excessive, eg, because the heating system is inefficient (*Metropolitan Properties Co Ltd v Noble* [1968] 1 WLR 838).

The alternative, but less common, way for a rent to be registered is as a sum variable according to the cost from time to time of services the landlord or a superior landlord provides, or of any works of maintenance or repair that either of them carries out. The rent officer or the rent assessment committee must be satisfied that the contractual terms as to the variation of the rent are reasonable (Rent Act 1977, s 71(4)). This is a matter within their discretion. The only reported case of the court's intervention was to order a variable rent where the landlord was a self financing tenants' cooperative subject to the accounting and audit rules of the Industrial and Provident Societies Acts (*Re Heathview Tenants' Cooperative Ltd* (1981) 258 EG 644). A tenant whose rent is registered in this way has the statutory right to information about costs that go to make up the service charge.

4.10 Varying contract terms

4.10.1 By statute

Statute gives the court jurisdiction to intervene to vary lease provisions relating to service charges (Landlord and Tenant Act 1987, s 35). This applies to a long lease of a flat, granted for over twenty-one years but not including any business premises. The property let by the lease must not include more than one flat, nor common parts as well as a flat.

A party to the lease can apply to vary it if it fails to make satisfactory provision on certain matters. They are:

(1) the provision or maintenance of services reasonably necessary to afford the occupiers a reasonable standard of accommodation (including safety and security and the condition of the common parts);

(2) the recovery from one party to the lease of another party's expenditure for the benefit of the first, with or without others; and

(3) the computation of a service charge. Computation provisions are expressly declared unsatisfactory where the total service charge which the landlord can collect exceeds, or is less than (Leasehold Reform, Housing and Urban Development Act 1993, s 86), his expenditure.

In a block of flats, it will often be desirable to be sure that all the leases stay in the same form, particularly when dealing with the calculation and collection of service charges. The Act has two provisions designed to cover that (Landlord and Tenant Act 1987, ss 36, 37). First, the respondent to a variation application can ask for corresponding variations to other specified leases if the court makes the order originally requested. This will normally mean that if one tenant applies to vary his lease, the landlord will ask for the same changes to other leases in the block if the first tenant succeeds. However, although the landlord must be the same in respect of all the leases, the flats need not be in the same building. Secondly, a specified majority of the parties to leases from the same landlord may apply to vary all of them where the object cannot be achieved unless all are varied. Counting the tenant of each flat as one party and the landlord as one, an application in respect of fewer than nine leases must be made by all parties or all but one. If there are more than eight leases, at least 75 per cent of the parties must consent to the application and no more than ten per cent oppose it.

4.10.2 Changes of circumstances

There is also one case, reported before the introduction of the statutory provisions, where the basis of the tenant's contributions to the central heating costs incurred by the landlord was altered after the landlord had linked the central heating system of the block in which the flat was to that of an adjoining block, where the extent of heating inside the individual flats was greater (*Pole Properties Ltd v Feinberg* (1982) 43 P&CR 121). The Court of Appeal held that if the change in circumstances is great enough there is an inherent jurisdiction to vary the original bargain, shifting it to a basis which is then fair and reasonable.

This jurisdiction remains available for cases which the statute would not cover, although its precise extent is uncertain.

4.11 Demands for payment

4.11.1 Form

A written service charge demand must contain certain basic information if the sum demanded is to be payable. It must state the name and address of the landlord. If that address is not in England and Wales, an address which is must be given for service on the landlord (Landlord and Tenant Act 1987, s 47). The name and address of the landlord's agent does not satisfy this requirement.

No part of any service charge which is demanded is considered due until the requirement has been met. The only exception is where the court has appointed a receiver or manager whose functions include receiving service charges.

4.11.2 Time limit

There is a time limit for making service charge demands. The tenant is not normally liable to pay any charge relating to costs incurred more than eighteen months before he receives the demand. He does have to pay, however, if within that period he is notified in writing that the costs have been incurred and he will later be required to contribute (Landlord and Tenant Act 1985, s 20B).

Chapter 5

Repairs

5.1 Repairs scheme

Whenever flats are let or sold it is desirable that the document by which they are disposed of should incorporate a scheme to regulate the repair and maintenance of the whole block. This is essential where the flats are disposed of freehold or on long leases. In the more common leasehold case, the arrangements to be made should be considered both from the landlord's point of view, and from the tenant's. The freehold owners of flats will have the same interests as tenants under long leases.

5.1.1 Landlord's view

The landlord is concerned to ensure that the whole block is kept in a reasonable state of repair. When the flats are let on short tenancies, they will revert to him comparatively quickly, and only with proper maintenance will he be able to continue to charge full rents. Even where the flats are disposed of on long leases, the good repair of the block protects the security on which his ground rents are charged and will be of direct concern if any lease has to be forfeited.

The simplest way for a landlord to ensure that repairs are done and done well is to do them himself. For jobs which affect more than one flat this is most practical, and it also ensures consistency in the standard of work. Even where the tenants reimburse the cost of the work, the landlord can choose any proper way to remedy defects, even if it is not the cheapest, albeit temporary, solution (*Manor House Drive Ltd v Shahbazian* (1965) 195 EG 283). Unless the landlord covenants to do the work, he will need to reserve a right of entry to give him the necessary facilities. He has no implied right to enter voluntarily to do work, even if the work is admittedly necessary (*Stocker v Planet Building Society* (1879) 27 WR 877). But if he covenants to repair, he may enter for that purpose (*Saner v Bilton* (1878) 7 ChD 815). This remains so even if the lease merely contains a tenant's covenant to reimburse the landlord for the cost of repairs, without the landlord actually undertaking to do the work (*Edmonton Corporation v W M Knowles & Son Ltd* (1962) 60 LGR 124).

The landlord who accepts responsibility for repairs, whether all or just major ones, will have to arrange to know what is needed. A power of entry to inspect should be reserved. An express covenant to do work on property demised is construed as an obligation to do so only on being given notice that there is a defect (*Torrens v Walker* [1906] 2 Ch 166). It is useful to reinforce this with an express covenant by the tenant to notify wants of repair to the landlord. Failure to notify the landlord of the need for work will then not simply exonerate the landlord from any duty to do it, but may also make the tenant liable for the consequences of neglect.

The landlord will generally want to recoup the cost of repairs from the tenants, although there is a statutory restriction on this in the case of short lettings. This can be done either by contributions to a service charge, or it can be reflected in the rent. The fact that the landlord covenants to repair does not automatically imply a tenant's covenant to repay the cost (*Riverlate Properties Ltd v Paul* [1975] Ch 133). On a short letting, where the landlord has implied statutory repairing obligations, the second method—reflecting the value of the covenant to repair in the rent—is the only one available for work within the statutory covenant (*Campden Hill Towers Ltd v Gardner* [1977] QB 823).

5.1.2 Tenant's view

The flat owner is also concerned to ensure that the whole block is in repair, because unless it is the physical stability and the value of his flat may be prejudiced. From his point of view, the matter can be divided into three parts. First, as regards his own flat, any work which is not his responsibility should be taken on as an obligation by someone else, normally the landlord. Secondly, the other flats in the block should be maintained to a standard that will ensure that their condition does not damage his flat. Thirdly, the common parts must be maintained not only to protect structural stability, but also so that they are in a satisfactory state to use.

The flat owner will want the landlord, or whoever else is responsible for repairs to the rest of the block, to undertake an enforceable obligation to do so, rather than merely reserving the right. As there can be no easement for the protection of a building against the elements (*Phipps v Pears* [1965] 1 QB 76; except possibly, it has been suggested without being decided, in respect of a roof: *Sedgwick Forbes Bland Payne Group Ltd v Regional Properties Ltd* (1981) 257 EG 64, 70) that right will not arise by implication. The possibility of other parts of the block changing hands, and the leases of other flats coming to an end, must be covered.

The tenant will also be concerned to ensure that the obligation to do the work is one on which he can rely. If the duty is undertaken by a third party created for the purpose, without assets, he should consider the desirability of an express guarantee from the landlord. There is no implied covenant by the landlord to do the work on the third party's default (*Hafton Properties Ltd v Camp* [1994] 03 EG 129).

5.2 Flat owner's responsibility as tenant

Normally a tenant's duty to repair the premises demised to him is set out in some detail in the lease or tenancy agreement. Unless the document seeks to transfer to the tenant responsibilities that statute lays on the landlord, the extent of the tenant's responsibility is a matter of interpretation of the document. Repairing covenants run with the land and the reversion, and therefore can be enforced by and against successors to the original parties to the lease (*Martyn v Clue* (1852) 18 QB 661).

Some repairing obligations are implied where none is expressly stated. The extent of the tenant's duty in those circumstances depends on the length of the letting. All that a weekly tenant need do is to use the flat in a tenant-like manner (*Warren v Keen* [1954] 1 QB 15). This means making minor running repairs like mending fuses, clearing blocked sinks and cleaning chimneys. It also covers such routine precautions as draining down the water system if leaving the flat when freezing temperatures are likely. A yearly tenant has the further obligation to keep the flat wind and weather proof (*Wedd v Porter* [1916] 2 KB 91).

A tenant may effectively have a further implied repairing obligation by the operation of the law of waste, which is an act which changes the nature of a property, and can render the tenant liable to his landlord in tort. A tenant for a term of years is liable for permissive waste, ie, allowing property to deteriorate to an extent that its nature changes. Yearly tenants may also be liable for permissive waste. They are certainly liable for voluntary waste, which is a wilful or negligent act which tends to the destruction of the demised premises. Tenants for terms of years are liable for voluntary waste. Periodic tenants for less than a term from year to year are liable only for permissive waste.

5.3 Landlord's responsibility for flat

A landlord does not as a general rule have any liability to repair premises he lets, unless there is an express provision in the lease or tenancy agreement (*Arden v Pullen* (1842) 10 M&W 321). But if the tenant has a duty to repair, the landlord may have an implied correlative duty. This means that if the tenant's obligation (eg to repair the interior) can only be performed satisfactorily if other work (eg, on the exterior) is done, the landlord has a duty to do that other work (*Barrett v Lounova (1982) Ltd* [1990] 1 QB 348).

Where he does enter into a covenant for repair, eg, in respect of structural parts of the flat, it is subject to the implied condition that he has notice of the need for repair (*Torrens v Walker* [1906] 2 Ch 166). The landlord is not under any obligation to inspect the flat for defects, so the tenant should make a point of drawing his attention to work that needs to be done. However, a landlord is liable to do a repair even if he learns of the need for it from a third party (*Dinefwr Borough Council v Janes* [1987] 2 EGLR 58).

Leases of flats frequently impose another condition precedent to the landlord's obligation: that the tenant has made the contributions to repair costs or service charge payments due from him. Tenants should beware of the variant of that condition, which makes the landlord's duty dependent on all the tenants of flats in the block paying what is due from them. Although it is understandable that the landlord does not wish to be out of pocket, it means that one tenant does not have it within his own control to determine whether the landlord's obligation to him is to be enforceable. However, the two obligations—to repair and to pay the service charge—may well be construed as independent, so that each must be performed whether or not the other has been. That will generally be the position if the service charge relates to more than the repairs (*Yorkbrook Investments Ltd v Batten* [1985] 2 EGLR 100). If the landlord's duty is conditional only on the tenant in question having paid his service charge, default by any other tenant is irrelevant (*Marenco v Jacramel Co Ltd* [1964] EGD 349).

In two cases, the landlord has obligations to repair that are imposed by statute. These are: first, where a flat is let for less than seven years; secondly, on a letting at a very low rent, where he gives a warranty that it is fit for human habitation.

5.4 Landlord's implied covenant: short leases

5.4.1 When implied

The Landlord and Tenant Act 1985 imposes repairing obligations on the landlord of a flat let for a term of less than seven years. To assess the length of a letting for this purpose, any part of the term falling before the lease is granted is disregarded, unless the tenant was then in possession under an agreement for lease (*Brikom Investments Ltd v Seaford* [1981] 1 WLR 863). Options can also alter the length taken into account for this purpose, whether or not they are exercised. If the landlord has power to end the lease before seven years of the term have expired, that is deemed to be a letting for less than seven years. This does not apply to an option to determine on the tenant's death, because in that case the landlord cannot control when the lease will end (*Parker v O'Connor* [1974] 1 WLR 1160). On the other hand, an option to renew a lease, so that the original lease and the new one would together total at least seven years, takes the original letting outside these provisions.

The parties are not at liberty to reduce the landlord's obligations by agreement. Any contractual term that purports to do so is void. What they can do is to apply to the county court for a consent order to approve the modification or exclusion of the landlord's responsibilities. The court must consider it reasonable, having regard to all the circumstances. Such orders are not common.

There are no implied repairing covenants on letting a flat on or after 3 October 1980 to any of the following (Landlord and Tenant Act 1985, s 14(4), (5)):

(1) Specified educational bodies and named student hostel organisations (Assured and Protected Tenancies (Lettings to Students Regulations) 1988, as amended);

(2) Registered and cooperative housing associations;

(3) County district and London borough councils, the Common Council of the City of London, the Commission for the New Towns, a new town or urban development corporation, the Development Board for Rural Wales and the Broads Authority (Norfolk and Suffolk Broads Act 1988, Sched 6);

(4) The Crown, unless the property is to be managed by the Crown Estate Commissioners, and a government department.

5.4.2 Extent of obligation

The landlord's duty under the statutory implied repairing covenant falls into two parts. First, he is to keep in repair the structure and exterior of the flat, including drains, gutters and external pipes. Windows, including frames and sashes, can be included (*Irvine v Moran* [1991] 1 EGLR 261). This obligation extends to other parts of the block in which the tenant has an interest, in cases where any want of repair affects the tenant's enjoyment of the flat or any common parts he is entitled to use. Secondly, the landlord must keep in repair and proper working order the installations for space and water heating, and for the supply of water, gas, electricity and sanitation. This includes basins, sinks, baths and sanitary conveniences (although lagging internal pipes is not required: *Wycombe Area Health Authority v Barnett* (1982) 264 EG 619), but it does not cover other fixtures, fittings and appliances for using water, gas and electricity. The installations in question must be in the flat, or, to the extent that the tenant's enjoyment of the flat or the common parts is affected, those which serve the flat and are in another part of the building in which the landlord has an interest, are owned by the landlord or are under his control.

The obligation may involve the landlord in doing work not in the flat. If he does not have the right to insist, it is a defence to any claim for not carrying it out to show that he used all reasonable endeavours to obtain the necessary rights, but was unable to do so.

Where the lease of the flat was granted before 15 January 1989, or pursuant to an agreement made earlier, the repair obligation is restricted to the flat. However, the landlord could not cut his responsibility down by defining the flat as excluding the exterior walls. The outside was still included (*Camden Hill Towers Ltd v Gardner* [1977] QB 823) and so was the roof over a top floor flat (*Douglas-Scott v Scorgie* [1984] 1 WLR 716).

The standard of repair has regard to the age, character and prospective life of the flat, and the locality in which it is situated. In the case of an appliance, eg, a cistern, it can extend to rectifying an original design fault (*Liverpool City Council v Irwin* [1977] AC 239). There are three matters expressly excluded: first, anything within the tenant's duty to use the flat in a tenant-like manner; secondly, rebuilding or reinstatement after destruction or damage by fire, tempest, flood or other inevitable accident; thirdly, repair or maintenance of anything the tenant is entitled to remove from the flat.

A tenant who is seeking to enforce the landlord's implied covenant must prove that the defect in question does come within the scope of the statute, and does not, eg, require work which is not a repair (*Foster v Day* (1968) 208 EG 495). Further, the landlord must have been notified that something needed to be done, because, as with other repairing responsibilities, his duty only arises when he has notice (*O'Brien v Robinson* [1973] AC 912). It is enough that the landlord should have known that a repair was needed (*Sheldon v West Bromwich Corporation* (1973) 117 SJ 486). So a landlord whose plumbers inspected a forty year old cold water tank and observed that the water was discoloured, was liable for the damage caused when it burst. The plumbers did not actually have to find it weeping to give the landlord sufficient notice to establish liability.

5.5 Landlord's implied covenant: right to buy lease

Where the long lease of a flat has been granted under the right to buy, statute imposes certain repairing obligations on the landlord (Housing Act 1985, Sched 6, para 14). He is responsible for the structure and exterior of the flat and the block of which it forms part. The duty extends to drains, gutters and external pipes. Furthermore he must repair any other property over which the tenant has rights.

This is primarily a duty to do the work, because—subject to an exception—the landlord is entitled (subject to limits during the first five years) to require the tenant to bear a reasonable part of the cost of doing the work, or insuring against it. The exception, where the expense must fall on the landlord, is work on structural defects, unless the landlord only became aware of them more than ten years after the lease was granted or unless the tenant was told of them before taking the lease.

The county court may authorise an agreement varying these terms if it is reasonable to do so. In the absence of an order, an agreement penalising the tenant if he enforces or seeks to rely on the landlord's duties is void.

5.6 Fitness for human habitation

5.6.1 Landlord's consent

The landlord of a flat let at a low rent—for lettings since 6 July 1957: up to £80 pa in London (until 31 March 1965, the administrative county, and after that, Greater London excluding the outer London boroughs) and up to £52 pa elsewhere—gives a statutory implied undertaking to keep it fit for human habitation (Landlord and Tenant Act 1985, s 8). He cannot contract out of this undertaking. There is no distinction between lettings at a rack rent and those at a ground rent. This is a reason for fixing a ground rent above the statutory limits.

There is one exception. There is no undertaking on a letting for a period of at least three years on terms that the tenant makes the flat reasonably fit for human habitation. Neither party must have the option to end the term before the end of the three years.

Fitness for human habitation is judged on a number of separate criteria (Landlord and Tenant Act 1985, s 10). They are: repair, stability, freedom from damp, internal arrangement, natural ventilation, water supply, drainage and sanitary conveniences, and facilities for the preparation and cooking of food, and the disposal of waste water. Defects must be very serious: plaster ceilings that have partly collapsed may not be sufficiently so (*Maclean v Currie* (1884) Cab & El 361). Again, the landlord's liability does not arise until he is notified that something is wrong (*McCarrick v Liverpool Corporation* [1947] AC 219), and does not apply if the flat cannot be made fit at reasonable expense (*Buswell v Goodwin* [1971] 1 WLR 92).

5.6.2 Public health

The person having control of a building containing flats is responsible for ensuring that it is fit for human habitation (Housing Act 1985, s 190; Housing Act 1988, s 130). The duty falls on the person who is in receipt of a rack rent, or who is entitled to let at such a rent (*White v Barnet London Borough Council* [1989] 2 EGLR 31).

The local housing authority has power to serve a repair notice if it is satisfied that a flat is unfit for human habitation either in itself or because of the condition of part of the block outside the flat. The only exception is if they consider that repair is not possible at reasonable expense. The notice specifies the works required and gives a reasonable time for doing them. A repair notice which has become operative is a local land charge (Housing Act 1985, s 189). There is an alternative form of notice where substantial repairs are needed to bring the property up to standard, although it is not unfit for human habitation (s 190). An appeal against a repair notice lies to the county court. One of the grounds is that someone else, the owner of that part of the premises, ought to do the work or pay for it; that other person has to be served with a copy of the notice of appeal (s 191).

If repair is not possible at reasonable expense, there are compulsory purchase powers (Housing Act 1985, s 192). However, if a notice is not complied with, the authority can do the work and charge the cost to the defaulter (ss 193–197). A person who intentionally fails to comply with a notice commits an offence and, on summary conviction, is liable to a fine of up to £2,500 (s 198A).

5.7 Repairs by other flat owners

The interest that one flat owner has in the state of repair of other flats in the block is clear. Yet it may be less easy to find an appropriate method by which one can oblige another to repair. The ideal when flats are let on long lease is for the landlord to covenant to repair the rest of the block, or to do so if other flat owners default. Many landlords are not willing to undertake this responsibility. Other possibilities will therefore be examined.

If the owner of the flat which is out of repair has covenanted to repair it directly with the flat owner who is complaining, there should be no difficulty in enforcing that obligation. Where there is no direct contractual relationship because one or the other flat has changed hands, the problems of enforcing positive covenants have to be considered. There is also uncertainty about what remedy a flat owner could obtain. There is no reported case as yet in which a decree of specific performance has been awarded in such a case. Part of the reasoning for making such an order against a landlord in *Jeune v Queens Cross Properties Ltd* [1974] Ch 97, that the part of the building concerned was one to which the plaintiff tenants had no right of access, would apply here. Perhaps therefore the remedy of specific performance will be extended. Otherwise, the remedy would be damages.

Long leases of flats frequently contain a covenant by the landlord to enforce the tenants' covenants in similar leases of other flats in the block. To enforce a repairing covenant at second hand through a common landlord should be effective, as the landlord can use the threat of forfeiture. However, unless there are more than three years of the lease term left to run, the landlord may well have to obtain the leave of the court under the Leasehold Property (Repairs) Act 1938 before proceeding. That means he will only be able to take action in respect of serious breaches of covenant. Even in the absence of a landlord's covenant to enforce the obligations under other leases, a tenant may be able to oblige a common landlord to take action if he is being deprived of the use of part of the demised premises or is being seriously prejudiced (*Hilton v James Smith & Sons (Norwood) Ltd* (1979) 251 EG 1063). That decision— which concerned the obstruction of a right of way, which also made a parking area unusable—is open to criticism, and has yet to be applied to the enforcement of repairing obligations.

Serious want of structural repair in one flat can prejudice the stability of a neighbouring one, which enjoys an easement of support. However, that does not mean that the owner of the first flat has a duty to repair (*Sack v Jones* [1925] Ch 235). On the contrary, an easement of support does not place any obligation on the owner of the servient tenement to replace it, even if its deterioration eventually results in the support being withdrawn (*Jones v Pritchard* [1908] 1 Ch 630, 637, 638). But it does entitle the owner of the dominant tenement to go in and do any necessary work, at his own expense (*Bond v Nottingham Corporation* [1940] Ch 429, 438–9).

In addition, a flat owner may enjoy express rights of entry for this purpose, and if so their exercise and the degree to which he is entitled to repayment for the cost of work, if at all, depends on the construction of the document concerned.

It may be important for a flat owner to have a right of entry into other flats for the purpose of repairs to ensure that he has the full benefit of the NHBC guarantee on a new flat.

The tort of nuisance is committed by an occupier of property who wrongly causes or allows something deleterious to escape onto someone else's property which either causes physical damage or interferes with the beneficial use of the other property. Knowingly permitting the spread of dry rot (see *Gordon v Selico Co Ltd* [1986] 1 EGLR 71) or woodworm infestation from one flat to another could well be actionable on this basis. Where a nuisance does not arise from a human agency, there is no liability unless the defendant had, or ought to have had, notice of the danger (*Leakey v National Trust* [1980] 1 QB 485).

There is a limitation. The occupier of the other flat is not liable in nuisance for damage caused by an independent contractor whom he employs, unless the damage was foreseeable when the contract was made (*Petter v Metropolitan Properties Co (Chelsea) Ltd* (1974) 231 EG 491). In that case, a builder pierced a water pipe under the floor of a flat, and water damaged the flat underneath. At the time, the flat was unlet and the builder was employed by the landlord in modernisation work, but the result would have been the same had he been employed by another tenant. The builder was himself liable.

A property owner's responsibility for negligence is wider. Negligence is to do something without regard to its consequences, or to omit to do something, which a prudent person would have realised would damage the property of someone who should have been within his contemplation. Clearly, the acts or omissions of a flat owner in connection with the structural maintenance of his flat are likely to affect the owners of other flats in the same block. Disrepair, if serious enough to prejudice other flats, offers a cause of action independent of the flat owner's contractual duties.

5.8 Common parts

The obligation to repair the common parts of a block of flats will normally fall on the landlord or some party other than the individual flat owners. That third party may be a tenants' company, which is effectively a tenants' cooperative. Although commonly such a company is formed to hold the reversions to the leases of the individual flats, it may operate simply to provide the services required including repairs to the common parts. It may also be the leaseholder of the common parts.

5.8.1 Means of access

Occasionally it is possible to divide the areas used for access, which would otherwise be common parts, between the flat owners. In a converted house, eg, where there is one flat on each floor, each flat may be allocated the landing or hall on the same floor and a portion of the stairs. In that case, those access areas are equally part of the flats, although subject to easements for the benefit of the other flat owners, and the considerations applying to them are the same as those relating to the repair of the flats proper.

If a landlord retains the common parts and covenants to repair them, his liability is not, as it is in other cases, conditional on his being given notice that a repair is needed (*Melles & Co v Holme* [1918] 2 KB 100). This is because he is in occupation of the common parts, and there should therefore be no impediment to his observing defects as soon as they become apparent. The landlord's covenant to repair the common parts will normally be in the same terms with each of the flat owners, and in that case each of them can enforce it. For each, the measure of damage will be the effect of the landlord's default on the plaintiff's flat. That may well amount to the full cost of the work required (*Marenco v Jacramel Co Ltd* [1964] EGD 349). That others are also affected by the default does not reduce the amount recoverable, nor does it mean that they must join in the action to enforce the landlord's covenant.

The fact that the landlord grants a right of way over passages and staircases which are retained by him does not imply any obligation to keep them in repair. Where there is no express undertaking to repair, it is the person in whose favour a right of way is granted, ie the flat owner, who is entitled although not obliged to do repairs. He has a right of entry for that purpose (*Newcomen v Coulson* (1877) 5 ChD 133).

A lease may contain a term under which the tenant indemnifies the landlord against claims made by visitors to his flat in respect of personal injury or damage to goods while on the common parts. This can have the effect of exonerating the landlord from all or part of his repairing responsibility, or at least from the results of not fulfilling it. Not all such indemnities are enforceable. As occupier of the common parts, the landlord owes a common duty of care to lawful visitors to the flats

(Occupiers' Liability Act 1957). The Unfair Contract Terms Act 1977, s 4, makes an indemnity against the landlord's liability unenforceable if a number of conditions are met. These are: first, that the landlord occupies the common parts for his business purposes (s 1(3)); secondly, that the tenant 'deals as a consumer', which means that the landlord enters into the lease in the course of business, but the tenant does not (s 12); thirdly, that the indemnity does not satisfy the reasonableness test, ie, it is not fair and reasonable having regard to what the parties know or ought to have known when the lease was granted (s 11(1)); fourthly, that the indemnity is not a part of the lease which relates to the creation of the leasehold interest in land (Sched 1, para 1(b)); and fifthly, that the lease was granted on or after 1 February 1978 (s 31(1), (2)).

5.8.2 Roof

A landlord who retains possession and control of the roof of a block of flats has an obligation to repair it, unless the lease otherwise provides. A term expressly dealing with repairs to other common parts does not, even by implication, affect that duty (*Cockburn v Smith* [1924] 2 KB 119). The precise extent of this duty is not clear. In one case it was held to be an absolute duty, which made the landlord liable for damage even though he had taken reasonable care to do repairs (*Hart v Rogers* [1916] 1 KB 646). Later, the liability was limited to taking reasonable care (*Cockburn v Smith*, supra).

5.8.3 Lift

The landlord, or indeed his managing agent, can incur liability under the Health and Safety at Work etc Act 1974 involving the repair of a lift in a block of flats (*Westminster City Council v Select Managements Ltd* [1985] 1 WLR 576). The statutory duty is 'to take such measures as it is reasonable for a person in his position to take to ensure, so far as is reasonably practicable, that . . . [the lift] . . . is . . . safe and without risk to health' (s 4(2)).

5.9 Enforcement of repairing obligations

5.9.1 Appointment of manager

Tenants of flats who find that their landlord is not doing the repairs which he has a duty to do, even in cases where the tenants are obliged to pay the cost of the work and are willing to do so, may apply to the court for the appointment of a manager. The objective is to appoint someone to take the landlord's place to organise the work and collect payments for it. Such arrangements were first made under the court's inherent jurisdiction to appoint a receiver (*Hart v Emelkirk Ltd* [1987] 1 WLR 1289), but has now been put on a statutory basis (Landlord and Tenant Act 1987, ss 21–24) which, in cases where it applies, supersedes other powers. The same arrangements apply where the landlord fails to insure.

There are some cases in which this does not apply. Some landlords are exempt: resident landlords, local authorities, some other public bodies and certain housing associations. A tenant under a business tenancy cannot apply. Flats which are the functional land of a charity are not covered.

The procedure involves first giving a preliminary notice to the landlord, although the court can dispense with this requirement if it is not reasonably practicable. If the landlord does not rectify matters, the tenants must apply to the court for the appointment of someone to act as manager and/or receiver. The person nominated may well be a professional managing agent or surveyor, but can be a company formed by the tenants to manage on their behalf (*Howard v Midrome Ltd* [1991] 1 EGLR 58). The court's order can deal with the manager's remuneration.

Once an order has been made, it should be registered as a writ or order affecting land.

5.9.2 Traditional remedies

A tenant's principal remedy against a landlord who fails to repair is to sue for damages. There are alternatives. He can do the work and deduct the cost from future payments of rent (*Lee-Parker v Izzett* [1971] 1 WLR 1688), and in some circumstances may be able to deduct the cost from rent even before doing the work (*Melville v Grape Lodge Developments Ltd* (1978) 39 P&CR 179). The basis of damages may depend on the tenant's purpose in acquiring the flat. If it was to be the tenant's home, the amount is properly based on the cost of repairs done by the tenant and compensation for discomfort, loss of enjoyment and ill-health while living in a deteriorating property. When the flat was acquired as an investment, the diminution in its market value is an appropriate measure of damages (*Calabar Properties Ltd v Stitcher* [1984] 1 WLR 287). In some cases, the tenant can obtain a decree of specific performance requiring that the work be done.

By statute, a tenant can seek specific performance against a landlord or anyone else in breach of a repairing covenant (Housing Act 1974, s 125). The covenant can relate to any part of the premises of which the flat forms part, so the order could result not only from a failure to repair the plaintiff's flat, but also from disrepair to another flat or to the common parts. It could be made against the landlord, or against a fellow tenant. Despite the intervention of statute, the remedy is still a discretionary one.

Statute apart, specific performance is available against a landlord if it is clear precisely what work must be done and if the balance of convenience favours such an order (*Jeune v Queens Cross Properties Ltd* [1974] Ch 97). There is authority that the reverse does not apply: a landlord cannot obtain an order for specific performance against a tenant (*Hill v Barclay* (1810) 16 Ves Jun 402). As this decision rested at least partly on a lack of mutuality, perhaps the fact that a tenant can now obtain an order for specific performance will allow the court to grant one to a landlord.

A landlord's remedies against his tenant for breach of a repairing covenant are subject to various restraints. Forfeiture must be preceded by notice requiring the tenant to remedy the breaches (Law of Property Act 1925, s 146). That action, and an action for damages, may require the leave of the court under the Leasehold Property (Repairs) Act 1938. Any action for forfeiture, and an application for leave to commence one, should be registered by the landlord against the tenant as a pending land action (*Selim Ltd v Bickenhall Engineering Ltd* [1981] 1 WLR 1318). The amount of damages that the landlord can recover from a tenant is restricted to the amount of the diminution in the value of the reversion (Landlord and Tenant Act 1927, s 18).

Nevertheless, a flagrant breach of covenant (removing part of a parapet wall in contravention of the terms of the lease and against the landlord's known wishes) was enforced by a mandatory injunction for reinstatement granted under Order 14 (*Viscount Chelsea v Muscatt* [1990] 2 EGLR 48).

The restrictions on landlords' actions against tenants have no application to the enforcement of covenants attaching to freehold flats.

5.9.3 Secure tenants of local housing authorities

New regulations give additional rights to secure tenants of flats let by local housing authorities, but not to all secure tenants, eg not to tenants of housing associations (Secure Tenants of Local Housing Authorities (Right to Repair) Regulations 1994). They apply to large landlords, letting at least 100 houses or flats to secure tenants, and to small repairs, not likely to cost more than £250.

The landlord must promptly issue instructions to a contractor giving a limited time within which the work should be done. Different times, up to seven working days, are prescribed for different items of work. If the work is not done, the tenant may require the landlord to appoint a second contractor, who has the same period again within which to do the work. In either case, if there are exceptional circumstances beyond the control of the landlord or the contractor, the prescribed period for the work is suspended.

If the work is not done within the second period, the tenant is entitled to compensation—minimum £12, maximum £50—from the landlord.

5.10 Right of entry for inspection and repair

A flat owner will sometimes need to go onto someone else's property
in order to repair his flat. This may be the common parts over which
he has a right of way, or another flat. Even though the only reasonable
way to carry out the repair is from the other property, as when repairing
the wiring to a ceiling light to which access is obtained from under
the floor of the flat above, there is no automatic right to go in (*John
Trenberth Ltd v National Westminster Bank Ltd* (1979) 39 P&CR 104).
It is a right that can exist as an easement (*Ward v Kirkland* [1967] Ch
194). That means that the flat owner must show that an easement has
been granted to him either expressly, and in any well arranged repairing
scheme for flats that will be the case, or impliedly because a right was
exercised before the dominant tenement was sold off from joint ownership
(Law of Property Act 1925, s 62), or that it arose by prescription.

An easement of support carries with it a limited right for the owner
of the dominant tenement to repair the flat that is the servient tenement,
and the flat owner has the necessary right of entry for that purpose.
Again, the lease may grant him an express right.

To the extent that the flat owner has the right to use pipes and wires
running through other flats or the common parts, as distinct from those
in his own flat that can only be reached from elsewhere, that right carries
with it the right to enter to repair as necessary (*Pwllbach Colliery Co
Ltd v Woodman* [1915] AC 634). It makes no difference that the flat
owner does not enjoy the exclusive use of those pipes and wires.

Landlords generally reserve a right of entry to carry out repairs to
the demised premises that are their responsibility. Even if they do not
do so, the fact that they undertake repairing obligations automatically
gives them an implied licence to enter at reasonable times to carry out
the work (*Saner v Bilton* (1878) 7 ChD 815). This extends to cases where
the landlord does not positively covenant to do repairs, but where the
tenant agrees to pay him the cost of doing the work. That gives him
the right to enter to do what is required, within the scope of the tenant's
covenant to reimburse him (*Edmonton Corporation v W M Knowles &
Son Ltd* (1962) 60 LGR 124). This has been stretched even further, to
a case where there was no covenant about repairs. Both parties expected
the landlord to do the work voluntarily, and that was enough to give
him the right to enter for the purpose (*Mint v Good* [1951] 1 KB 517).

A landlord also enjoys some statutory rights of entry. If the flat is
let on an assured tenancy or a protected tenancy he has a right of access
and to all reasonable facilities for carrying out any repairs he is entitled
to do (Rent Act 1977, s 148, Housing Act 1988, s 16). Again, if the
flat is in a general improvement area or a housing action area, the landlord
has a right of entry to do repairs that are required by an improvement
notice, or under an undertaking he gives in lieu (Housing Act 1985,
s 224).

The two statutory implied repairing duties—on short lettings and under the warranty of fitness for human habitation—also give a landlord powers of entry to inspect the condition of the premises (Landlord and Tenant Act 1985, ss 8(2), 11(6)). The landlord can carry out the inspection himself, or he can give anyone else written authority to do so. He must give the tenant at least twenty-four hours' notice, and he must carry out his inspection at a reasonable time of day.

5.11 Alternative accommodation

If the state of repair resulting from the landlord's breach of covenant is so bad that the tenant has to move out, the tenant can claim the reasonable cost of alternative accommodation as part of his damages (*Calabar Properties Ltd v Stitcher* [1984] 1 WLR 287).

5.12 Buildmark scheme

The Buildmark scheme is the combined warranty and protection scheme offered by the National House-Building Council. It applies to newly built flats, as well as houses. There is a separate scheme for flats created by the conversion of existing buildings.

If damage occurs or defects become apparent that might be covered, care must be taken to ascertain just what is within the guarantee of the flat in question. The details which follow refer to the current scheme, introduced on 1 April 1988.

After completing an acceptance form (BM2), the purchaser of a new flat should receive three documents:

(1) Buildmark booklet (BM3);
(2) a Ten Year Notice (BM4); and,
(3) if applicable, a Ten Year Common Parts Notice (BM5).

Copies of the last two documents are supplied for the buyer's mortgagee.

The guarantee falls into two parts: the first is the responsibility of the seller, the second of the NHBC.

5.12.1 Cover provided

The builder is responsible, within a reasonable time and at his own expense, to put right any defect or damage reported to him within the first two years from the issue of the Ten Year Notice ('initial period'). If the flat is unoccupied and unsold for twelve months after the notice is issued, that initial period runs for twelve months from the date of the first sale of the flat. In relation to the common parts, there will be one notice for the whole block, and in most cases there will be a different initial period from that relating to the flat.

There are some exclusions from the builder's liability. Among these are: wear and tear; deterioration caused by neglect; normal dampness, condensation and shrinkage; effects of alterations or extensions after the issue of the notice. There are two exclusions of particular concern to those advising buyers. First, either of the ten year notices, relating to the flat or the common parts, may be endorsed with matters excluded from the cover. Secondly, if there has been a previous owner, anything which he could reasonably have reported, but did not, cannot be the subject of a claim by a later owner.

The builder's liability is underwritten by the NHBC, but only if he fails to honour a judgment or an arbitration award. However, if the builder is insolvent, the buyer may apply to have that condition lifted.

After the initial guarantee period, for the remainder of the ten years from the date of the ten year certificate ('structural guarantee period'), the NHBC takes responsibility. It pays the cost of rectifying major damage (extensive repairs, or complete or partial rebuilding). Again, there are exclusions. They include matters endorsed on the Ten Year Notice and damage of which notice was or could reasonably have been given to the builder during the initial guarantee period.

The NHBC cover does have financial limits. Claims must be made in writing to the NHBC at Chiltern Avenue, Amersham, Bucks HP6 5AP. Disputes are settled by arbitration.

5.12.2 Other flats

There is an extension of cover which is particularly valuable in the case of flats. Damage to one flat caused by defective work, not complying with NHBC requirements, in an adjacent building—commonly another flat—built by the same builder will be put right. However, the use of the word 'adjacent' must mean that this refers only to the flats immediately above, below or beside the one affected. That is not wholly satisfactory, because it does not, eg, cover the result of a water overflow resulting from defective workmanship from a third floor flat which damages one on the first floor. However, subject to that limitation, one flat owner can claim for the results of poor work outside his flat, whether or not a claim is made by the other owner.

The builder's obligation extends to putting right the defective work in the other flat, but only if he can gain access. For this reason, the buyer of a new flat should seek to ensure that he is granted a right to enter other flats to do repairs.

5.12.3 Common parts

Common parts are defined widely for the purposes of the NHBC Buildmark scheme. They cover all parts of the building which contain the flat which are neither within the exclusive possession of the buyer nor of any other person. That definition may result in parts of the building which are common parts so far as the leases of the flats are concerned not being covered by the guarantee, or, not so commonly, vice versa.

5.12.4 Conversions

For conversions, the NHBC insurance scheme follows the pattern of that for new flats, but for a limited period. The builder gives a guarantee for one year rather than two, and this is followed by five years' responsibility on the part of the NHBC.

5.13 Rebuilding

There is some theoretical doubt as to the extent of the right to rebuild flats that are destroyed. It has been suggested that on the total destruction of an upper floor flat let on a lease, the lease automatically comes to an end because there is no longer any subject matter of the demise. If that is the correct rule, the consequences would be serious. It would prevent rebuilding by leaseholders, and would put in jeopardy the capital value of flats held on long lease at a low rent, not only for the flat owners but also for mortgagees lending on security of them.

Although there seems to be no reported case in which the destruction of a flat has of itself brought a lease to an end, there are dicta indicating that it is possible. '. . . it is very difficult to imagine an event which could prematurely determine the lease by frustration—though I am not prepared to deny the possibility, if, eg, some vast convulsion of nature swallows up the property altogether, or buried it in the depths of the sea' (*Cricklewood Property and Investment Trust Ltd v Leighton's Investment Trust Ltd* [1945] AC 221, 229 per Viscount Simon LC). This concept receives support from the House of Lords' acceptance that the doctrine of frustration can apply to leases, although it rarely will (*National Carriers Ltd v Panalpina* (*Northern*) *Ltd* [1981] AC 675).

However, such authority as there is seems to be against a lease coming to an end on the destruction of a flat. Where the two upper floors of a warehouse were sublet and subsequently wholly consumed by fire, the subletting did not determine and the subtenant remained liable to pay the rent (*Izon v Gorton* (1839) 5 Bing NC 501). This view has also received academic support ('Impossibility and Property Law', E O Walford (1941) 57 LQR 339, 340).

In practice, it is certainly assumed by all dealing with flats that the destruction of one does not end the lease of it, so that there is a right to rebuild. That conclusion is certainly convenient. As it is not inconsistent with authority, it is suggested that it would be the view adopted by the courts.

There are difficulties all the same. These relate not only to leasehold flats, but also to those sold freehold. What is the position if, after total destruction, rebuilding becomes unlawful, eg because planning permission is refused? Clearly, the owner suffers a loss that can be compensated by insurance. But what of the flat owner's legal estate? It is no longer accepted that the ownership of a piece of land includes the ownership of a column of air above it *ad coelum*. It normally extends merely to cover any building or structure on the land, together with any space above them needed for their ordinary use (*Baron Bernstein of Leigh v Skyviews & General Ltd* [1978] QB 479). In effect, therefore, the upper boundary is flexible, accommodating such structures as are on the land for the time being. The destruction of a block of flats would normally, if it were in single ownership, bring the volume of air space in private ownership down nearer to ground level.

It is conceivable that the fact that the block had been in multiple ownership would allow of the concept of continuing ownership of blocks of airspace during a normal rebuilding period. It seems to be contrary to general principle that that should continue indefinitely without a new building. What would be the position if the block were not rebuilt and the site was compulsorily acquired ten years later? Would it be necessary for all the separate interests in the non existent flats to be bought out? These questions remain unanswered.

Chapter 6

Enforcement of Covenants

6.1 The problem

Every satisfactory scheme for managing flats involves the flat owners entering into obligations—relating, eg, to use, repairs and maintenance—that constitute a permanent code of regulations for the block. Their enforcement must not be prejudiced if the flats, the common parts or any reversion change hands. In many cases it is desirable that the covenants should be mutually enforceable by flat owners against each other.

The difficulty in the way of this is that at common law the burden of a covenant did not pass when the person who made it conveyed his freehold land to someone else. In equity, the burden of restrictive covenants, but not positive ones, bound successors in title if certain conditions were satisfied (*Tulk v Moxhay* (1848) 2 Ph 774). The most serious drawback to the common law rule, when dealing with flats, is that a positive covenant to repair or to contribute towards the cost of repairs cannot be enforced against the successors in title of the original owner of a freehold flat.

There are a number of possible ways round this difficulty, all to some extent artificial, and the result has been to reduce the number of freehold flats to a tiny minority. Of the possible solutions to the problem, which are examined below, the commonest is to let flats on long lease. Even this may not suit all circumstances, and its limitations are discussed below.

Not only must the burden of a covenant pass to successors in title, so also must the benefit. For successful enforcement by a successor to the person in whose favour a covenant was originally made, the plaintiff must show that he has the benefit of it. There should be no difficulty in this. The common law recognised that a positive covenant intended to benefit land of the covenantee ran with that land (*Sharp v Waterhouse* (1857) 7 E&B 817), and covenants are now in favour of successors in title even though not expressed to be (Law of Property Act 1925, s 78). The conveyance of the land, even without any reference to the covenant, is probably sufficient to vest the benefit in the transferee (*Griffith v*

56

Pelton [1958] Ch 205). Certainly, successors in title can sue to enforce
a covenant, even though not parties to the original document (Law of
Property Act 1925, s 56).

The position of a third party without an interest in the property must
also be considered. Flat schemes are sometimes administered by
management companies which are neither in the position of landlords,
nor do they own the common parts. Their right to collect service charge
contributions from the flat owners for the time being, notwithstanding
transfers of the flats, is essential to the viability of the arrangement.

6.2 Leases

Leases provide the most common, and probably the most adaptable,
means to ensure that the flat owners' covenants remain enforceable.
The liability for all strictly relevant covenants, whether made by the
flat owner as tenant or by the landlord, passes to the covenantor's
successors in title. This is because the landlord for the time being and
the tenant for the time being enjoy privity of estate. In addition, by
privity of contract, the original parties to the lease remain bound to
each other for the whole of the term of the lease. The wording of the
lease can restrict this last liability of one or both of the original parties
after they have parted with the interests in the property. A provision
to that effect is rarely found, and then generally only in the case of
the landlord.

Covenants that remain enforceable throughout the lease, binding and
benefiting those who for the time being are interested in it, are variously
described as 'touching and concerning the land' and 'having reference
to the subject matter of the lease'. These phrases mean the same thing
(*Breams Property Investment Co Ltd v Stroulger* [1948] 2 KB 1). The
category includes all the usual basic lease terms, eg, the covenants: to
pay rent (*Williams v Bosanquet* (1819) 1 Brod & B 238); to repair (*Martyn
v Clue* (1852) 18 QB 661); to insure (*Vernon v Smith* (1821) 5 B&Ald
1); to use the premises only as a private dwellinghouse (*Wilkinson v
Rogers* (1863) 3 New Rep 145); to obtain consent before assigning (*Hooper
v Clark* (1867) LR 2 QB 200); to supply water (*Jourdain v Wilson* (1821)
4 B&Ald 266); to appoint a housekeeper to clean the premises (*Barnes
v City of London Real Property Co* [1918] 2 Ch 18).

This category must be contrasted with covenants that are collateral.
Among covenants that have been held not to bind assignees are: to
pay a premium by instalments (*Hill v Booth* [1930] 1 KB 381); giving
an offer of first refusal of the landlord's adjoining property (*Collison
v Lettsom* (1815) 6 Taunt 224); to pay the landlord's taxes in respect
of other property (*Gower v Postmaster General* (1887) 57 LT 527). That
last decision can hardly cover a tenant's obligation to contribute to the
landlord's outgoings, including taxes, on common parts, because the

enjoyment of the facilities that they provide is certainly an integral part of the demise of the flat.

As long as the covenants in question come into the category of those immediately relevant to the property they bind successors in title, whether the covenantor is the tenant (*Spencer's Case* (1583) 5 Co Rep 16a) or the landlord (Law of Property Act 1925, s 142). Similarly, successors in title of the original covenantor can enforce them, whether they were in favour of the landlord (s 141) or of the tenant (*Spencer's Case*, supra). There is no distinction here between positive covenants and restrictive ones.

In one case, however, it can make a difference: where the flat is sublet. On a subletting, whether of the whole block or a single flat, best practice is to repeat in the sublease all the relevant covenants that appear in the head lease. Even if they are not repeated, those head lease covenants that are restrictive will bind the sub-tenant as long as he has, or is deemed to have, notice of them (*Hill v Harris* [1965] 2 QB 601). Those restrictive covenants do not require registration, as they are covenants between landlord and tenant (Land Charges Act 1972, s 2(5)).

The difficulty that using a lease does not of itself solve is making enforceable covenants by people other than the landlord or the tenant, ie, other flat owners or an independent management company. In these cases the doctrine of privity of estate does not help, because it is strictly confined to the relationship of landlord and tenant. As far as restrictive covenants are concerned, mutual enforcement between flat owners may be possible, under the general provisions relating to restrictive covenants, and the existence of leases of each of the individual flats in identical form will be helpful in establishing that there was a letting scheme.

In other cases, the best that can be done is to use the landlord as a form of guarantor. This works in two ways. First, he can covenant with the tenant to undertake the obligations in question—eg to repair other flats or to clean the common parts—if and so far as they are not performed by other flat owners or the management company. Secondly, the landlord can covenant to enforce the covenants in other tenants' leases, perhaps at the expense of the tenant calling upon him to do so. The landlord should restrict that obligation to covenants in the other leases that touch and concern the land. If it could be construed as extending, eg, to a covenant to contribute to the costs of a management company, the landlord would not be able to take enforcement action once the lease had been assigned. To have an obligation, in another lease, to enforce that covenant could therefore leave him in a difficult position.

6.3 Restrictive covenants

Covenants affecting a specified property, which are negative in nature, and are entered into to benefit other specified property, can be enforced against the successors in title of the original covenantor, subject to requirements about registration or notice (*Tulk v Moxhay* (1848) 2 Ph 774). This is an important means of controlling the use of flats. Such covenants can be used to curb excessive noise, unauthorised business use, indiscriminate parking and the like. They are, however, no help in requiring proper repairs, even if phrased negatively, eg, 'not to allow the flat to fall into disrepair'. Covenants that are essentially positive— to comply with that covenant would require repair work to be done— do not come into this category.

A scheme, a 'letting scheme' equivalent to a building scheme, applying a standard set of restrictions to all the properties covered, is appropriate for flats. This entitles the flat owners for the time being to enforce the restrictions against each other (*Elliston v Reacher* [1908] 2 Ch 665). It applies equally to freehold or leasehold dispositions. There are five conditions with which a restrictive covenant scheme must comply:

(1) The title to the flats must derive from a common seller or landlord;

(2) The flats must have been intended to be sold or let subject to standard restrictions consistent only with a general scheme of development;

(3) The party initiating the scheme must intend each flat to benefit from the scheme;

(4) The flats concerned must originally have been acquired from the person imposing the restrictions, on the basis that they were intended to benefit the other flats;

(5) The area affected by the covenants must be clear (*Reid v Bickerstaff* [1909] 2 Ch 305). This point can cause difficulty where a scheme covers a housing estate, but there should be no difficulty about boundaries where it is confined to a block of flats.

It is an advantage to have a recital in the conveyance, transfer or lease which imposes the restrictions, to help to establish that there is a scheme. It does not affect the substance of the position, but it helps to provide evidence of what is largely a matter of intention. The recital should say that the parties' intention is to impose like covenants when each flat is sold or let, in order to regulate the block in question for the mutual benefit of the flat owners.

Restrictive covenants imposed since 1925 should be registered (Land Charges Act 1972, s 2(5); Land Registration Act 1925, s 50). They will not be binding on successors in title if this is not done. The one exception is covenants between landlord and tenant, including covenants in a lease relating to property that is not demised by it (*Dartstone Ltd v Cleveland Petroleum Co Ltd* [1969] 1 WLR 1807). Although the last case is considered something of an anomaly in respect of most property, it is convenient in connection with flats. It means, eg, that a covenant by a landlord who retains the common parts that he will not permit a communal garage to be used except by residents of the flats does not require to be registered to ensure that it binds a buyer of the reversion.

Restrictive covenants that do not need to be registered bind successors in title if they have notice. A buyer must have notice of the covenants before he acquires the lease or the reversion, as the case may be. That notice can be either actual or constructive. He is taken to have notice of matters that should have come to his attention. It is hardly conceivable that anyone could purchase a lease, or a property subject to a lease, without having notice of the terms of the lease. If he did not require to see the lease in circumstances when that would be the normal thing to do, he would still have constructive notice of its contents. The question of notice should not therefore cause difficulty.

6.4 Estate rentcharges

A major step towards the satisfactory enforcement of positive covenants against successors in title to freehold properties was the introduction of the estate rentcharge by the Rentcharges Act 1977. This is a rent-charge of one of two types (s 2). It is either one to make covenants enforceable against the owner of the land for the time being, in which case the rentcharge must be for no more than a nominal amount, or, it is a rentcharge to meet or contribute to the cost of services, maintenance, repairs or insurance, of a sum no more than reasonable for that purpose. The figure can fluctuate from year to year (*Beachway Management Ltd v Wisewell* [1971] Ch 610). This type of payment was earlier held to be a rentcharge, eg, where there was a covenant to contribute to the cost of sea defences on the partition of land that benefited from them (*Morland v Cook* (1868) LR 6 Eq 252). But as covenants to pay maintenance costs have not always been similarly construed (*Halsall v Brizell* [1957] Ch 169), the rentcharge should be expressly created. The importance of the estate rentcharge is that it is exempt from the statutory provisions relating to the redemption and extinguishment of rentcharges (ss 3(3)(*b*), 8(4)).

This means that a perpetual rentcharge can be created out of a freehold flat, subject to covenants that will be permanently binding. There are various methods of enforcement. The most effective sanction is probably a right of re-entry. As an alternative, the owner of a rentcharge can distrain, which should also be effective in cases where more than a nominal sum is payable. These rights are not subject to the law against perpetuities (Perpetuities and Accumulations Act 1964, s 11(1)).

A rentcharge does not offer a simple way for flat owners to enforce covenants against each other. Only the rentcharge owner will have the power of enforcement. Rentcharges created to collect the cost of services will presumably all be vested in a single person, possibly a tenants' company. That company provides the services, incurs the cost and collects the contributions. It also provides a convenient vehicle to enforce the covenants against a recalcitrant flat owner. Effectively, that is enforcement by the majority of the flat owners. But where the obligation to provide services, and therefore the benefit of the rentcharges, is in someone else without any interest in enforcing the general covenants relating to the flats, this will not work.

If the rentcharges are only for nominal amounts, created simply for the enforcement of covenants, in whom should they be vested? Initially, they will be in the hands of the developer, but the normal reason for selling flats freehold is to rid oneself of all connection with them. As a rentcharge falls within the definition of land (Law of Property Act 1925, s 205(1)(ix)), no more than four people can hold a legal estate in it (s 34(2)). It cannot therefore be owned by more than four flat owners jointly.

The rentcharges can be conveyed to a body, be it a company or a trust, formed specially for the purpose. The beneficial owners will be the flat owners. The mechanics of transferring shares each time a flat changed hands will be daunting. As the body would be of no importance until the need arises to enforce a covenant, it seems likely that sooner or later the transfer formalities will be neglected, so that the benefit of the rentcharges will cease to be held on behalf of the flat owners for the time being. A trust may not suffer from this drawback, because the beneficiaries can be the owners of the flats for the time being, and no transfers of beneficial interests will be needed. The trustees could however be faced with difficult questions as to the extent to which the enforcement of a covenant—demanded by one flat owner—is in the interests of their beneficiaries as a whole.

For a form of deed of trust, see Precedent B:3, p 223.

This type of estate rentcharge seems unlikely to be satisfactory in practice for a block of flats. It may, however, be ideal for a pair of maisonettes where each owner is to be responsible for the repairs to his own half. No money contribution is required. Each owner could have vested in him the rentcharge issuing out of the other maisonette. It would still be necessary to ensure that the maisonette and the benefit of the rentcharge from the other one were conveyed together, but that should be easier when no third party is involved.

It has been suggested that as the Rentcharges Act 1977 makes enforceable both positive and negative covenants attached to estate rentcharges, it is not necessary to register the negative ones as restrictive covenants. This suggestion is regarded as wrong. It is not correct to say that the 1977 Act makes the covenants enforceable by statute. It merely saves certain types of rentcharge from its general policy of gradual abolition of rentcharges, and recognises the long established practice of securing rentcharges by taking covenants from the chargor. A negative covenant attached to a rentcharge is no less 'a covenant . . . restrictive of the user of land', which is the statutory definition of a restrictive covenant (Land Charges Act 1972, s 2(5)), and is therefore void against a buyer of a legal estate for money or money's worth if not registered (s 4(6)).

6.5 Enlargement of long leases

Enlarging a long lease is a method of making positive covenants enforceable against successors in title which has been suggested over many years, but seems still to be untested in the courts. It would take advantage of s 153 of the Law of Property Act 1925.

That section empowers the tenant under a long lease of a certain type to enlarge his interest into a freehold by executing a deed poll. The reason for the use of this procedure here is that 'the estate in fee simple so acquired by enlargement shall be subject to all the same . . . covenants and provisions relating to user and enjoyment, and to all the same obligations of every kind, as the term would have been if it had not been so enlarged' (s 153(8)). The argument therefore is that all that needs to be done is to demise flats on very long leases, relying on the tenants to enlarge. Covenants that touch and concern the land, the burden of which would have passed to assignees of the lease even though they were positive covenants, will then survive the enlargement and be fully enforceable.

For the section to apply, the flats have to be demised for at least 300 years, rent free or virtually so, and without any right of re-entry exercisable on breach of a condition. Probably this demonstrates the greatest snag. Without a right of re-entry, there would be no effective sanction on breach of covenant after enlargement. The covenantee would, by definition, have no reversion that a breach of covenant would damage, and so would not be able to claim damages. Further, it is not clear whether the benefit of the covenants could be effectively assigned.

Because of these uncertainties, it is not recommended that this suggested method of dealing with covenants on freehold flats be adopted.

6.6 Mutual deeds of covenant

Positive and restrictive covenants are fully enforceable between the original contracting parties. If therefore every successive flat owner covenants with every other flat owner, it ensures that the covenants are fully enforceable. Difficulties in respect of successors in title to the original covenantors are eliminated.

There are two major drawbacks to this system. The first is the proliferation of documentation. If all flat owners are to have rights against each other, all need to be involved to execute documents every time any of the flats changes hands. The second drawback is the policing of the arrangements, how to make sure that all incoming flat owners do in fact enter into the covenants. It may be that a succession of mutual deeds would be satisfactory where there is a pair of freehold maisonettes, or a very small block of flats.

Ideally, every freehold flat owner would want to have in his hands an original or duplicate deed of covenant executed by every other flat owner. In that way, he could be sure of his right to enforce the covenants, and could convince a buyer of his flat that the position was totally satisfactory. Only in the smallest blocks of flats could that number of deeds be contemplated.

The way to reduce the number of deeds required in larger blocks is to have a master deed to which incoming flat owners subscribe. This is only likely to work well when there is some central authority—such as a tenants' company or trustees responsible for maintenance—who can hold the deeds and organise the arrangements. Such a central authority could be given the duty of enforcing the covenants on behalf of the other flat owners. If it is not, each flat owner would still need proof that every newcomer had adhered to the terms of the master deed, so it would probably be necessary to circulate copies of the deeds they executed.

Ensuring that incoming flat owners execute deeds can be a problem. Even if one of the covenants is to ensure that one's successor executes a deed, the conveyance of the flat would not be invalidated if that covenant were ignored. In cases where covenants are linked to services provided regularly, or to rights of access, an effective sanction is to make them conditional on the deed having been executed. When the title is registered, a restriction can be entered on the register preventing registration of a transfer without the consent of a named person. That would allow a management company to keep control of matters. Cases involving involuntary transfer, on death or bankruptcy, could still cause problems, particularly while the flat is empty so that no-one is interested in availing themselves of the services and access rights.

6.7 Conditional easements

Where rights are granted on condition that a payment is made, the court will enforce that payment against anyone taking advantage of the right. This can be used to make the obligation to pay a service charge follow the ownership of a flat. It is not suitable for enforcing a positive duty to repair, as distinct from paying for repairs done by someone else. It does provide a way to enforce covenants to pay against the successor in title to a freehold flat.

What is not clear is how closely connected the rights and the payments have to be. In one case, plots of land were sold subject to a covenant to pay a proportion of the cost of maintaining roads, sewers and a promenade along a sea wall. The same deed gave the owners of the plots the right to use the roads and sewers. The landowners who took advantage of those rights had the obligation to make the payments, even though they were not the original covenantors (*Halsall v Brizell* [1957] Ch 169). There is no doubt that in this way a right of access to a flat granted conditionally on the flat owner for the time being contributing to the repair and maintenance of the hall and staircases would bind the flat owner for the time being to make those payments. But, what if the right of access was also subject to the flat owner paying a contribution to the cost of maintaining the roof of the whole block? The principle is that a person cannot take a benefit conferred by a deed without accepting its full terms. However, it seems reasonable to assume that the right and the obligation should have some closer link than merely appearing in the same deed. The degree of connection that may be necessary has not been decided.

There may also be problems when the flat is empty. If a flat owner simply does not occupy the property when he is entitled to, there seems no reason why he should escape his responsibilities. But if he cannot occupy the flat, because he has died, that argument is weaker. Certainly, the legal estate in the flat continues. Yet, executors might argue that although the ownership is vested in them, it is not realistic to treat them as occupiers taking advantage of access rights. It is suggested that the proper approach is, again, that they can if they choose have the benefit of the rights, and probably do very occasionally exercise them, so they should accept the obligations. However, the point has yet to be settled. The result might vary according to the particular facts of any particular case.

Chapter 7

Use

7.1 Use of flat

7.1.1 Residential use

Normally the only use which the planning legislation authorises for a flat is as a private dwellinghouse. Indeed, to subdivide a flat into more than one dwellinghouse is a material change of use that requires planning permission (Town and Country Planning Act 1990, s 55(3)(*a*)). This applies if it is used as 'two or more separate dwellinghouses'. Although the mere change of use, without physical alterations, is enough to require permission, it seems likely that some division of the flat would be needed, to create 'separate' dwellinghouses. A subletting of part of a flat does not necessarily involve any element of separation.

Planning considerations aside, and in the absence of covenants in the lease of a flat or restrictive covenants limiting its use, the flat owner is at liberty to use it for whatever purpose he likes. Indeed, a partial business use may not even deprive a tenant of statutory protection (*Royal Life Saving Society v Page* [1978] 1 WLR 1329), although this is a matter of degree.

A covenant to use the flat 'only as a private dwellinghouse' is broken by a partial business use, such as running a day school and giving dancing lessons in premises that are nevertheless still used as a residence (*Wickenden v Webster* (1856) 6 E&B 387). It is not contravened by holding an auction sale there of the occupier's furniture (*Reeves v Cattell* (1876) 24 WR 485), nor by a flat owner who shares with a friend living as a member of the family (*Segal Securities Ltd v Thoseby* [1963] 1 QB 88).

A company tenant can comply with a covenant to use a flat as its own residence if its directors, its staff or its own guests live there. However, if, as a matter of business, it grants licences to residential occupiers, that is in breach of covenant (*Falgar Commercial SA v Alsabahia inc* [1986] 1 EGLR 41).

A flat may be expressly intended for both residential and business use. A covenant in a tenancy agreement to use a flat as a residential flat and partly for dental practice is a positive covenant to do both, although the tenant need not practise the dentistry personally. The user covenant does not override other covenants. A covenant not to install machinery without the landlord's consent must be complied with, even though the machinery is essential for the practice (*A Peachey & Co Ltd v Smeyatsky* (1974) 231 EG 243).

The appropriate remedy against a flat owner who breaks a covenant restricting the use of his flat is generally an injunction.

7.1.2 Immoral use

There is no implied covenant by a tenant against using a flat for immoral purposes (*Burfort Financial Investments Ltd v Chotard* (1976) 239 EG 891). An express covenant to that effect is often imposed on tenants. There may be some difficulty in interpreting such a covenant, because it is to be understood in the context of the modern use of the expression. Changing views are illustrated by a decision in 1911 that to let a flat to a man's mistress on the basis that the lover would pay the rent was to let for an immoral purpose (*Upfill v Wright* [1911] 1 KB 506). This was doubted in 1977 when a tenant who allowed his son and the son's mistress to occupy premises as man and wife did not use them for an immoral purpose (*Heglibiston Establishment v Heyman* (1977) 36 P&CR 351).

There may be an overlap with a covenant not to use the flat for an illegal purpose. It is an offence knowingly to permit all or part of the premises that the accused occupies to be used as a brothel (Sexual Offences Act 1956, s 35(1)).

7.1.3 Illegal use

On any letting of a flat, there is an implied covenant not to use it for an illegal purpose. There is often an express covenant to that effect too. The illegality must be in the use of the flat itself. If the tenant is convicted of the illegal possession of drugs, there is only a breach of covenant if the flat has been used as a hiding place, as distinct from the tenant having them about his person when he happened to be in the flat (*Abrahams v Wilson* [1971] 2 QB 88).

Apart from criminal offences, a covenant against illegal use can be broken by using the flat in contravention of planning law.

7.2 Interference with enjoyment

7.2.1 Nuisance

Nuisance is the use of one property in a manner which unreasonably interferes with the use and enjoyment of another. It is of particular concern in connection with flats, where properties in separate occupation are grouped together. Actions which can constitute nuisance are both those which affect the fabric of the flat, and also those which interfere with the flat owner's lifestyle there. In the latter category comes shouting, banging and ringing doorbells (*Palmar v Loder* [1962] CLY 2233). But there is a limit to personal liability. A flat owner pestered in a similar manner by an unwanted admirer is not liable to other flat owners in the block if she does everything she can to deter the man (*Commercial General Administration Ltd v Thomsett* (1979) 250 EG 547).

Neighbours have to show some tolerance of one another. The use to which a complainant seeks to put his flat, and complains that he cannot, must be 'not merely according to elegant or dainty modes and habit of living, but according to plain and sober and simple notions among English people' (*Walter v Selfe* (1851) 4 DeG&Sm 315, 322 per Knight-Bruce VC). The standard can vary according to the circumstances. 'What would be a nuisance in Belgrave Square would not necessarily be so in Bermondsey' (*Sturges v Bridgman* (1879) 11 ChD 852, 865 per Thesiger LJ). Minor interferences are not actionable. 'The convenience of such a rule may be indicated by calling it a rule of give and take, and live and let live' (*Bamford v Turnley* (1852) 3 B&S 62, 84 per Bramwell B).

Accordingly, noise which is necessary although inconvenient, made in the course of executing repairs, is not generally a nuisance. Interference with health and physical comfort is treated more seriously than things of lesser importance, eg television reception (*Bridlington Relay Ltd v Yorkshire Electricity Board* [1965] Ch 436). If a flat owner is unusually sensitive, that added vulnerability does not justify complaints about matters that would otherwise not be a nuisance (*Robinson v Kilvert* (1889) 41 ChD 88). Deliberate and malicious acts intended to discomfort a neighbour cannot be justified on the basis of normal reciprocity (*Christie v Davey* [1893] 1 Ch 316).

A flat owner taking an action for nuisance may sue for damages or for an injunction to stop the action of which he is complaining. An injunction can be granted not only against specific acts, but also against doing any act that will involve any injurious result. A flat owner was enjoined against doing any act which might create noise which was or would become a nuisance to the occupier of the flat below (*Charles v Trott* (1973) 227 EG 1857). A neighbour who persists in creating a nuisance in defiance of an injunction is guilty of contempt of court, and in an extreme case he may be ordered not to occupy his own flat (*Liburd v Cork* (1981) 78 LSG 566).

A flat owner with a valid complaint about the use of another flat sometimes has a right of action not only against the other flat owner, but also against their common landlord. In one case, a flat roof above the sitting room in one flat, already let on a long lease, was converted by the landlord into a terrace and roof garden for the flat above, which he then let on a long lease. The use of the terrace caused noise which

was a nuisance to the owner of the lower flat. He was successful in
an action against the common landlord, for breach of his covenant for
quiet enjoyment. The Court of Appeal added that had the action for
nuisance against the owner of the upper flat not been abandoned, he
would have been entitled to an indemnity from the landlord (*Sampson
v Hodson-Pressinger* [1981] 3 All ER 710). The principle is that the landlord
is liable if he has expressly or impliedly authorised his tenant to create
or continue a nuisance (*Harris v James* (1876) 45 LJQB 545). He is
not responsible where the tenant chooses a course of conduct that creates
a nuisance, when he could perfectly well have carried out the purpose
of the letting in another way which would not have had that result
(*Rich v Basterfield* (1847) 4 CB 783).

7.2.2 Quiet enjoyment

In most leases the landlord covenants that the tenant will have 'quiet
enjoyment', and a covenant to that effect will be implied if the lease
is silent (*Kenny v Preen* [1963] 1 QB 499). In principle, this guarantees
the tenant against disturbance caused by people exercising legitimate
rights, ie doing lawful acts, not unlawful ones for which there would
be other sanctions such as an action for nuisance. However, it has also
extended to unlawful acts.

Examples of acts which have been held to break a covenant for quiet
enjoyment are: failing to stop adjoining flats being used for immoral
purposes, when the landlord had enforceable covenants forbidding such
use from the tenants of those flats (*Jaeger v Mansions Consolidated Ltd*
(1903) 87 LT 690); removing doors and windows to make a flat
uninhabitable (*Lavender v Betts* [1942] 2 All ER 72); erecting a tall building
next door which caused smoke to blow down the tenant's chimneys
and made rooms uninhabitable (*Tebb v Cave* [1900] 1 Ch 642).

The covenant specifies the people for whose acts the landlord is
responsible. The most common form of covenant is a qualified one,
which limits responsibility to the acts of the landlord, and anyone claiming
through, under or in trust for him. Implied covenants are limited in
this way (*Jones v Lavington* [1903] 1 KB 253). A person 'claims under'
the landlord if the landlord created his interest, but not if he merely
holds under him. So, for example, a tenant of a flat whose lease was
granted by the landlord's predecessor in title does not claim through
the current landlord (*Celsteel Ltd v Alton House Holdings Ltd (No 2)*
[1987] 2 EGLR 48).

7.3 Physical interference

7.3.1 Water overflow

A particular cause of difficulty in flats, which can constitute a nuisance, is damage caused by water overflowing from a flat above. The occupier of the upper flat must be negligent if he is to be liable. Even though water does escape and does cause damage, there is no liability where the defendant genuinely believes that the system has been turned off (*Tilley v Stevenson* [1939] 4 All ER 207), nor where the cause is a cistern that overflows because a valve develops a fault without warning (*Ross v Fedden* (1872) LR 7 QB 661). Even if the defendant is negligent, he is not liable for the resulting damage if the immediate cause of the overflow is some third party's malicious act (*Rickards v Lothian* [1913] AC 263). Further, a flat owner is not negligent simply because he does not regularly inspect the overflow pipe from a wash basin which later overflows (*Hawkins v Dhawan* [1987] 2 EGLR 157).

Although in some cases there is strict liability for damage caused by the escape of water artificially accumulated on property, under the rule in *Rylands v Fletcher* (1868) LR 3 HL 330, this will not apply here, even where the damage results from a burst cistern. Where the water is collected on the property for the benefit of tenants and with their knowledge, this head of liability does not apply (*Anderson v Oppenheimer* (1880) 5 QBD 602). But the deemed consent does not apply where the installation is basically faulty (*A Prosser & Son Ltd v Levy* [1955] 1 WLR 1224).

A flat owner is not liable for the escape of water from his flat caused by an independent contractor, provided that he is not negligent in choosing the contractor (*Blake v Woolf* [1898] 2 QB 426) and that the damage was not foreseeable when the contract with the contractor was made (*Petter v Metropolitan Properties Co (Chelsea) Ltd* (1974) 231 EG 491). The contractor may well be liable himself.

This contrasts with the case of a water overflow caused by an employee. The employer is liable for the employee's actions in the course of his employment (*Ruddiman & Co v Smith* (1889) 60 LT 708).

A flat owner will often be insured against damage to his flat and its contents from water coming from a flat above, and also against his liability to others arising from an overflow of water from his own flat.

7.3.2 Fire

At common law, a property owner was absolutely liable for the consequences of fire escaping from his premises, unless it was started by act of God or a stranger. This liability is now restricted by the Fires Prevention (Metropolis) Act 1774, which is not restricted to London (*Sinott v Bowden* [1912] 2 Ch 414). It exonerates a property owner from liability for a fire that begins on his property 'accidentally' (s 86). This has been interpreted to refer only to fires caused by mere chance (*Filliter v Phippard* (1847) 11 QB 347), or where the cause is unknown. The defendant must show that he has the benefit of the Act's protection (*I&J Hyman (Sales) Ltd v A Benedyk & Co Ltd* [1957] 2 Lloyd's Rep

601). The Act does not affect a flat owner's liability for a fire caused by negligence (*Musgrove v Pandelis* [1919] 2 KB 43), or as a result of a nuisance (*Williams v Owen* [1955] 1 WLR 1293). A fire started by an independent contractor can even make a flat owner liable if he had a degree of control over what the independent contractor was doing (*Balfour v Barty-King* [1957] 1 QB 496).

7.4 Use of other flats

7.4.1 Residential use

Where all the flats in a block are let for residential purposes, and this is done to implement a scheme of letting for that purpose, the effect is to impose a restriction to residential use on the whole block. Each flat owner is entitled to ensure that the rest of the block is not put to any other use, even though there is no express covenant to that effect in his favour.

There must be some evidence that there was a scheme for the general management of the building. The use of standard agreements may provide that evidence: '. . . where the landlord enters into such an agreement with each tenant it is obviously intended to be and is, as a matter of fact, for the benefit of all the tenants' (*Hudson v Cripps* [1896] 1 Ch 265, 268 per North J). However, this does not inevitably follow from the use of a standard agreement if there is another reason for adopting such agreements, eg compliance with head lease covenants (*Kelly v Battershell* [1949] 2 All ER 830).

Once there is evidence of a residential letting scheme, a flat owner can take action if the remainder of the block is put to some other use, eg a hotel (*Alexander v Mansions Property Ltd* (1900) 16 TLR 431) or offices (*Gedge v Bartlett* (1900) 17 TLR 43). The remedy will be either an injunction or damages.

7.4.2 Immoral use

A landlord who lets all the flats in a block on agreements in which each individual tenant covenants not to use his flat for immoral purposes may be in breach of his covenant for quiet enjoyment to one tenant, if he does not enforce another tenant's covenant against immoral use. 'It is perfectly clear that the landlord himself, having all these covenants, the object of which is to secure that those premises shall be properly and respectably occupied, cannot be allowed himself to violate that obligation and assist in conducting them as brothels' (*Jaeger v Mansions Consolidated Ltd* (1903) 87 LT 690, 697 per Collins MR).

7.5 Common parts

The principles governing the use of the common parts are the same
as those that apply to the rest of the building. Where there is a letting
scheme, their use as contemplated by the scheme must remain
undisturbed. If all the flat owners covenant in the same terms with a
common landlord only to use the common parts in certain ways, the
landlord may be obliged to enforce one flat owner's covenant at the
suit of another.

The occupier of the common parts, often the landlord or perhaps
a tenants' company to whom they have been let, can also be liable for
nuisance created by the use of them. This is unusual. A further source
of liability is illustrated by the conviction of a management company
under the Control of Pollution Act 1974 as a result of the excessive
noise coming from the lift in a block of flats that they managed (*A
Lambert Flat Management Ltd v Lomas* [1981] 2 All ER 280). The
conviction was upheld notwithstanding that the flat owners might not,
in that particular case, have had any civil action.

7.6 Building flats

Restrictive covenants imposed on freehold land, or by long leases, may
prevent the building of flats. Restrictions may limit what is built on
land to houses, or to no more than a specified number of dwellings.

The general jurisdiction of the Lands Tribunal to discharge or modify
restrictive covenants (Law of Property Act 1925, s 84; Law of Property
Act 1969, s 28) can be invoked to seek authority to build flats where
they would otherwise be forbidden. The grounds upon which an order
can be made are:
(a) that changes in the character of the property or the neighbourhood,
    or other material circumstances, make the restriction obsolete;
(b) where a restriction is contrary to the public interest or does not
    secure to those entitled to its benefit any practical benefits of
    substantial value, that its continued existence will impede some
    reasonable user of the land for public or private use;
(c) that those of full age and capacity entitled to the benefit of it
    agree;
(d) that the discharge or modification will not injure those entitled
    to the benefit of it.

Even if the development of flats on the land would be reasonable,
success in an application to the Lands Tribunal is not assured. Certainly
the fact that planning consent has been granted is not conclusive. Ground
(b) was introduced in 1969 with the object of increasing the number
of cases in which a discharge or modification would be ordered. In
considering applications in connection with proposals to build flats, the
tribunal has placed a wide interpretation on the expression 'practical

benefits of substantial value'. It includes the peace and quiet of a garden (*Re Beardsley's Application* (1972) 25 P&CR 233 (*LT*)) and space, quiet and light (*Re Wards Construction* (*Medway*) *Ltd's Application* (1973) 25 P&CR 223 (*LT*)). Even where no-one was entitled to object to the modification, because the original covenant to build no more than three private dwellinghouses was imposed only for the benefit of the then sellers and not for the benefit of other parts of the estate once sold off, the tribunal exercised its discretion and refused the application because it would be injurious to neighbouring owners (*Re Wrightson's Application* (1961) P&CR 189 (*LT*)).

There is an alternative course for a developer who wants to do a conversion. The county court has jurisdiction to vary the terms of a restrictive covenant or a lease prohibiting or restricting the conversion of a house into two or more flats (Housing Act 1985, s 610). The court must be satisfied that changes in the neighbourhood render the house as a whole no longer readily capable of being let as a single unit. This section cannot be used where two houses are to be converted into flats that will extend across the old boundary and will consist of parts of both of the old houses (*Josephine Trust Co Ltd v Champagne* [1963] 2 QB 160).

Chapter 8

Insurance

8.1 The fabric

Insurance is an area of particular concern in a block of flats. Each flat owner is vitally interested in the continuing repair, and indeed existence, of all the other parts of the block, both the other flats and the common parts. Insurance gives the most satisfactory guarantee of performance of obligations with that aim. Insurance arrangements are most easily made in the leases of individual flats, but if flats are sold freehold they are one of the matters to be dealt with in mutual covenants.

When flats are let on short leases, the landlord normally insures although the lease often does not mention the point. The landlord treats the insurance premium as one of his overheads in letting the flat and does not expressly recharge it to the tenant. In long leases the insurance obligation should be expressly imposed. The premium is normally the responsiblity of the tenant, either because he effects the policy or because he is required to reimburse the landlord. The question whether it is better to provide for the landlord to insure or whether the tenant should do so, resolves itself into a choice between having a single policy to cover the whole block, or a separate policy for each flat. This is considered in the next section.

Whichever party has obligation to insure, the matters with which the covenant should deal are the same.

8.1.1 Sum insured

The proper insurance cover is the full rebuilding cost, which is the amount of damages that would be recovered on default (*Burt v British Transport Commission* (1955) 166 EG 4). This may differ significantly from the market value, which may be lower than the current rebuilding cost (*Reynolds v Phoenix Assurance Co Ltd* (1978) 247 EG 995), or higher (*C R Taylor (Wholesale) Ltd v Hepworths Ltd* [1977] 1 WLR 659). It is prudent and permissible to include an allowance for inflation which will increase the cost during the period before rebuilding can start (*Gleniffer Finance Corporation Ltd v Bamar Wood & Products Ltd* (1978)

73

37 P&CR 208). The sum insured is also generally increased by percentages to cover professional fees and site clearance costs. For large blocks of flats, it should be remembered that more professional services may be required than in reconstructing a smaller building. It may be necessary to employ, eg, structural engineers. The percentage allowance for fees should cover such contingencies.

8.1.2 Risks covered

The covenant must state the risks the policy is to cover. It is best to list the risks, but two points should be kept in mind. First, the requirements should not go wider than insurance is from time to time available in the market. For example insurance against subsidence is universally offered subject to an excess borne by the insured. An unqualified covenant to insure against subsidence would result in the party who covenants underwriting the remainder of the risk (*Enlayde Ltd v Roberts* [1917] 1 Ch 109). Secondly, if the landlord insures and the tenant pays the premium, there should be the chance to add new risks as the need arises and cover becomes available. Unless the lease makes provision for this, the tenant will not be liable to pay the premium attributable to any additional risk (*Upjohn v Hitchens* [1918] 2 KB 48). It is suggested that the lease should list the risks, subject to the qualification 'to the extent that insurance is for the time being generally available against such risks to flats' and with an extension to such other risks as the landlord may reasonably require.

8.1.3 Parties

Who is to effect the insurance policy will be considered further in the next section. It should be noted, however, that where a lease specifies the names in which a policy is to be taken out, it is a breach of covenant to add a further name (*Nokes v Gibbon* (1856) 26 LJ Ch 433). If it is decided that the tenant shall insure, the landlord will generally require that the policy is taken out in their joint names. It is as well to add that either party may require others to be named as joint insured persons if it is reasonable to do so. That allows mortgagees of the lease of the flat, and of the reversion, to be named on the policy.

8.2 Insurance of block or each flat

In granting long leases of flats, the developer must decide whether the flats will be insured individually by the lessees, or whether the block will be insured as a whole by the landlord. Where flats are sold freehold, there is generally no practicable way to ensure that the block is insured as such, so there is no choice to be made. The decision in leasehold developments depends on a number of factors, not all of which point to the same conclusion. These will be dealt with in turn.

8.2.1 Amount of cover

A single policy covering the whole building is the easiest way to ensure that the block is fully insured. When building costs are constantly rising, the amount of cover should be regularly adjusted. Ideally this will involve a professional valuation. An inexpensive alternative is a policy which index links the sum insured, eg to the 'Building' housing cost index prepared by the Royal Institution of Chartered Surveyors.

A landlord, whether the developer or a tenants' company, can ensure that separate policies covering the individual flats comply with these criteria. However, monitoring compliance, particularly when flats change hands, can be burdensome.

There are occasions, if a single policy is effected, when individual flat owners consider that their particular flat is underinsured. When costs rise particularly steeply, the buyer of a flat in the course of a year of insurance can find his mortgagee demanding that the flat be insured for more than its proportion of the sum insured under the block policy. Landlords are generally reluctant to adjust the sum insured between policy renewals, if only because of the work that would then be involved in collecting contributions from other flat owners to the increased premium. There are two possible solutions to this problem.

The first of these is that the sum insured under the block policy can be stated in the policy to be allocated between the flats in a specified way. This allows the amount of cover for one flat to be adjusted separately. This is troublesome, because detailed consideration should be given to the relative costs of building flats at the different levels. The second solution is that the tenant can effect supplementary insurance. Provided the new policy is expressly written to provide additional cover, there will be no overlap which could result in an abatement of the sums payable under each policy. Supplementary insurance should be relatively cheap, and presumably will be temporary until the next renewal of the block policy.

8.2.2 Payment of premiums

If the flats are separately insured, the landlord will wish to assure himself that the premiums are paid promptly to keep the policies in force. He can do this by inspecting the policies and premium receipts—the lease needs to give him power to require them to be produced (*Chaplin v Reid* (1858) 1 F&F 315)—but this is a burdensome chore. From the landlord's point of view, this argues for a single policy.

The interest of the tenants is not the precise reverse of this. They are also concerned that the whole building remains insured, because damage to a part that was not insured could prevent or delay reinstatement of their own flats. A lease which requires the landlord to insure the whole block can also require him to provide the tenant with proof that he has complied with his covenant. It is not feasible to arrange for each tenant to prove to every other tenant that he has insured his flat with a separate policy. Here again, therefore, the advantage lies in a single policy for the whole block.

8.2.3 Insurer

It is better to have a single insurer responsible for the cover on the whole block. If a claim arises, and more than one insurer has issued policies covering the property, there is the danger of a dispute between them as to the division of responsibility. This can delay settlement as effectively as if liability were contested. A single policy covering the block is one way to ensure that there will be no inter-insurer disputes.

To achieve the same effect, a lease which requires the tenant to insure may also require that he does so with a named insurer, or one whom the landlord nominates or approves. In such a case, there are statutory safeguards for the tenant, who may otherwise be required to take out an unnecessarily expensive policy. A tenant may challenge his landlord's nomination of an insurer on the ground that the insurance available from that source is unsatisfactory in any respect or that the premium is excessive. If the tenant's challenge succeeds, a court may order the landlord to nominate a different, specified, insurer or one who satisfies requirements which the order lays down (Landlord and Tenant Act 1987, Sched 3, para 8). This does not apply in the case of a short letting of a flat by a local authority and some other public authority landlords (para 9).

8.2.4 Claims

If the landlord takes out a single insurance policy on the block, flat owners will wish to be assured that their rights are not prejudiced, above all their rights to claim the money to reinstate their own property if it is destroyed or damaged. In a small block, it may be possible to effect a single policy in the joint names of all those interested in the property. This gives each flat owner direct contractual rights against the insurer. It also means that the insurer will not be able to exercise any right of subrogation against a flat owner. The disadvantage is that any settlement of a claim will be a payment in favour of all the policyholders jointly.

An alternative adopted in practice is for the names of the flat owners, and indeed their mortgagees, to be noted on the policy as persons interested in the property. The legal significance of this arrangement is not clear. There is no contract between the insurers and those with their names endorsed on the policy. The insurer's obligation remains one to pay the insurance moneys to the insured person on a claim arising. This does not seem to be displaced or supplemented by any form of trust in favour of those whose names are noted. Again, the insurers have no duty to tell them if the policy is allowed to lapse. Possibly, the insurer is prevented from denying that those whose names are noted have an interest in the property for the purposes of s 83 of the Fires Prevention (Metropolis) Act 1774, but this is a very limited advantage.

A particular difficulty in which tenants may find themselves is now ameliorated by statute. A policy taken out by the landlord may require that notice be given of any claim within a limited period. Breach of that condition could mean the chance to claim being lost. As a matter of contract, it is for the landlord to claim, because the tenant is not party to the policy, and if he does not, the benefit of the insurance is lost. However, it is now open to a tenant to notify the insurer of any insured damage to the flat, or any other part of the building in which it is. He must give notice within six months, or any longer period allowed by the policy. Forms of notice may be prescribed (Landlord and Tenant Act 1987, Sched 3, para 7). This does not apply to short leases where the landlord is a local authority or certain other public authorities (para 9).

8.2.5 Mortgagees' rights

The position of a flat owner's mortgagee is similar to that of the flat owner himself. He will wish to be sure that the flat in which he is interested is adequately insured, and that if it comes to it he can enforce payment of the insurance moneys. Many large lending institutions prefer to arrange the insurance of all the properties mortgaged to them under their own block policy. Among the advantages to them of this arrangement are: they can negotiate the precise terms of the policy, they can be sure that the premiums are promptly paid and they can earn commission on the premiums paid by the borrowers. Formerly, some building societies sought to insist on their own insurance arrangements, even where the lease of the flat to be mortgaged provided for the landlord to insure the whole block under a single policy. It is now normal for building societies to fall in with the arrangements envisaged in the lease.

8.2.6 Policy conditions

Before settling upon a single insurance policy to cover a block of flats, it is prudent to consider the effect of the general law of insurance and the conditions of the proposed policy. Every policy is a contract *uberrimae fidei*. If the landlord effects the policy he must be in a position to ensure that he is able to disclose all the information that the insurers will require. If he cannot, there is a danger of the policy being voidable. Although it cannot be infallible, the leases of the flats should contain a tenant's covenant to disclose to the landlord anything relevant. That may at least bring the matter to the tenant's attention.

The greater the extent of the policy, the greater the risk of something that may lead to the repudiation of a claim. A policy may well, eg, contain a condition that the amount paid on claims shall abate rateably to the extent that there is any other insurance covering the same loss. This type of clause can take effect even if the other policy was taken out by someone else. So the landlord's claim under the policy taken out on the block could be prejudiced by insurance taken out by the tenant. Or again, a condition that the insured must not admit or negotiate any claim is common. In some policies on blocks of flats, 'the insured' means not only the landlord who took out the policy, but also the flat owners.

The point can also be covered by a tenant's covenant, but for two reasons it is better that a more satisfactory policy wording be negotiated. The principle should be that neither the landlord nor any flat owner is prejudiced by any act or omission of any other flat owner. To rely only on a lease covenant to comply with the policy conditions means that on contravention, the landlord is being forced back onto reliance on the estate of the tenant instead of having the backing of the insurers. Also, it may be difficult to guarantee passing the benefit of any such covenants to other flat owners.

8.3 Common parts

The fabric of the common parts should be insured against the same risks as the flats, and if a single policy is effected for the block it will automatically be included.

Extra insurance will often be needed for the common parts. Specialist plant, particularly lifts and boilers, is generally subject to separate policies which require regular maintenance inspections, and may be linked to a service providing them. The contents of the common parts should also be insured. This policy will generally cover not only furniture and carpets, but also television aerials.

8.4 Information

A tenant can require the landlord to whom he pays a service charge which includes a sum payable for insurance to supply him with a written summary of the insurance then covering the block. With the tenant's agreement, the request can be made by the secretary of a recognised tenants' association which represents him. The request is duly made if served on the landlord's agent, or the person who receives rent for him. The landlord has a month in which to supply the summary.

The summary must include the sum insured, any amount of cover attributed to the flat, the insurer's name and the risks covered. Instead of a summary, the landlord may supply a copy of the policy (Landlord and Tenant Act 1985, Schedule, para 2).

Within six months after obtaining a summary or a copy of the policy, the tenant or the secretary of the association may require from the landlord reasonable facilities for inspecting and taking copies or extracts of the policy and documents providing evidence of payment of premiums (Landlord and Tenant Act 1985, Schedule, para 3). If it is a head landlord who insures, the request must be passed on to him and he has to provide the immediate landlord with a summary or copy policy and give inspection and copying facilities (para 4).

Failure to comply with these duties without reasonable excuse is a summary offence, carrying a fine of up to £2,500 (Landlord and Tenant Act 1985, Schedule, para 6).

8.5 Rebuilding impossible

There are circumstances in which, although premises are insured, rebuilding or reinstatement of damage is impossible. An example is when planning permission to rebuild is refused, perhaps because of a change in the allocation of the land following a revision of the structure plan for the area.

If the lease does not say what is to happen in such a case, the insurance proceeds will go to the party who paid the premiums, whatever name the policy was in (*Re King decd, Robinson v Grey* [1963] Ch 459). But if the parties agree to abandon rebuilding, the money will be divided between them in the proportions of the value of their interests immediately before the damage (*Beacon Carpets Ltd v Kirby* [1985] QB 755).

It may nevertheless be wise to make express provision in a lease.

If the block was covered by a single policy, there will have to be a division between the flat owners, as well as one between the landlord and the tenants. The leases can provide that an equal share should be attributed to each flat. If the flats are of different sizes, this will not be acceptable, and there will have to be a valuation. Logically, this would relate to the comparative building costs of each flat—because the total insurance figure should be the total rebuilding cost—but this would involve the artificial and unrealistic concept of building each of the flats individually. A comparison of open market value, and division in those ratios, is likely to be more acceptable to the flat owners.

Where the landlord is a tenants' company, so that any part of the insurance money allocated to the landlord will subsequently fall to be divided between the tenants as part of the company's assets, there is no point in allocating any part to the landlord. In that case, it is best expressly to provide that the whole of the proceeds is to go to the tenants, to avoid dispute. The argument applies particularly to the part of the proceeds attributable to the common parts. If they are, in effect, owned cooperatively by the tenants, then if they cannot be rebuilt their value might as well be distributed to the tenants as quickly as possible.

8.6 Loss of use

Insurance policies covering residential premises do not usually offer cover against loss of use. A landlord may have cover against loss of rent as a result of damage from any insured risk, but in the case of a ground rent this is minimal. A rack rent tenant may be indemnified against rent due during a period when the flat is unusable. This cover is generally provided as an extension to a policy covering the contents of a flat. If the lease includes a cesser of rent proviso, suspending the rent during any period when the flat is unusable because of insured damage, the insurance cover will be unnecesary for the tenant, to the extent that they overlap.

Exceptionally, there are policies which offer flat owners indemnity against the cost of alternative accommodation if a flat is rendered uninhabitable or access to it is denied, subject to certain limits.

8.7 Escape of water

One of the commonest causes of damage originating in one flat and taking its toll in another is water, whether from damaged or defective plumbing or simply from an overflowing bath.

Subject to exclusions for premises left empty, comprehensive insurance policies generally cover the escape of water from tanks and pipes. This normally covers damage resulting from freezing and from defective heating systems. It would not cover carelessness. The owner of the flat from which the water escapes will often be liable for damages for creating a nuisance. His contents insurance policy may well include an extension indemnifying him against any claim against him.

Although it is not usual, it is for consideration whether the lease of a flat should oblige the flat owner to effect such insurance, in order to reduce the possible causes of dissent amongst occupiers of the block.

8.8 Public and employee liability

The person in whom the common parts are vested should insure against liability to third parties. Even though this may be a tenants' company, it may incur liability, as occupier of defective premises, to one of the flat owners who is injured as a consequence. When a single policy covers the fabric of the whole block, and extends to public liability, it is important to ensure that this is covered. Under such a policy, the insurers may be indemnifying the flat owner, as an insured person, in respect of damage to his flat. A public liability policy normally covers third party claims, rather than a claim by one of the insured persons against another. If damage to individual flats is covered in this way, the policy wording should clearly show that the leaseholder of one flat may be regarded as a third party in pursuing a claim against the landlord holding common parts, or indeed against any other flat owner.

A landlord who employs anyone to perform duties in connection with the flats, eg porters, cleaners, gardeners, maintenance men, must insure against his liability for personal injury to the employees (Employers' Liability (Compulsory Insurance) Act 1969, s 1(1)). This does not apply where an independent contractor is engaged for the purpose (s 2(1)). The Act covers 'every employer carrying on any business', but the very wide definition of 'business' found in the Landlord and Tenant Act 1954, s 23(2), is adopted for this purpose (s 1(3)(c)). The result is that the only landlord likely not to be covered by the provision is a single individual.

Chapter 9

Dispositions

9.1 General principles

The general rule is that the tenant of a flat is fully entitled to dispose of his flat, whether by assigning the lease or subletting, unless one of the terms of the lease or tenancy agreement restricts that freedom (*Keeves v Dunn, Nunn v Pellegrini* [1924] 1 KB 685; *Leith Properties Ltd v Byrne* [1983] QB 433). Short leases frequently vary this position. The tenant covenants not to assign, to sublet or both ('an absolute covenant'), or not to do so without the landlord's consent ('a qualified covenant'). A breach of this covenant renders the lease subject to forfeiture, if the landlord reserved a right to forfeit which he normally will have done. The same variations are found, although not so frequently, in long leases.

9.2 Special cases

9.2.1 Assured tenancies

With certain exceptions, a term is implied by statute into every periodic statutory tenancy that the tenant will not assign, underlet or part with possession of the whole or any part of the property (Housing Act 1988, s 15). The proviso that consent is not to be unreasonably withheld, usually implied by s 19(1) of the Landlord and Tenant Act 1927, does not apply. The cases in which this does not apply are certain contractual, not statutory, periodic tenancies. They are those which contain an express provision prohibiting disposals by the tenant, whether absolutely or conditionally, and those for which a premium was charged.

9.2.2 Regulated tenancies

Until the contractual protected tenancy comes to an end, whether the tenant may assign or sublet depends on the tenancy terms. All the same, if without the landlord's consent the tenant assigns the tenancy or sublets the whole of the flat, or all that had not already been sublet, the landlord has a statutory ground for possession if it is reasonable for the court to make an order (Rent Act 1977, Sched 15, Pt I, Case 6). Subletting for only a limited period, and not necessarily at the date of the court hearing, suffices to provide grounds for possession (*Finkle v Strzelczyk* [1961] 1 WLR 1201). However, a landlord who unconditionally accepts rent after an assignment, and in full knowledge of the facts, sufficiently consents to preclude any right to possession (*Hyde v Pimley* [1952] 2 QB 506).

A statutory tenancy of a flat cannot be assigned. A purported assignment ends the tenancy, although if the landlord agrees to it the effect is of a surrender followed by the grant of a new tenancy (*Collins v Claughton* [1959] 1 WLR 145).

9.2.3 Secure tenancies

With a few exceptions, it is not possible to assign a secure tenancy of a flat (Housing Act 1985, s 91(1)). The Act does not spell out the consequences of purporting to do so, but presumably there is no legal effect. The exceptions to this general rule are, first, fixed term tenancies granted before 5 November 1982, and secondly, assignments under a property adjustment order, to a person to whom the tenancy could have been transmitted on the death of the tenant and in the course of an authorised exchange.

It is automatically a term of a secure tenancy of a flat that the tenant may not sublet or part with possession of it without the landlord's written consent, although there is a statutory right to take lodgers (Housing Act 1985, s 93(1)).

9.2.4 Right to buy leases

A lease of a flat granted as a result of a secure tenant exercising his right to buy cannot normally include any restriction on the tenant's right to assign or sublet. If it does, the provision is void (Housing Act 1985, Sched 6, para 17(1)). The exception relates to flats in special rural areas, which can contain either a restriction or a right of first refusal in favour of the former landlord.

The rule is different where the tenant opted for a shared ownership lease. Until the tenant owns a 100 per cent share, he is not entitled to make any disposal (Housing Act 1985, Sched 8, para 9).

9.3 Landlord's consent

Where the landlord has the right to give consent before the tenant assigns or sublets, whether under the terms of the lease or tenancy agreement or by statute, there are a number of constraints on how he exercises that right.

9.3.1 No charge

The landlord is not allowed to charge for giving his consent (Law of Property Act 1925, s 144). It has to be said that this is not a very strong prohibition. If there is express authority to charge in the lease, that is in order, so the Act applies only where nothing is said, and even so the landlord can require the tenant to pay his legal and other expenses.

In the case of a protected tenancy, charging for consent may be a criminal offence, subject to a fine of up to £1,000 (Rent Act 1977, s 120).

9.3.2 No discrimination

A landlord of a flat is not entitled to withhold consent to an assignment or subletting on grounds which amount to racial or sexual discrimination (Race Relations Act 1976, s 24; Sex Discrimination Act 1975, s 31). Doing so renders the landlord liable to pay damages to the person discriminated against.

There is an important exception, where these rules do not apply, in the case of small properties. Three conditions must be met. First, the landlord or a close relative must live there and intend to continue to do so; secondly, that occupier must share accommodation, other than storage or means of access, with residents outside his household; thirdly, within the property there is not normally, in addition to household of the landlord or his relative, either separately let accommodation for no more than two households or other accommodation for more than six people.

9.3.3 No unreasonable refusal

Whether or not the lease or agreement says so, a landlord whose consent must be sought to an assignment or subletting is not entitled unreasonably to withhold it (Landlord and Tenant Act 1927, s 19(1)). This applies only where there is a qualified covenant against disposals, not in the case of absolute covenants.

In such a case, the landlord has a statutory duty as long as the application for consent was in writing. Within a reasonable time, he must give consent and serve a notice of his decision, specifying any conditions attached to a consent or reasons for a refusal (Landlord and Tenant Act 1988, s 1).

In judging whether the landlord is being unreasonable, all the circumstances have to be taken into account. The primary test of the acceptability of an assignee will be his financial position, and the landlord will be entitled to references before he makes up his mind.

What a landlord is not entitled to do is to use the requirement for consent to gain himself an advantage he would not otherwise have had. For example, in one case a flat had already been sublet separately from commercial premises beneath it and the subtenant had Rent Act protection. The landlord could not validly withhold consent to assign the flat separately, so as to get both parts of the property to come back into the same hands which would defeat the Rent Act protection (*Bromley Park Garden Estate Ltd v Moss* [1982] 1 WLR 1019). Again, a landlord was unable reasonably to refuse consent to an assignment to an American on the ground that he was unlikely to occupy the flat for twenty years and would sublet in the meantime, because the lease provided a procedure for subletting which was obviously contemplated (*Rayburn v Wolf* (1985) 50 P&CR 463).

9.3.4 Consequences of unreasonable refusal

A tenant of a flat has three courses of action when faced with a landlord who refuses to consent to an assignment or subletting in circumstances the tenant considers unreasonable.

First, he can ignore the landlord and proceed without the consent. The landlord's sanction, forfeiture of the lease, will not be available to him in those circumstances (*Treloar v Bigge* (1874) LR 9 Exch 151; *Lewis & Allenby (1909) Ltd v Pegge* [1914] 1 Ch 782). Clearly, this course needs the co-operation of the other party to the transaction, and that may prove a stumbling block because there may be uncertainty whether or not the landlord is in fact justified in not consenting.

Secondly, the tenant may apply to the court for a declaration that the landlord's refusal is indeed unreasonable (Landlord and Tenant Act 1954, s 53(1)).

Thirdly, he is entitled to damages for breach of the landlord's statutory duty (Landlord and Tenant Act 1988, s 4). The amount of damages will depend entirely on the amount of his pecuniary loss resulting from the landlord's default.

Chapter 10

Landlord's Identity

10.1 General

There has been growing concern in recent years that tenants should know who their landlords are. Various statutory provisions have been introduced, but none has yet proved wholly successful. The result has been further legislation, and the measures now overlap each other.

10.2 Discovering who is landlord

10.2.1 Statutory notice

The tenant of a flat has a statutory right to know the identity of his landlord. He can make a written request to the person who demands the rent, or who last received it, or who acts as the landlord's agent in connection with the tenancy. The recipient then has 21 days in which to supply a written statement of the landlord's name and address. Failure to do so without reasonable excuse is an offence, carrying a fine of up to £2,500 (Landlord and Tenant Act 1985, s 1).

If the result of that request is to find that the landlord is a body corporate, the tenant may make a further written request for the name and address of every director and of the secretary. That request may be made to the landlord, its agent or the person who demands rent. It is an offence (punishable by a fine of up to £2,500) if, without reasonable excuse, the landlord does not give the information in writing within 21 days, or an agent or rent collector does not pass the request on to the landlord (Landlord and Tenant Act 1985, s 2).

10.2.2 Address for service

Every landlord of a flat—except one let with business premises—has a duty to furnish his tenant with an address for service in England and Wales (Landlord and Tenant Act 1987, s 48). If he does not do so, the tenant's obligation to pay rent and service charge is suspended. The only exception is where a receiver or manager has been appointed by court order and his functions include collecting rent or service charge as the case may be.

10.2.3 Rent books

Where the tenant of a flat pays rent weekly, the landlord must provide a rent book. Information has been prescribed which has to go into it, and this includes the name and address of the landlord. Failure to do so is an offence carrying a fine of up to £2,500 (Landlord and Tenant Act 1985, ss 4, 5, 7).

10.3 Change of landlord

10.3.1 Statutory notice

When the landlord's interest in a flat changes hands, the new landlord has a duty to give the tenant written notice of the assignment and of his name and address (Landlord and Tenant Act 1985, s 3). Failure to do so without reasonable excuse is an offence, making the new landlord subject to a fine of up to £2,500. Where trustees become landlord, they may give a collective description ('the trustees of . . .') and the address from which the affairs of the trust are conducted. That may well be convenient, because in that case there is no need to notify later changes in the identity of the trustees.

10.3.2 Consequences of no notification

In addition to the criminal sanction on the new landlord for failing to give the tenant notice of an assignment, there is also an incentive for the former landlord to ensure it is given. Until it is, or until the old landlord gives notice of the assignment with the new landlord's name and last known address, the old landlord remains liable to the tenant for any breach of covenant (Landlord and Tenant Act 1985, s 3(3A), (3B); Landlord and Tenant Act 1987, s 50).

It should also be noted that until the tenant has received notice of assignment he is entitled to continue to pay rent to the old landlord (Law of Property Act 1925, s 151(1)).

Part 2

Disposal of Flats

Chapter 11

Sale on Long Lease

11.1 General principles

It is clearly important for the owner of a block of flats who decides
to sell off the individual flats on long lease to settle on the form of
the transactions and the details of the documentation before he starts.
With flats, there is every reason for adopting standard documents, and
for not allowing amendments in individual cases. For ease of selling,
the form of lease should be reasonably even handed, between landlord
and tenant. Even if some flats sell on a lease that unduly favours the
landlord, there is always the danger that there will be delay and difficulty
in selling others of them; and the developer's profit will come from
the final sales.

For a form of lease, see Precedent A:3, p 175.

11.1.1 Developer's options

The developer must decide what final outcome he wants to achieve,
so that the documents may be drafted appropriately. His choices are:
  (1) To retain the reversions to the leases of the flats and the
       responsibility for management, albeit with the cost reimbursed
       by the tenants;
  (2) To create ground rents without involvement in the management
       of the property. This gives the developer an investment which
       he can either retain or subsequently sell;
  (3) To transfer the whole of his interest in the property to the tenants
       of the flats, ie not only granting leases but also vesting the
       reversions in the tenants, as a body.
These objects are best achieved by aiming at a final position in which
everyone who is then to be involved will have a legal estate in the property.
In every case the individual flats will be leased to the buyers. The only
difference is in the treatment of the reversions.

In the first case—the developer retaining the reversion—there is no
difficulty. Appropriate leases of the flats are granted, and the matter
is left there. The maintenance and repairing responsibilities on the one

hand, and the obligation to contribute towards their cost on the other, are dealt with by covenants in the leases.

The second option—retaining only ground rents, without further involvement—is best achieved by granting a single lease of the whole block, reserving the desired final ground rent, to a company in which the flat owners are the shareholders. That company is then the immediate landlord of the individual flat owners. A similar result comes from granting leases of the flats to the flat owners and a lease of the common parts to a tenants' company.

Finally, the third possibility, where the developer divests himself of all interest in the property, also involves having a company in which the flat owners are shareholders. In this case, it acquires the developer's reversionary interest.

11.1.2 Break up operations

A break up operation is the name given to a sale on long lease of individual flats in a block where they have previously been let on short terms. If all the flats are empty before the operation starts it does not differ from a sale of new flats. If some are still let on rack rents, the problem is to ensure that the management and service charge arrangements applicable to each type of letting can run simultaneously until all the flats are sold.

The recommended way to achieve this is to create all the long leases immediately. Those which cannot immediately be sold are vested in the developer or his nominee, and the rack rent tenancies are treated as sublettings.

11.2 Tenants' companies

A tenants' company is a limited company created as a type of tenants' cooperative, to allow all the flat owners of flats in a particular block to be treated as a body. Normally all the flat owners will be members, and they will be the only members. In schemes for the sale of flats, a company of this type may be used to hold the reversion to the leases of the flats, or to take a lease of the common parts. Whatever their role in the scheme for disposing of the flats, certain general points arise for consideration.

For a form of memorandum and articles for a tenants' company, see Precedent A:4, p 193.

11.2.1 Incorporation

A tenants' company will normally be incorporated as a company limited by guarantee or as a private company limited by shares. The advantages of limitation by guarantee are: the number of members can fluctuate, which makes it easier for the original subscribers to resign without having to transfer their shares to someone else; and it facilitates mortgages of the leases of the flats, because it is not necessary to ensure that the mortgagee can vest the flat owner's share in the purchaser if he has to exercise his power of sale.

On the other hand, the advantages of a company limited by shares are: joint owners of a flat can be made joint owners of the share(s) allocated to that flat, thus ensuring that they do not have more than their share of the votes; conversely, the owner of more than one flat can have a correspondingly larger number of shares and that number of votes; flats of different sizes can carry with them varying numbers of shares; the developer's initial interests can be safeguarded by ensuring that he retains a majority of shares or a class of shares with special rights. On balance, the greater flexibility of a company limited by shares recommends its use.

To limit the class of shareholders to flat owners, a requirement can be inserted in the memorandum of association to this effect. Making that stipulation in the memorandum, rather than in the articles, renders it permanent and unalterable if the memorandum also prohibits any alteration of it (Companies Act 1985, s 17). The original subscribers to the memorandum and articles, who will be nominees of the developer, will have to be excluded from this qualifying condition. To ensure that the final number of shares issued is correct—ie the same number of shares as there are flats, or whatever other ratio of the two figures has been decided upon—the original subscribers' shares can be dealt with in one of two ways. Either the directors named in the articles of association can allot all the authorised shares to flat owners, so that there are no shares left for the subscribers, or shares can be issued to the subscribers and transferred to flat owners on completion of sales.

The intention is normally that the board of directors also only consists of flat owners. They may well need professional assistance, but the feeling of co-operative management is better fostered if managing agents, solicitors and accountants are retained by the company, rather than joining its board. The simplest way to ensure that directors are flat owners is to impose a share qualification, assuming that the memorandum requires that shareholders be flat owners. To require that a director own at least one share then means that the director will have to be a flat owner. To allow for the launching of the company by the developer, the first directors named in the articles of association could be exempt from the qualification. Alternatively, and this would be a way to guarantee that the management was handed over by the developer, the qualification could become operative, say, eighteen months after the company's incorporation.

11.2.2 Solvency

A tenants' company normally has no realisable assets. Accordingly, if it is responsible for services and doing repairs, it must be in a position to collect in all the money it needs for that purpose. The primary source of funds will be the tenants, paying under the covenants in their leases. This is not infallible. The financial difficulties of one tenant, or simple recalcitrance, may affect the company's cash flow, or the amount it can finally collect. The danger of a shortfall is enhanced by the opportunity to contest service charges under the Landlord and Tenant Act 1985, the terms of which extend, as some earlier legislation did not, to tenants' companies.

To counter this, the company's articles should give it power to require additional payments from members. In effect, this is a power to levy a supplementary service charge from the tenants, to cover the default of a minority. In fairness, those who pay a supplementary levy should be allowed a credit if the uncollected amount is subsequently paid.

11.2.3 Compulsory membership

The development scheme will require that all flat owners are members of the company. Although this is generally readily accepted, there are two ways in which the scheme could falter. The documents should cope with both so far as they can. On the one hand the buyer of a flat will wish to be assured that he can insist on becoming a member of the company. On the other, the company will want to have reserve power to compel a flat owner to become a member.

A buyer of a flat will normally ensure that his contract entitles him to buy the share allocated to the flat, and that on completion he collects the share certificate and an executed share transfer. There will be rare occasions on which this is not possible. For these some alternative must be provided, bearing in mind that it is not lawful to register a transfer unless an instrument of transfer is presented to the company (Companies Act 1985, s 183(1)).

The company's articles can provide a fall back machinery. They can incorporate a power of attorney granted by the former flat owner, authorising someone else to transfer his share. A power of attorney must be granted by deed (Powers of Attorney Act 1971, s 1). Although a company's memorandum and articles are not a deed, they bind the members in the same way (Companies Act 1985, s 14(1)), and it is assumed that this justifies the not uncommon practice of writing a power of attorney into a company's articles.

Two alternative forms of power of attorney may be suggested, although neither is without problems. The directors or their nominee can be appointed a member's attorney for this purpose. The drawback to this is that a power of attorney normally lapses when the person granting it dies, although this only has an effect if the fact of the death is known (Powers of Attorney Act 1971, s 5(1), (2)). The same applies where the grantor of the power ceases to have legal capacity, as a company's articles cannot comply with the requirements for an enduring power. This therefore is no solution if, to the knowledge of those concerned, the shareholder has died, even if he died after disposing of the flat but before the power of attorney was exercised.

The donor's death does not revoke a power of attorney given to secure a proprietary interest of the attorney when it is expressed to be irrevocable (Powers of Attorney Act 1971, s 4(1)). So, the danger of the power lapsing on the shareholder's death after disposing of the flat disappears if the company's articles make a shareholder automatically appoint any subsequent owner of his flat as his attorney to transfer the share. The ownership of the flat is clearly secured by the power of attorney, because it enables the donee to comply with a covenant or condition in the lease requiring that he becomes a member of the company. Such a power can be granted in favour of the new owner of the flat 'and those deriving title under him' (s 4(2)), which secures the position on any further devolution of title.

Even this solution is not ideal. The appointment of the attorney has to be delayed until the flat changes hands, because until that moment it is not possible to identify the attorney. No problem arises where the flat owner executes an assignment or transfer of the lease of the flat, but the share transfer is at that point overlooked. But it does mean that if the registered member of the company dies before he transfers the flat the power of attorney is ineffective. For the power to take effect at all the donor must have capacity at the moment it is granted. Nevertheless of the two alternatives, this seems the better solution.

The articles of association will also need to provide that on the execution of a transfer pursuant to it, the recipient will pay a consideration equal to the nominal value of the share. That consideration will be held by the company as trustee for the former member or his estate.

The converse problem to ensuring that an incoming flat owner can acquire a share in the company is: can the company oblige a flat owner to become a member? Normally, a company has no power to force anyone to become a member of it. The memorandum and articles cannot validly give it that power, because a person only becomes bound by them when he becomes a member. Assuming that the outgoing flat owner wants to transfer his share—and he may be anxious to, so as to divest himself of his duty to contribute to the residual cost of repairs and services—all that is needed is a way to oblige the new flat owner to apply for registration, or a grant of authority to someone else to do so on his behalf. The only document to which the new owner will have been a party is the assignment or transfer of the lease, and even that may not have been executed by him. He is bound by the terms of the lease by privity of estate, but it seems likely that any provision in the lease relating to the share would not touch and concern the property and would not therefore automatically bind the assignee.

The normal method of coping with the problem is to include a tenant's covenant in the lease not to assign otherwise than to someone who simultaneously takes a transfer of the share. This is less than satisfactory because any covenant restricting assignment applies only to voluntary assignments and not, eg, on bankruptcy (*Re Riggs, ex p Lovell* [1901] 2 KB 16). Further, it does nothing to compel the assignee to apply for registration of the share transfer. There may be a further requirement that there is no assignment except to a person who enters into a direct covenant with the company. This could include a covenant to register a transfer, but the concept of a direct covenant is really only appropriate where the company collects the service charge but has no estate in the property. It increases the complication and cost of a sale of a flat.

The suggested solution is to include in the lease a condition, rather than a covenant. A condition qualifies the extent of the estate granted by a lease, so that the term comes to an end if it is broken. A condition controlling the assignment of a lease has been held to be effective (*Doe d Henniker v Watt* (1828) 8 B&C 308), and it seems ideal here. The term of the lease would be limited until such time as it is vested for, say, two months in a person who is not and has not applied to be registered as a member of the tenants' company.

11.3 Contract

The contract for the sale of a flat to be held on a long lease will normally be simple, because it will provide for the grant of a standard form of lease in a form of an annexed draft. For a form of contract, see Precedent A:1, p 165.

11.3.1 Title

On the grant of a lease, the title to which the tenant is automatically entitled by statute may not satisfy a purchaser paying a premium. If the landlord is the freeholder, the tenant is not entitled to call for any title (Law of Property Act 1925, s 44(2)). If the landlord is a leaseholder, the tenant is entitled to the title to the leasehold reversion, ie the lease under which the landlord holds and, if applicable, at least fifteen years title to it (s 44(1), (3); Law of Property Act 1969, s 23).

Buyers of flats, and indeed their mortgagees, normally require full proof of title. The Standard Conditions of Sale (2nd ed) make provision for title to be deduced. When the lease is to be granted for over 21 years, the title must be such as will enable the buyer to be registered with an absolute title (cond 8.2.4).

Where the landlord's title is registered, he can have an estate layout plan officially approved. This allows the Land Registry to issue a certificate of official search of the filed plan (Form 102) confirming that the property is within the title and stating which if any of the colourings on the filed plan affect that flat. It also obviates the necessity of sending a plan with an application for an official search (Form 94B).

11.3.2 Insurance

Special provision should normally be made for insurance. Neither of the normal rules—either that the seller remains responsible for the state of the property until completion (Standard Conditions of Sale, 2nd ed, cond 5.1.1) or that on exchange of contracts the buyer assumes responsibility for any loss or damage to the property (*Rayner v Preston* (1881) 18 ChD 1)—will be appropriate.

If the block is still being erected, insurance will normally be the builder's responsibility. Even if it is complete and ready for occupation, the lease will generally provide that after completion the block will be covered by a single policy with the tenant contributing an appropriate proportion of the premium. What the contract should provide in such circumstances is that the seller will effect a policy in the terms of the lease. It should also state that from the date of exchange the lease provisions will apply, so far as they relate to the disposal of any insurance moneys and to the liability to contribute to the cost of premiums.

11.3.3 NHBC guarantee

The National House-Building Council 'buildmark' guarantee scheme applies to newly built flats, although they have a similar but more limited insurance scheme for converted or renovated flats.

For the buyer of a new flat, obtaining the guarantee is initiated by completing the acceptance form (BM2) issued by the NHBC. For conversions or renovations, the builder has to apply to the NHBC before work begins. When the provision of a guarantee or insurance is part of the buyer's bargain, the contract should contain an appropriate term if nothing has been provided by that stage.

11.4 Grant of lease

Where the leases of flats are sold for the first time, it is normally assumed that each will be granted on the completion of the sale of that flat. There are two arguments for granting them earlier, and all at the same time.

First, some developers grant the leases to a nominee so that when it comes to the sales, they are selling existing leases. This rules out arguments about the form of the lease, as the buyer is not dealing with the landlord and cannot therefore expect to negotiate alterations in the terms. Secondly, where the sales of leases are likely to extend over an appreciable period—and this will particularly be the case on a break up operation, when some flats are still occupied under rack rent leases— to grant the leases simultaneously ensures that they will all have the same effect. Various proposals for the reform of the law of landlord and tenant are under consideration, some of which involve implying terms into leases. It is possible that these changes will be made so as to apply only to leases granted after the date that the new legislation takes effect. The inconvenient result, unless the leases are granted simultaneously, could be a block of flats let on leases in identical terms, some of which had to be interpreted differently.

Stamp duty will be chargeable in respect of the rent reserved. The original tenant would normally have to pay that, so it may be possible to pass the amount on to him. There is a real increase in cost if the lease in favour of the nominee has to be registered before it is transferred to the buyer. Land registry fees will have to be paid both on the registration of the grant of the lease and on the registration of the transfer.

11.5 Vesting reversion in tenants' company

If the reversion to the leases of the individual flats is to be vested in a tenants' company—whether it is a freehold reversion or a leasehold reversion—the timing has to be considered. The developer frequently wishes to ensure two results:

(1) The transfer must take place according to plan;
(2) He must retain control of the management of the property until all the flats have been sold.

Two alternative methods may be adopted. In the first, the reversion is transferred after all the flats have been sold. Before the first sale the developer enters into a contract with the tenants' company, which he has formed and which is then wholly under his control. That contract provides for the transfer of the freehold or the grant of a concurrent lease, with completion fixed for the day immediately after the grant of the final individual flat lease. On the sale of each flat a share in the tenants' company is issued to the flat owner. The control of the company therefore soon passes to the flat owners, but it is already committed to taking the reversionary interest.

The other method is to vest the reversion in the tenants' company at once, while keeping the control of the tenants' company in the hands of the developer until all the flats are sold. This could be done by delaying the issue of shares to the flat owners until all the flats are disposed of. This is unlikely to be acceptable to buyers or their mortgagees. It would also, in the interim, nullify any provision in the articles of association of the company to make up any deficit in service charge contributions.

The same effect can be achieved by a two class share capital. There can be 'A' shares, of which there is one per flat, each with one vote and liable to contribute to any service charge deficit. In addition, there are 'B' shares, of which there are three per flat, each with one vote but without liability to contribute to any shortfall in the service charge. All the shares are initially issued to the developer, or his nominees. On the sale of a flat, the appropriate 'A' share is transferred to that flat owner. The developer also contracts that as soon as the flats are sold, he will distribute his holding of 'B' shares between the holders of 'A' shares pro rata.

The result of this is that while the sale of the flats is proceeding, the fall back arrangements for the service charge operate as intended, with the flat owners—whether the developer or the purchasers—making appropriate contributions. The developer retains control of the company because until he disposes of the last flat, and therefore his last 'A' share, he has over seventy-five per cent of the votes in a general meeting of the company.

The first method, transferring the reversion after all the flats have been sold, has the merit of greater simplicity. It is not recommended where there is likely to be an extended selling period. Difficulties may result from the delay in establishing the permanent repair and service charge machinery. There is also the danger that once the tenants have control of the tenants' company, they may seek to repudiate the contract to acquire the reversion. The developer is in a position to enforce the contract by proceedings, but he will not want to be put in the position of having to do so. That danger may be considered more theoretical than practical.

The second method, with the split capital structure, is useful where the selling time may be long. This particularly applies to a break up operation. Some of the flats may still be let at rack rents, and the developer will have to undertake the repairing and service charge responsibility in respect of them.

11.6 Vesting common parts in tenants' company

Another arrangement sometimes adopted to regulate repairs to the structure and common parts of a block of flats, to provide services and to collect service charges is for the developer to grant a lease to a tenants' company of all the parts of the block for which the flat owners are not directly responsible. This offers the developer a greater degree of direct control. The lease of each flat is granted by the developer to the flat owner, and therefore the developer is the one to take enforcement action on any breach of the tenant's covenants. When the reversions to the leases of the flats are vested in the tenants' company, any pressure by the developer must be indirect.

As the means of access to the flats and the pipes and wires for the services are vested in the tenants' company, it is easy to ensure that the obligation to pay service charge contributions binds all the flat owners.

There need be no contractual relationship between them and the company other than as shareholders. By making a right (eg a right of way through the common parts to reach the flat) conditional on making a payment, anyone exercising the right becomes liable to pay (*Halsall v Brizell* [1957] Ch 169). There is some doubt as to the extent that this device can success-fully be used for payments not directly connected with the rights granted.

It is more difficult to ensure that flat owners will be able to enforce the tenants' company's repairing and other obligations. The company can be made a party to the leases, in order to covenant to do the work, but that may not benefit an assignee of the lease. An assignee of the company's lease of the common parts might not be bound. The flat owner and the company do not stand in the relationship of landlord and tenant; they are fellow tenants of different parts of the same building.

The flat owner will want the developer, as landlord, to covenant to repair and provide services, while allowing the work done by the company to fulfil that obligation. That means that the developer effectively guarantees the performance by the company of its obligations. If the company defaults, the developer will have remedies against the company as its landlord.

Difficult questions could arise if the developer sought to exercise his ultimate sanction, to forfeit the lease of the common parts. Could a flat owner who had in fact complied with all his obligations, including paying service charges to the company, argue that any action by the developer against the company might constitute a breach of the landlord's covenant for quiet enjoyment in the lease of the flat? The flat owner might not be prejudiced, but that would generally mean that the developer had been obliged to assume responsibility for the company's duties.

11.7 Break up operations

In a break up operation, where the developer seeks to sell long leases of flats that were formerly let at rack rents and some still are, the most satisfactory way to proceed is to create immediately the structure that will apply when the operation has been completed. Early buyers of flats will wish to be assured not only that repair and service charge provisions will operate satisfactorily immediately, but also that they will not bear unduly heavily on flat owners who have bought long leases. If the final arrangements come into force at once, with the developer taking the place of the flat owner of every flat as yet unsold, this can be achieved. The expenditure is divided between the flats, and the developer either makes an appropriate contribution, or has to do the work while being entitled only to collect part of its cost. The rack rent occupiers of unsold flats will be the developer's subtenants, and any service charges they pay go to the developer in his capacity as their landlord. Those service charges help him to defray his contributions to the service charges due under the long leases, but do not come into the calculations made to determine what the flat owners must pay.

The documentation for and stages of a break up operation can be as follows:

(1) The developer establishes a tenants' company with two classes of share capital;

(2) The developer transfers his interest in the block of flats to the tenants' company;

(3) The tenants' company grants individual leases of all the flats to the developer;

(4) On negotiating a sale of a flat, the developer sells his lease of that flat and transfers one 'A' share in the tenants' company to that buyer;

(5) On completing the sale of the last flat, the developer transfers three 'B' shares in the tenants' company to the then owner of each 'A' share.

The intention is that the initial transfer of the developer's interest to the company and the subsequent grant of leases back to the developer should not bear stamp duty on the capital value, although it would have to be paid on the rent reserved.

Chapter 12

Sale Freehold

12.1 General

12.1.1 When appropriate

Selling the freehold of individual flats has not been a popular method of developing blocks of flats. The principal reason has been the difficulty of enforcing covenants to repair and to contribute to the upkeep of the common parts. This difficulty has led some building societies to take a general policy decision that they will not lend money on freehold flats. That in turn has reduced their marketability and consequently their value.

The developer of a block of flats may well wish to divest himself of his entire interest in the property. Normally, he can do so without difficulty by granting long leases of flats and vesting the freehold reversion to those leases in a tenants' company. There are cases in which that is not a practical solution. In very small developments, perhaps of only four or six flats in the block, the imposition of a company structure is cumbersome and disproportionately expensive.

As on sales of long leases, the developer must determine in advance what form of documentation is going to be used. The arrangements will only work satisfactorily if standard documents apply to all flats.

12.1.2 Common parts

The developer who sells flats freehold as a means of ensuring that he parts with all his interest in the block must also dispose of the common parts. The convenient way to do this depends on the layout of the block. In some cases it will be possible to divide the common parts between the individual flats, eg conveying the foundations with the ground floor flat, the roof with the top floor flat, and parts of the staircase and landings with the flats on each floor. The necessary mutual rights can then be granted and reserved or excepted. In other cases this cannot be done. It would not be appropriate where there was a lift, or where flats were

102

not totally compact but included extra luggage rooms or basement stores. The common parts then have to be vested in a tenants' company.

12.1.3 Expenses on creating rentcharges

In deciding whether to use an estate rentcharge as the means of enforcing repairing obligations and collecting service charges, possible extra expenses must be considered.

Stamp duty is charged on a document creating a rentcharge to repay maintenance expenditure under s 57 of the Stamp Act 1891. This provides that:

> Where any property is conveyed to any person in consideration, wholly or in part, . . . subject either certainly or contingently to the payment . . . of any money . . . the money . . . is to be deemed the whole, or part, as the case may be, of the consideration in respect whereof the conveyance is chargeable with *ad valorem* duty.

In principle, therefore, to calculate the duty payable on the conveyance the price must be increased by the value of the sums payable under the rentcharge. It is impossible to say what will be paid. All the same, it is submitted that it must necessarily be of no value, because it will be calculated on a repayment basis for what the flat owner receives in the form of work or services. Alternatively, it could be argued that the sums payable are not a consideration for the flat, but for the services to be received later. It is suggested that no increase in stamp duty is appropriate. Should any be payable, it will be the responsibility of the buyer, as it is payable on the consideration for what he is acquiring, in the same way as the duty on the stated price.

The formalities in connection with the creation and registration of a rentcharge will inevitably involve extra professional fees on the sale and purchase of the flat.

12.2 Contract

For a form of contract for selling a freehold flat, see Precedent B:1, p 213.

12.2.1 Defining the flat

It is if anything more important to be precise in defining the extent of a flat sold freehold than when granting a long lease of it. Difficulties can particularly arise where flats are created on a conversion, because they are often irregular in size and layout. The danger lies in the possibility that part of the block may remain unsold.

Once all the flats have been sold, the developer will believe that he has no further interest in the property. Say a question then arises as to whether, eg, a top floor flat includes the roof void, where the flat owner would like to create an extra room, and the conveyance of the flat is not clear on the point. It could be rectified with the cooperation of the developer, but it may not be possible to trace him. This contrasts with the position of the landlord of the whole block who retains a permanent interest, in whom any residual part not demised must still be vested.

The contract should therefore precisely define the extent of the flat, and also the appurtenant rights and the rights reserved. They can be set out *in extenso* in the agreement, or it may be convenient to refer to the form of conveyance or transfer to be used, and set them out there.

12.2.2 Insurance

The seller should continue to insure the flat until completion, as will normally be the case under the Standard Conditions of Sale, 2nd ed (cond 5.1.1). There are two reasons for this. First, unlike the sellers of most freehold property, the developer of a block of flats will have a continuing interest in the building after completion, unless it is the last flat that is being sold. Secondly, there is at least an element of doubt whether, if an upper storey flat is being sold and it is completely destroyed by fire, the seller can perform his contract by conveying the 'site' of it. If total destruction frustrates a contract of this type, the seller will not be able to enforce payment of the contract price.

12.2.3 Conveyance or transfer

Whatever development scheme is decided upon, the contract will have to require the buyer to accept a transfer in a standard form. It may be useful to require the buyer to execute a duplicate assurance for the seller to retain. This is a necessity if an estate rentcharge is created.

The covenants for repairs and the like may well be set out in the transfer. If there is to be a separate deed of covenant, the contract will need to require the buyer to execute it.

For a form of transfer reserving an estate rentcharge, see Precedent B:2, p 215.

12.2.4 Registration of rentcharge

The flat and any estate rentcharge are separately registered under different titles. The two are cross-referenced, by notes on the register (Land Registration Rules 1925, r 108). It is convenient for the registration applications—for the first registration or the transfer of the flat and for the first registration of the rentcharge—to be dealt with together. The contract can require the buyer to apply for the registration of the rentcharge on behalf of the tenants' company, as the owner of it. He can also be required to pay the registration fee, on the basis that the rentcharges are being created for the benefit of the flat owners collectively.

12.3 Maisonettes

The flats or maisonettes in a building divided into only two units are particularly suitable for disposal freehold, above all if they are completely self contained. No elaborate development scheme involving a tenants' company is appropriate or even feasible with only two properties.

12.3.1 Repairs

The simplest way to arrange for repair and maintenance work to be done is to divide the building into two—the foundations going with the lower maisonette and the roof with the upper one—and to give each flat owner the duty to do all the work needed to his half. Some practical disadvantages may result. Some major jobs involve work on both halves of the building. The possibility of non co-operation by one party can be countered by a power granted to the other party to enter the half that is not his to do the work, and to recover the cost.

Again, people may feel that unless the flat owners agree on a single colour for exterior decoration, the colour clashes that can result may reduce the value of both properties. Little is gained by writing an obligation to agree into the documents. If the parties can agree, they will do so voluntarily. If they do not, the only alternative would be to have the colour chosen by an independent third party. This seems ridiculously elaborate in the circumstances. If the owners prefer polychromatic individualism to monochromatic profit, who is the developer to disagree?

There are two ways in which payment for repairs and maintenance can be arranged, where each owner does the work on his half of the building. Either, each owner pays for the work that he has to do. Or, the cost of all work is halved, each owner contributing to what the other does. The latter system is probably fairer, although it involves more paperwork. Many owner-occupiers will do much of the work themselves, paying only for materials. To avoid arguments, it may be best to make clear whether an owner is entitled to make a charge for his own labour.

12.3.2 Development schemes

Either of two similar schemes can be used for selling maisonettes. One is technically leasehold, but is included here both for convenience, and because the employment of the leasehold format is perhaps even more a matter of mechanical convenience than with other flats.

In one case, each maisonette is sold freehold, subject to the reservation of an estate rentcharge which is vested in the owner of the other. The form of transfer in Precedent B:2, p 215, could be adapted for this purpose. Alternatively, a lease is granted of each maisonette and the freehold reversion to each lease is vested in the tenant of the other property. That is, the owner of the ground floor maisonette is tenant under a long lease of that property and is the freeholder landlord of the upper maisonette, and *vice versa*.

The latter, leasehold, system is probably better because of the greater familiarity with the landlord and tenant relationship. In either case, the documents should seek to link each owner's interests in both maisonettes, by making neither assignable without the other. The effectiveness of such restrictions is not certain, but as it is in the owners' interests to maintain the link, the provision in the documents is of use more as a reminder.

The contract for the disposal of the first maisonette should contain a condition requiring the seller to dispose of the other one on the same basis.

For forms for the sale of leasehold maisonettes see Precedent A:5, p 199 (contract for the sale of the first maisonette); Precedent A:6, p 203 (contract for the sale of the second maisonette); Precedent A:7, p 205 (long lease of a maisonette).

Chapter 13

Right of First Refusal

13.1 Outline

Before the introduction of collective enfranchisement, statute had given long leaseholders of flats the collective right to buy their landlord's freehold, or his leasehold reversion, if he decided to sell. This right of first refusal continues to apply—and is important in dictating the procedure to be followed by a landlord who wishes to sell the reversion in a block of flats—but is now considerably diminished in its significance for tenants.

The fundamental difference between the two rights is that collective enfranchisement allows the tenants to take the initiative, and allows them to buy the freehold compulsorily when they wish to do so. By contrast, the right to buy leaves the initiative with the landlord: should he decide to sell, which he is not obliged to do, he has to offer the property to the tenants at the same price as he is seeking elsewhere. Furthermore, if what the tenants' immediate landlord has for sale is a leasehold reversion, that is all the tenants have the chance to buy.

Collective enfranchisement is not only a right to acquire the freehold, but also all intermediate interests. The right of first refusal relates to the immediate landlord's interest, as long as the reversion is for at least seven years.

The right to first refusal procedure may make the sale of the freehold take longer than it otherwise would, so it may be unattractive for the landlord. However, there is a sanction against his artificially inflating the offer price so as to deter the tenants from buying. If the sale to the tenants does not go through, there is a restriction on the owner's selling it to someone else for less during the following 12 months.

A landlord who ignores the tenants' first refusal rights commits no offence and suffers no penalty. But the tenants may have the right to follow the property into the buyer's hands, and to acquire it compulsorily from him at the price he paid. That is a powerful deterrent against buying the freehold of a block if the tenants' rights have been disregarded. For a buyer who wants to ensure that those rights have been respected, so that he buys free from claims by the tenants, there is a statutory clearance procedure.

The qualifications for tenants to exercise the right of first refusal and to join in a claim for collective enfranchisement overlap, but are not the same. The statutory provisions for collective enfranchisement are much more detailed. This is a summary of some of the principal differences.

	First refusal	*Collective enfranchisement*
Length of tenancy	Can be short letting, unless assured or protected shorthold.	Must be long tenancy.
Resident landlords	Not affected if flat in a converted block, occupied as only or main residence for 12 months.	Same conditions, but only apply if block contains no more than four flats. A relative can occupy.
Public sector landlords	Following are exempt: Crown, local authorities, most other public authorities, charitable housing trusts and housing associations.	Following are exempt: Crown (may voluntarily agree), charitable housing trusts (if flat provided for charitable purpose) and National Trust.
Subletting	Subtenant of qualifying tenant has no right, even if also qualifying.	Tenant at the end of a subletting chain has statutory right, even if his landlord would qualify.
Use	Does not apply if over 50 per cent of block has non-residential use.	Does not apply if over ten per cent of block has non-residential use.

13.2 Qualifications

The right of first refusal is for qualifying tenants of flats in a block to which the right applies, unless owned by an exempt landlord (Landlord and Tenant Act 1987, ss 1–3; Housing Act 1988, Sched 13, para 2). The various elements of these qualifications must be considered.

13.2.1 Qualifying tenant

Every tenant qualifies for the right of first refusal, except one whose tenancy is an assured tenancy, a protected shorthold tenancy, a business tenancy, an assured agricultural occupancy or a service tenancy which ends with his employment. A subtenant only qualifies if his landlord is not a qualifying tenant. A tenant does not qualify if he is tenant of more than two flats in the block, and for this purpose a company is treated as tenant of a flat let to an associated company.

13.2.2 Flat

The definition of a flat for this purpose is 'a separate set of premises, whether or not on the same floor, which:
 (a) forms part of a building, and
 (b) is divided horizontally from some other part of that building, and
 (c) is constructed or adapted for use for the purposes of a dwelling'
(Landlord and Tenant Act 1987, s 60(1)).

13.2.3 Block

The right of first refusal applies to a block in which qualifying tenants hold at least two flats and a total of more than half of them. If more than half of the internal floor area of the block, disregarding common parts, is used for non-residential purposes, the right of first refusal does not apply. The Act has been applied to a development of four blocks of flats with separate garages (*30 Upperton Gardens Management Ltd v Akano* [1990] 2 EGLR 232 (*LVT*)).

13.2.4 Landlord

Three types of landlord are not affected by the right of first refusal: those holding under short leases, resident landlords and exempt landlords. A landlord who holds under a short lease—a term of less than seven years or terminable at his landlord's option during the first seven years— is disregarded; the landlord's statutory responsibilities devolve on his landlord. A landlord resident in the block in question may not be bound by the right of first refusal. This applies if the block is one which was not purpose-built where the landlord occupies the flat as his only or main residence, and has done so for at least twelve months. Some public sector landlords are exempt. They include local authorities, charitable housing trusts and registered housing associations.

13.3 Procedure

The Act lays down an elaborate procedure to ensure that tenants are notified when their right of first refusal is going to arise, to give them the opportunity to exercise it and to fix the price. However, it should be emphasised that the whole statutory procedure only leads to an agreement subject to contract, which in accordance with the usual rules is not binding (Landlord and Tenant Act 1987, s 20(2)). The enforcement sanction lies in the reluctance that buyers are likely to feel in dealing with a landlord who has not followed the procedure, because they run the risk of the tenants claiming to buy the freehold compulsorily.

13.3.1 Relevant disposal

The landlord has to serve notice on the qualifying tenants when he proposes to make a relevant disposal. With some specified exceptions, the definition of relevant disposal is comprehensive (Landlord and Tenant Act 1987, s 4; Housing Act 1988, Sched 13, para 3). It covers every disposal and creation (which covers a new lease) of any legal or equitable estate or interest in the premises or merely in the common parts.

The major exceptions are: the grant of a tenancy of a single flat, the grant of a mortgage, a transfer by at least two members of a family to fewer of themselves or at least one of them and other members of the family, a disposal by a corporate body to an associated company and a gift to a member of the family or a charity. Among other cases which are not relevant disposals are disposals as a result of matrimonial proceedings, bankruptcy or compulsory purchase. Where there is no relevant disposal, the fact that the landlord has no obligation to serve a notice means that the tenants have no right of first refusal.

13.3.2 Landlord's notice

The notice the landlord has to serve on the qualifying tenants specifies the main terms of the proposed disposal, particularly defining the property and estate or interest affected and the consideration (Landlord and Tenant Act 1987, s 5). Where the landlord proposes to do a transaction affecting all or parts of more than one building, he must sever it for the purposes of the notice so that it relates only to terms for disposal of the building containing the recipient tenant's flat. The notice states that it is an offer to dispose of the property on those terms, open to acceptance by the requisite majority of qualifying tenants.

The notice specifies two periods. First, there must be a minimum of two months from the service of the notice for acceptance of the offer. Secondly, at least another two months has to be given for nominating persons to take the freehold (Landlord and Tenant Act 1987, s 5).

The landlord must give all the qualifying tenants notice, but if he serves at least 90 per cent of them (or all but one if there are fewer than ten) he is taken to have complied. The result of serving a number of tenants may be that the notices are given on different days. Even so, the period for accepting the offer is to end on the same date for all the tenants: all have the benefit of the latest date that applies to any of them. If the nominating period runs from the end of the acceptance period, it runs from that latest date.

13.3.3 Tenants' response

The procedure for tenants who want to take advantage of their landlord's offer is in two stages (Landlord and Tenant Act 1987, s 6). First, they have the period of at least two months given in the notice within which they have to accept. At least 50 per cent of qualifying tenants have to serve notice to that effect. This is, effectively, merely an acceptance in principle. Secondly, they have a further two months—from the end of the original period for acceptance, even if they replied earlier—within which to nominate a person to acquire the freehold.

This nominee has a central role in the rest of the purchase procedure. There is no restriction on whom the tenants nominate. In most cases it will probably be convenient for them to form or acquire a company for the purpose.

Tenants may be keen to buy the freehold, but may feel that the landlord is asking too much for it. In that case, 50 per cent of them can, during the period for acceptance, serve notice making a counter-offer (s 7). The landlord then has three options. He can accept the counter-offer, reject it or make a further offer himself. Accepting the counter-offer allows the matter to proceed as if the tenants had accepted the landlord's offer, but on the amended terms. A further offer by the landlord is open to acceptance or rejection by the tenants in the same way as the original offer.

13.3.4 Purchase contract

As already mentioned, the landlord's offer and the tenants' acceptance are both subject to contract, so they do not result in a binding agreement. What the statutory procedure does is to give the nominated person a further three months, from the end of the two month nominating period, within which to enter into a contract with the landlord. It assumes that the terms of that contract will be as outlined in the notices, but there is no bar on varying them by negotiation. Only if no binding contract is concluded is there any sanction on the landlord.

13.3.5 Restrictions on landlord

The Act places a number of restrictions on a landlord where there is no sale to the tenants, although the only effective sanction backing them may be the possibility of the tenants having a compulsory right to buy from a subsequent owner.

The primary restriction on a landlord is that he is forbidden to make a relevant disposal unless he has served notice on the tenants. A disposal without serving notice may be restrained by injunction. If he duly served notice, there are various circumstances in which for twelve months he is not entitled to dispose of the property to anyone else for a consideration less than he offered to or agreed with the tenants, and on corresponding terms. This one year restriction applies in five cases (where procedural steps are involved, if they are not taken within the prescribed time limits):

(1) If the tenants do not name a nominated person;

(2) When the landlord makes a fresh offer in response to the tenants' counter-offer, if the tenants do not accept it or make another counter-offer;

(3) If the nominated person serves notice of not intending to proceed;

(4) If the landlord serves notice that he has not obtained a necessary consent to sell to the tenants, or a declaration that the consent was unreasonably withheld, even though the landlord has a duty to take active steps to obtain that consent;

(5) If no binding contract is entered into, and the landlord serves notice to that effect.

What the tenants can do, by buying from the subsequent buyer when the landlord is in breach, is dealt with below.

13.4 Buyers from landlord

13.4.1 Change of landlord

The tenants' rights to take further action, if the freehold in their block is disposed of without their being offered first refusal of it, necessarily depend on their knowing that it has changed hands. They have the general right of all tenants of residential property to be informed that there has been a change of landlord (Landlord and Tenant Act 1985, s 3). In addition, they have a right to find out particulars of the disposal.

Within two months of receiving notice of a change of landlord, or any other document indicating that there has been a disposal, at least 50 per cent of the qualifying tenants may serve notice asking for details (Landlord and Tenant Act 1987, s 11). The tenants' notice must give the name and address of some person to whom the information is to be supplied. In reply, the new landlord must, within one month, give the date of the disposal and its terms including the consideration. If he no longer owns the property, he must pass a copy of the notice to the new owner and give the tenants his name and address.

13.4.2 Compulsory purchase from new landlord

The major sanction available to tenants whose right of first refusal is ignored, is their right to insist on buying the reversion back from the new landlord (Landlord and Tenant Act 1987, s 12). If they act within a limited time—three months either after they were entitled to information about the change of ownership or after they received it—they can buy from the new landlord at the same price as he paid. Fixing the price may be troublesome, eg because the first sale was of a number of properties together (*Sullivan v Safeland Investments Ltd* [1990] 2 EGLR 227 (*LVT*)), or because there was more than one previous sale in quick succession (*Tyson v Carlyle Estates Ltd* [1990] 2 EGLR 229 (*LVT*)).

In some circumstances, the price is to be adjusted. If the premises have increased in value, but not simply because of a change in the value of money, the price is the market value at the date the new landlord acquired, had the circumstances then already been changed. This would apply, eg, where the property had been improved. In cases of dispute this, and other purchase terms, are settled by a rent assessment committee. The valuation date in a contested case is probably the date of the tribunal hearing (*139 Finborough Road Management Ltd v Mansoor* [1990] 2 EGLR 225 (*LVT*)).

The tenants are not entitled unreasonably to delay. The new landlord can call the sale off if there is no binding contract within three months of the tenants' original notice, unless a related court or rent assessment committee application is pending. After the application is settled, the tenants have a further two months.

If the new landlord passes the reversion on, the tenants' rights are carried over against the buyer.

13.4.3 Clearance procedure

There is a way in which a prospective buyer of the freehold of a block of flats can be sure that the tenants have no claim to buy it (Landlord and Tenant Act 1987, s 18). It involves the buyer serving notices on the tenants.

He has to serve notices on at least 80 per cent of the tenants (not merely the qualifying tenants, as he may well not know which they are). The notice must state the general nature of the main terms of the disposal which is envisaged, including particularly the property concerned and the estate or interest being disposed of and the consideration. It invites the tenant to respond in one of three ways: to say that the landlord has served him with notice of the disposal; or to say that there is a reason why he is not entitled to notice from the landlord; or, if he is entitled, to say whether he would wish to avail himself of a right of first refusal. The tenants have twenty-eight days for reply.

The statutory right of first refusal does not apply in either of two cases: first, if only 50 per cent, or fewer, of the tenants whom the buyer served with notices replied; secondly, if more than half of them replied, but indicated either that they were not entitled to, or would not wish to avail themselves of, a right of first refusal.

The proportions of tenants for this purpose all assume one tenant per flat.

Chapter 14

Shared Ownership

14.1 Object

Shared ownership is a method of disposal aimed at providing a way to acquire a flat at a lower cost, in terms of regular outgoings, than would normally be possible. The buyer pays only a proportion of the capital value of the flat. In addition, he pays a rack rent in respect of the remainder of the value. If he chooses to buy 60 per cent of the ownership of the flat, he pays the landlord seller 60 per cent of its market price. Thereafter, he also pays him 40 per cent of what the rack rent of the flat would have been.

The system assumes that mortgage instalments, comprising both capital and interest, payable in respect of a loan of any particular sum exceed the rent that would be payable for a flat of the same capital value. The buyer retains part of the benefit of the fact that renting is cheaper than buying. In return he sacrifices a proportionate part of the equity and the possibility of a gain in its capital value.

A shared ownership lease can give the tenant the option to acquire further tranches of the equity, on making more capital payments related to the then market value of the flat. When the tenant wants to part with the flat, the lease can provide for a number of possible courses of action. It may contain pre-emption provisions, requiring the tenant to offer to surrender it to the landlord. The tenant may be entitled to assign the lease as it is, ie still reserving a partial rack rent. Or, the tenant may either be able, or indeed may be obliged, to exercise his option to become full owner of the lease. Once that option has been exercised, no unusual restraint upon assignment would be appropriate.

14.2 Use in different cases

14.2.1 Local authority landlords

Shared ownership is a method of disposal primarily suited to local authorities. They have a social interest in encouraging the purchase of flats by those who would not otherwise be able to afford them. They have the organisation to cope with repeated valuations needed if the tenant buys by instalments. They are free from certain legislative restrictions that generally inhibit the use of this method.

However, the former right of secure tenants who could have exercised the right to buy to have a shared ownership lease instead has been withdrawn (Leasehold Reform, Housing and Urban Development Act 1993, s 107(c)).

14.2.2 Private landlords

At first sight, the granting of shared ownership leases appears to be ideal for the private landlord wishing to speed the progress of a break up operation. It could enable a sitting rack rent tenant to buy a long lease when he could not otherwise afford it. However, there is a difficulty. If the current tenancy is subject to the Rent Act, the new lease can also be a protected tenancy (Housing Act 1988, s 34(1)(b)). That means that there will be a restriction on charging a premium for the lease if both assignment and underletting the whole property are inhibited (Rent Act 1977, s 127). A landlord would normally want such a restriction where any part of the rack rent remained payable.

Developers who are prepared to dispose of a flat on concessionary terms do better to consider the possibilities open if they leave some or all of the purchase price on mortgage. If they had been prepared to accept less than a commercial return on part of the value of the flat, they might make an equivalent gesture simply by reducing the interest rate charged on the money advanced. It may also be possible for them to secure part of the equity benefit that they would have retained under a shared ownership lease. Following *Multiservice Bookbinding Ltd v Marden* [1979] Ch 84, it has been assumed that a mortgagee can make an agreement for repayment of capital that will result in the mortgagor having to repay more than he borrowed, without it being a clog on the equity of redemption. The arrangement might, eg, be that 10 per cent of the purchase price is left outstanding, and that the borrower will pay back 10 per cent of the market value of the flat on the date of repayment. The full range of possibilities has not been tested in court.

A developer choosing, as an alternative, to accept payment of the price by more than two instalments must remember that this will be a 'rental purchase agreement' if completion is delayed until all or a specified part of the price is paid. This gives the court a wide discretion in dealing with any possession application the developer might make on the tenant's default (Housing Act 1980, s 88).

14.2.3 Housing association landlords

A housing association can grant a shared ownership lease provided its rules give it the power to do so. This applies to those associations whose tenancies are not protected tenancies, ie those registered under the Housing Associations Act 1985, or within that Act's definition of a co-operative housing association, ie one with rules restricting membership to tenants and prospective tenants and precluding the grant or assignment of tenancies to non members and registered under the Industrial and Provident Societies Act 1965 (Rent Act 1977, s 15(1), (3)).

Clauses for inclusion in a lease granted by a housing association are set out in Precedent C:1, p 227.

14.3 Documentation

14.3.1 Final purchase

The simplest way in which to put a shared ownership disposal of a flat into effect is to grant a lease in the intended permanent form, with extra provisions. These will graft onto it the tenant's option to acquire what was previously left outstanding and his obligation to pay the proportion of the rack rent in the meantime.

When the tenant exercises his option to purchase the outstanding interest, a brief supplementary deed can be executed to record the fact. This will have the effect of cancelling those parts of the lease dealing with the share ownership position. The deed itself need not be elaborate, because the lease can state that this will be the effect of exercising the option.

An alternative method is illustrated by the model clauses for local authority shared ownership leases. This involves surrendering the first lease when the tenant exercises his option, and granting another in conventional form. This seems an unnecessary complication. It is likely that that method has been suggested because it was modelled on the arrangements to acquire a freehold house, where the tenant buyer has to acquire the reversion and take a conveyance.

14.3.2 Stamp duty

Special provisions apply to the stamp duty charged on a shared ownership lease. They allow duty to be charged on the basis that the lease is granted at a premium equal to the market value or sum from which the initial premium is calculated and at the final ground rent reserved on the tenant exercising his purchase option (Finance Act 1980, s 97; Finance Act 1981, s 108). This offers the tenant two savings. First, the duty on the premium is restricted to the market value at the date of the lease and ignores the fact that any payment the tenant makes later may be calculated by reference to the then current market value. The total of the capital sums paid by the tenant may therefore exceed the sum on which duty is calculated. Secondly, the tenant does not have to pay duty on the partial rack rent reserved by the lease, but only on the final ground rent.

On a sale at a discount by a local authority, a registered housing association or one of a number of other official bodies, the duty on the premium is charged without reference to the obligation to repay all or part of the discount on an early resale (Finance Act 1981, s 107).

Various conditions have to be satisfied if a shared ownership lease is to qualify for the stamp duty concessions:

(1) *Landlord* The lease must be granted by one of the following bodies: a local authority with a duty to provide housing accommodation; a housing association on the register maintained by the Housing Corporation or Housing for Wales; a new town development corporation; the Commission for the New Towns; the Development Board for Rural Wales; or the Council of the Isles of Scilly;

(2) *Terms* The lease must demise a dwelling for the exclusive use of the tenant, or of the joint tenants. It must provide that on the tenant making a payment the rent will be reduced;

(3) *Consideration* The consideration for the lease must be partly a rent and partly a premium. The premium is to be calculated by reference to the open market value had the lease reserved the minimum rent—ie the lowest amount to which the tenant can opt to have the rent reduced—or by reference to a sum calculated from that value;

(4) *Statement* The lease must contain a special statement for stamp duty purposes. This gives the amount of the minimum rent, and the market value or the sum calculated from it. It must also say that the parties intend the duty to be charged under s 108 of the Finance Act 1981 by reference to those figures.

In drafting a lease to take advantage of this stamp duty concession, not only should the special statement be included, but the tenant should covenant to use the premises for his exclusive use to satisfy the second condition.

Chapter 15

Timeshare

15.1 Object

Timeshare (which is also given a number of other names) is a method of disposing of holiday accommodation. It is an outright sale of the right to occupy the property in question for one or more specified weeks for a stated number of years.

The buyer acquires his holiday flat for a number of years, usually between thirty and eighty, at a fraction of its full cost. He has nothing further to pay except for repairs, maintenance and services. He has an interest that he can sell or leave by will. Recognising that a buyer may not always want to spend holidays in the same place, there are organisations through which timeshare owners can exchange rights to occupy with others interested in different properties.

The developer should be able to realise considerably more for a flat by selling the right to occupy it on this piecemeal basis, instead of selling a normal lease of it. He generally has a continuing interest in the development, not only in organising maintenance and services, but also in providing ancillary catering, shop and entertainments on parts of the development that he retains.

15.2 Methods of disposal

15.2.1 Club membership

There are a number of legal problems in the way of a straightforward grant of timeshare rights to a buyer. The most common structure for a developer to adopt is to vest the whole development in a trustee who holds the property on behalf of a club for up to eighty years. Each buyer becomes a member of the club. His individual membership entitles him to the occupation rights for which he has paid. The club contracts, at least initially, with the developer to manage the estate.

This arrangement sidesteps a number of possible difficulties:
    (1)   As the club's right to the estate is as a beneficiary under a trust, and not as tenant, it will not enjoy renewal rights under Part

118

II of the Landlord and Tenant Act 1954, as it otherwise might (*Addiscombe Garden Estates Ltd v Crabbe* [1958] 1 QB 513). The developer's reversion is therefore safeguarded, as he can be made the remainderman under the trust;

(2) Making the flat owners' occupation rights into benefits of club membership takes the relationship with the buyer out of the realm of landlord and tenant. This avoids a whole series of possible difficulties, although there are arguments against a number of them being relevant: eg renewal rights under Part I of the Landlord and Tenant Act 1954, limits on the landlord's right of forfeiture, limits on service charge payments;

(3) As the flat owner is a licensee and not a tenant, and the licence is granted for holiday purposes, it is not unlawful to evict him summarily and without legal proceedings, if he does not quit at the end of one of his occupation periods (Protection from Eviction Act 1977, ss 3(2A), 3A(7));

(4) Resting the relationship between the club and the flat owner upon contract probably means that it must be restricted to the perpetuity period, hence the limit of eighty years.

This method of disposal is recommended. It avoids the legal imponderables implicit in the only other scheme that has been tried, revolving leases. The club provides some small measure of democratic structure in which members can voice and settle their discontents. In practice, properties occupied on a time sharing basis are unusual in the number of parties simultaneously interested in them. Most of those people will be unknown to each other. The imposition of the essentially bilateral landlord and tenant structure is to that extent unreal, and may be unhelpful in solving problems.

15.2.2 Revolving leases

There are two possible leasehold methods of timeshare disposal, neither of which seems wholly satisfactory. One is to grant each buyer a single lease for his chosen period in each of the years for which the arrangement lasts. A number of leases are therefore granted in respect of each of the flats, the leases taking effect in possession in turn. The other is to grant a series of separate tenancies, one for each period of intended occupation.

It is technically possible to grant a lease for a series of separate, non consecutive, periods (*Smallwood v Sheppards* [1895] 2 QB 627). However, such a lease is one for a term only of the aggregate of the separate periods: ie a lease for one week each year for eighty years is a lease for eighty weeks (*Cottage Holiday Associates Ltd v Customs and Excise Commissioners* [1983] QB 735). This inconveniently casts implied repairing duties on the landlord (Landlord and Tenant Act 1985, s 11). The landlord cannot therefore charge his tenant with the cost of those repairs, either directly or as part of a service charge (*Campden Hill Towers Ltd v Gardner* [1977] QB 823).

15.2.3 Series of tenancies

The other possibility does not yet seem to have been tried. This is to grant the buyer a series of tenancies, one to cover each of his intended occupation periods. Each would certainly be a short tenancy, but it would not be an assured tenancy because it would be at low rent (Housing Act 1988, Sch 1, para 3) and granted for holiday purposes (para 9).

There would still be the danger of imposing repairing obligations on the landlord which it was not intended that he should bear. That could be dealt with either by excluding the statutory control by court order (Landlord and Tenant Act 1985, s 12(2)), or by transferring the immediate reversion to a tenants' company so as to make repairs and maintenance a communal responsibility.

One danger to note is that no tenancy can be granted at the outset to take effect more than twenty-one years later. It will be void (Law of Property Act 1925, s 149(3)). However, a contract entered into initially to grant such tenancies when the time comes is quite valid (*Re Strand & Savoy Properties Ltd, D P Development Co Ltd v Cumbrae Properties Ltd* [1960] Ch 582).

15.3 Contract

Anyone contracting to acquire timeshare accommodation from a developer or dealer is entitled to a cooling off period within which to change his mind. A person who, in the course of business, enters into a contract conferring 'timeshare rights'—intermittent accommodation rights for leisure purposes exercisable for at least three years—must comply with statutory requirements (Timeshare Act 1992). The rules do not apply to a private owner of a timeshare when he disposes of it.

The person dealing with the professional must be given the right to cancel the timeshare agreement during a minimum of 14 days. The time runs from his being given a document setting out the terms of the agreement and a notice of the right to cancel. There is a similar right to cancel an agreement providing credit for acquiring the timeshare.

It is an offence not to comply with the statutory requirements about timeshare agreements (maximum fine £5,000 on summary conviction, unlimited fine on indictment).

15.4 Documentation

The recommended method of timeshare disposal—licences granted to club members—can conveniently be documented in this way:

(1) *Trust instrument*   This vests the property in a trustee, who holds it for the members of the flat owners' club for the duration of the timeshare scheme, and after that for the developer. A corporate trustee would be suitable for this purpose. Such a trustee will wish formally to be indemnified against any costs associated with owning the property. In practice, the outgoings will be paid by the club, from members' contributions. The trustee will also be protected by having recourse to the value of the property it holds. Nevertheless, further protection can be provided by the developer, as settlor, giving an indemnity in the trust instrument;

(2) *Club constitution*   The club rules have two functions. They regulate the rights of the flat owners in relation to their flats. These include: periods of use, manner of use, services enjoyed, payments for services. The rules must also deal with the structure of the club, which will need a steering committee, and members' rights to pass on membership, which in effect gives them the right to pass on their flats;

(3) *Membership certificate*   It is convenient to have a document in the flat owner's hands that records his entitlement. The contract between him and the club will be recorded partly by the club's rules, which define the detailed terms of general application, and the certificate which adds the matters referring specifically to him: his name and address, in which flat he is interested, and for what periods. This certificate performs the same function as a share certificate, which records a shareholder's entitlement to a share, for which the detailed regulations are governed by the company's memorandum and articles of association;

(4) *Management agreement*   Successful enjoyment of a timeshare flat depends upon satisfactory maintenance and service arrangements. The club has the obligation to make the necessary arrangements but, at least in the early years, it will not be an effective body. The developer normally undertakes management duties for an initial period, and there is a binding agreement covering this to reassure buyers and to set the pattern for the future;

(5) *Contract*   It will normally be convenient for the developer to enter into a preliminary contract with the buyer. This has the same function as a normal conveyancing contract: to formulate the parties' obligations and to fix a future time for them to be completed. As with other conveyancing contracts, this is a temporary document, superseded on completion by the others mentioned above. It will be subject to the statutory right to cancel during the cooling-off period.

Chapter 16

Short Term Letting

16.1 Assured tenancies

The protection of the Rent Acts, controlling rent and giving security of tenure to tenants under short lettings, has not applied to flats let since 15 January 1989 (with minor exceptions). A new statutory category of tenancies was then created, assured tenancies, which gives tenants more limited protection.

16.1.1 Qualifications

An assured tenancy is created when a flat is let (a licence is not included) by a private sector landlord as a separate dwelling to one or more individuals—but not to a company—at least one of whom occupies it as his only or principal home (Housing Act 1988, s 1(1)). A new tenancy of a flat which for any reason does not fall within this category is outside all statutory control on rent and security of tenure; the common law rules apply to it.

A landlord can legitimately pursue a policy of letting to companies in order to avoid the statutory protection (*Estavest Investments Ltd v Commercial Express Travel Ltd* [1988] 2 EGLR 91), but he should ensure that the company is actually the one who performs the tenant's covenants to avoid the arrangement being dismissed as a sham. The fact that a company is formed or acquired expressly for the purposes of the tenancy does not prevent the transaction from escaping from the statutory net (*Hilton v Plustitle Ltd* [1989] 1 EGLR 119).

A letting cannot be an assured tenancy if the rent payable is too high or too low. It must be neither over £25,000 a year nor under £1,000 a year in Greater London or £250 a year elsewhere (Housing Act 1988, Sched 1, paras 2–3C).

16.1.2 Tenant protection

A tenant under an assured tenancy has some security of tenure. When a fixed term tenancy comes to an end, a periodic tenancy automatically arises and to ensure that this is not on terms which would make the tenant quit, he has the right to have them fixed by a rent assessment committee. The court can only make an order for possession of a flat held on an assured tenancy on one of the grounds, some mandatory others discretionary, specified in the Act (Housing Act 1988, ss 5–7, Sched 2). The widow or widower of a sole tenant under an assured tenancy succeeds to the tenancy, unless the former tenant had himself succeeded to it (s 17).

There is no general rent control covering assured tenancies. However, when there is a statutory periodic tenancy, or any other periodic tenancy which does not contain a term permitting the rent to be adjusted, the landlord—but not the tenant—may serve notice to increase the rent. If the tenant does not agree the new figure, he may refer it to a rent assessment committee (Housing Act 1988, ss 13, 14). Accordingly, a landlord can avoid that control of rent by ensuring that the terms of the tenancy contain acceptable provisions for review. For this reason, even if a limited fixed term tenancy is to be granted, there may be advantage in adding a periodic tenancy to it, eg 'for three years and thereafter monthly'.

16.2 Assured shorthold tenancies

An assured shorthold tenancy is probably the most common form of short term letting of flats, because it offers the landlord a guarantee of possession at the end of the term. As far as rent is concerned, the only form of control is that the tenant may, on one occasion only, refer it to a rent assessment committee if it is 'significantly higher' than the landlord might be expected to charge (Housing Act 1988, s 22).

16.2.1 Qualifications

An assured shorthold tenancy is a particular type of assured tenancy, and the basic qualifications are therefore the same. There are additional requirements (Housing Act 1988, s 20):

(1) The tenancy must be granted for a term certain of at least six months, which the landlord has no power to end within the first six months;

(2) Before it is entered into, the landlord must give the tenant notice in a prescribed form.

Clearly, the landlord of an assured tenant who has security of tenure might wish to change to this arrangement instead. That obvious evasion of the assured tenancy rules is not allowed: the landlord of a sitting assured tenant cannot validly grant him an assured shorthold tenancy. Conversely, however, when an assured shorthold tenancy comes to an end, a further letting by the same landlord to the same tenant will, unless the landlord opts otherwise, be an assured shorthold tenancy even if it does not comply with the normal requirements. The later tenancy may, therefore, be a periodic tenancy, rather than a fixed term one, and no further statutory notice need be given.

16.2.2 Possession

The landlord is guaranteed possession once an assured shorthold tenancy has ended, even if the tenant has remained in the flat on a periodic basis. The landlord must give the tenant notice that possession is required. In the case of a fixed term tenancy, there must be at least two months' notice. It can be given while the tenancy is still current so that the landlord becomes entitled to possession promptly. Where the tenancy is a periodic one, the notice must give a date for possession. This date must meet three criteria: firstly, it must be the last day of a period of the tenancy; secondly, it must be at least two months after the date the notice was given; and thirdly, it must not be before the first date on which the tenancy could have been ended by notice to quit (had a notice to quit been appropriate for an assured tenancy) (Housing Act 1988, s 21).

There is an accelerated county court procedure for a landlord to regain possession from an assured shorthold tenant, so long as he does not seek any other relief, such as recovering arrears of rent. The application is supported by the landlord's affidavit, and judgment can be given by a district judge without a hearing.

16.3 Resident landlords

No assured tenancy is created if the owner-occupier of a flat lets part of it, nor if the owner-occupier of a building, which is not a purpose-built block of flats, lets a flat (Housing Act 1988, Sched 1, para 10). So the only case in which this exception does not apply is where the owner of a purpose-built block lives in one flat and lets another; that can create an assured tenancy, or an assured shorthold tenancy, in the normal way. For this purpose, an owner-occupier is someone who occupies the property as his only or principal home. If there are joint landlords, at least one of them must qualify in that way.

16.4 Shared flats

Flat sharing is common in inner city areas, and was for a time much favoured by property owners as a way to avoid the Rent Act. However, doubt was cast on its efficacy for that purpose. The legal distinction which was then drawn applies equally to assured tenancies, and arrangements which would be outside the Rent Act do not create assured tenancies: neither set of legislative rules applies to licences.

The transactions are put into effect in this way. When a number of people wish to share a flat, the owner enters into a separate contract with each. That contract is a licence permitting the sharer to occupy the flat in common with such others (a maximum number is often specified) as the landlord names. Each sharer is responsible for his own agreed payment.

The contention is that this creates a series of individual and independent licences, and no tenancy. Statutory restrictions on tenancies cannot therefore apply. However, the contrary argument is that the arrangement is a sham: what was intended by all parties was a joint tenancy and that is therefore what is created even though the agreements may appear to be licences on their face.

At one time it seemed that the House of Lords had stopped such sets of sharing agreements from escaping statutory regulation. As Lord Templeman put it, 'An occupier of residential accommodation at a rent is either a lodger or a tenant' (*Street v Mountford* [1985] AC 809, 817). Sharing agreements were held to create a joint tenancy. However, following reconsideration by the House of Lords, the position now appears to be as follows. Sharing licences are valid if the parties genuinely did not intend that the occupiers should have exclusive possession, the accommodation in the premises makes sharing a realistic possibility and the agreements are independent not interdependent. Failing this, the arrangements will create a tenancy (*A G Securities v Vaughan*; *Antoniades v Villiers* [1990] 1 AC 417).

The present position is far from certain. Sharing agreements may be effective as such, and therefore not create assured tenancies. For this to apply, the parties must intend to be bound by the terms expressed in the agreement, so that it is not a sham, and the accommodation must be such as to allow the contemplated sharing. However, even in such a case, it cannot be guaranteed that the sharing agreements will be construed as licences.

16.5 Student flats

Flats let to students are generally within the provisions relating to assured tenancies. However, certain educational institutions and bodies specified in regulations made by the Secretary of State are exempt (Assured and Protected Tenancies (Lettings to Students) Regulations 1988, as amended).

The exemption applies to a tenancy granted to a person who is pursuing, or intends to pursue a course of study provided by a specified educational institution. Once exempt, the tenancy remains outside the assured tenancy category even if the tenant ceases to be a student.

The owner of a house which is to be divided into students' flats can escape the statutory provisions by letting it as a whole to one of the specified educational institutions for them to sublet flat by flat. The letting of the house cannot be an assured tenancy, because the tenant is not an individual (Housing Act 1988, s 1); also the letting is not of a separate dwelling-house (*St Catherine's College v Dorling* [1980] 1 WLR 66).

When one of the privileged landlords has a flat that is temporarily surplus to its needs for students, it can grant a short term tenancy of it. On satisfying three conditions, the landlord has a mandatory ground for obtaining possession when the tenancy ends, for which an accelerated county court procedure is available. First, the tenancy must be for a fixed term of no longer than twelve months. Secondly, during the immediately preceding twelve months, the flat must have been let to a student on a tenancy which was not an assured tenancy under the provisions just discussed. Thirdly, on or before the beginning of the tenancy, the landlord must give the tenant written notice that possession might be recovered on this ground (Housing Act 1988, Sched 2, Ground 4).

16.6 Holiday flats

A person who takes a flat for a holiday does not receive an assured tenancy (Housing Act 1988, Sched 1, para 9). There is no definition of 'a holiday'. There is no reason to suppose that the term is limited to holidays of a particular length, at any particular time of year, or at places known to be holiday resorts. It is a question of fact whether a holiday is the purpose of the tenancy. Decisions on the similar Rent Act provisions are likely to be followed. A declaration that it is for a holiday is *prima facie* evidence that it is so (*Buchmann v May* [1978] 2 All ER 993), but the court will go into the surrounding circumstances (*R v Rent Officer for London Borough of Camden, ex p Plant* (1980) 257 EG 713).

One point on which there is no authority, although it was a common way to seek to avoid the Rent Act, is whether a letting for a 'working holiday' creates an assured tenancy. One county court judge was reported as accepting that a working holiday was a holiday for statutory purposes (*McHale v Daneham* (1979) 249 EG 969 (*CC*)). It is suggested that, whatever its name, a working holiday is merely a period of work in a different location from the usual one, and perhaps in a different job, and that this is not therefore a holiday for the purposes of the Act.

For a form of agreement to let a flat for holiday purposes, see Precedent D:2, p 237.

If a holiday flat is to be let off season, the object will be more to cover the overheads and to avoid physical deterioration than to make a substantial profit. That makes it vital to ensure that there is no delay in obtaining possession before the start of the high season. For this reason, the landlord has a mandatory ground for possession at the end of an off season assured tenancy, whatever the time of year (Housing Act 1988, Sched 2, Ground 3). Three conditions must be satisfied. First, the letting must be for a term certain of no more than eight months.

Secondly, at some time during the twelve months before it started, the flat must have been occupied under a right to occupy it for a holiday. (That occupation need not have been a tenancy, nor for consideration.) Thirdly, the landlord must have given the tenant notice, no later than the start of the tenancy, that possession could be recovered on this ground.

If the tenant refuses to leave, it will still be necessary for the landlord to take proceedings for eviction (Protection from Eviction Act 1977, s 1). There is an accelerated county court procedure available for their type of case.

16.7 Business use of flat

The tenant of a flat who uses it both as a residence and for business does not have an assured tenancy while the letting enjoys the protection of the Landlord and Tenant Act 1954, Pt II (Housing Act 1988, Sched 1, para 4).

Whether the letting of a flat with a mixed use is an assured tenancy or a business letting is a question of degree. The position was neatly illustrated by two contrasting cases heard together by the Court of Appeal. (They related to Rent Act protection, but the same rules apply.) In one case, a flat was let to a doctor, who had formally requested the landlord's consent to use it for professional purposes as well as for his residence. Nevertheless, the fact was that he only saw a patient there about once a year. That business use was minimal, so the tenancy counted as residential (*Royal Life Saving Society v Page* [1978] 1 WLR 1329). The other case concerned a flat mainly consisting of a single large room. The tenant adapted the hall for use as an office. He regularly conducted business from there and used the flat address for business correspondence. Even though the landlord had let the flat to him for residential purposes and, so far as the landlord was concerned, the business use was surreptitious, the letting had been converted into a business tenancy and the tenant had lost his residential protection (*Cheryl Investments Ltd v Saldanha* [1978] 1 WLR 1329).

16.8 Employees' flats

Tenancies of flats granted to employees by reason of their employment will be assured tenancies in the same way as other lettings, although the landlord may have a special ground on which he can recover possession. Three particular cases nevertheless need to be considered: flats let rent free, service occupancies and accommodation for agricultural workers.

16.8.1 Rent free lettings

Rent free lettings, and many at a concessionary rent, will not be assured tenancies. To come into that category, the rent must be less than £1,000 in Greater London or less than £250 elsewhere. An example of a tenant who fell outside the statute was the porter in a block of flats, employed to maintain the central heating, who occupied one of the flats without paying (*A L Ashway Ltd v French* (1952) 160 EG 465—a decision under the equivalent Rent Act rule).

The obvious manoeuvre for the employer anxious not to grant an assured tenancy is to charge no rent for the flat, and to reduce the tenant's pay by the amount which the rent would otherwise have been. Under the Rent Act that was held not to be effective, and it is assumed that the same will apply to assured tenancies. The point is that although no rent is paid, it has been quantified (*Montague v Browning* [1954] 1 WLR 1039). However, although there are judicial *dicta* casting some doubt, if no figure is placed, even indirectly, on the rent the tenancy is probably to be treated as one which is rent free (*Barnes v Barrett* [1970] 2 QB 657).

16.8.2 Service occupancies

A sure way to stop an employee's flat being subject to an assured tenancy is to grant a licence of it, rather than a formal tenancy (Housing Act 1988, s 1). The only exception is for agricultural workers, dealt with below.

There can be difficulty in ensuring that an arrangement is a licence, because the mere fact that an employer provides accommodation for an employee does not guarantee that it is. However, the employer-employee relationship often provides circumstances where a licence is appropriate. Such a licence is often called—both confusingly and inaccurately—a service tenancy. A better term is 'service occupancy'.

The flat has to be an integral element of that employee's job. Two types of case may be contrasted. On the one hand, there are caretakers and boarding school housemasters, of whom it can truly be said that they are required to occupy the flat for the better performance of their duties. That is the classic service occupancy. At the other extreme is the employee with a rare skill who is offered a flat as an inducement to take the job. Occupying that particular property has no effect on how he does his work, and his is not a service occupancy. However, it is always a question of fact. In one case, a school 'house parent' was granted a tenancy of a school house which had no direct bearing on his duties, and he had a true tenancy with full protection (*Royal Philanthropic Society v County* [1985] 2 EGLR 109).

16.8.3 Agricultural workers

An agricultural worker with a tied flat may have special rights, under an 'assured agricultural occupancy'. This applies when the reason why his right to the flat does not constitute an assured tenancy is because he pays no rent, or only a concessionary one, and/or the flat is comprised in an agricultural holding. It gives the farm worker the rights of an assured tenant (Housing Act 1988, s 24). There is, however, a procedure under which the landlord may induce the local housing authority to provide alternative accommodation, which will entitle him to possession (s 26).

16.8.4 Ground for possession

Even when a flat has been let to an employee on an assured tenancy, the landlord has the advantage of a special ground for possession. If it was let to the tenant in consequence of his employment (not merely, it should be noted, for the better performance of his duties), the court may order possession if it is reasonable to do so when the tenant has ceased to be in that employment (Housing Act 1988, Sched 2, Ground 16).

A change of landlord makes no difference, in that a new landlord can take advantage of the ground for possession once the job ends. However, if the tenant is still employed by the first landlord in the same job, the new landlord cannot use this ground for possession.

Chapter 17

Conveyancing

17.1 General

The procedure for buying, selling, letting and mortgaging flats is generally identical with that for other types of property. The only matters on which it is necessary to comment here are those which exclusively relate to flats or which are of particular concern to parties dealing with flats.

Clearly, in perusing title to flats, and particularly in assessing the acceptability of long leases of them, the general considerations discussed in the first Part of this book must be taken into account.

17.2 Precontract enquiries

17.2.1 Town and country planning

The erection of a block of flats requires planning permission in the usual way. It should be noted also that conversions that create two or more flats out of a building that was formerly a single dwellinghouse involve a material change of use of the building and of each of the new flats (Town and Country Planning Act 1990, s 55(3)(a)), which is a development that requires consent (s 55(1)). The statutory expression is, 'the use as two or more separate dwellinghouses'. There must be some doubt about the meaning of 'separate'. For the purposes of protected and no doubt also assured tenancies, the sharing of living accommodation prevents premises constituting a 'separate dwelling' (*Neale v Del Soto* [1945] KB 144). On the other hand, two physically separate flats could, for those purposes, form a single dwellinghouse (*Langford Property Co Ltd v Goldrich* [1949] 1 All ER 402). The subdivision of one flat into two completely separate ones requires planning permission as a conversion, even though the rest of the building remains unaltered.

17.2.2 Service charges

Where the statutory controls on service charges apply (Landlord and Tenant Act 1985, ss 18–30), a buyer should enquire what accounts and information the seller has already obtained from the landlord. Even if a flat changes hands, the landlord is not obliged to supply any summary of costs or to make available facilities for inspecting vouchers more than once in respect of the same period (s 24). Once the buyer takes over he may find that he has no chance to study details of expenses for earlier periods, if that duplicates enquiries the seller previously made. The buyer can still be concerned with expenditure made earlier, because those expenses may be reflected in current service charges. In particular, it is prudent to enquire whether the seller has been notified by the landlord of any costs incurred more than eighteen months earlier which are to be included in the service (s 20B(2); Landlord and Tenant Act 1987, Sched 2, para 4).

17.2.3 Rent

A lease granted before 15 January 1989 reserving more than a low rent will generally be a protected tenancy. This can mean that no premium or only a limited one may be charged when it is assigned. This difficulty normally only arises in the case of a lease which reserves a rent that will or may rise in the future, so that it exceeds the low rent limit. To buy a lease in respect of which there is then no restriction on premiums, but which will fall foul of the curbs later after the rent has been increased, may be to buy something that will become unmarketable.

The buyer should therefore ensure before exchanging contracts that the lease will not be caught. Two conditions must be satisfied (Rent Act 1977, s 127; Housing Act 1988, s 115):

(1) The lease is not and cannot become terminable, by notice given to the tenant, within twenty years of the date it was granted;

(2) The lease terms do not inhibit both assignment and underletting of the whole flat, ignoring restrictions during the final seven years of the term only. 'Inhibit' means preclude, permit subject to consent but allowing a payment in the nature of a fine excluding s 144 of the Law of Property Act 1925, or permit subject to consent while requiring an offer of surrender in connection with the request for consent.

17.3 Contract

For a form of contract for selling a leasehold flat, see Precedent E:1, p 247.

17.3.1 Insurance

On the purchase of a leasehold flat, the buyer should seek to ensure that the risk remains with the seller until completion, as the Standard Conditions of Sale (2nd ed, cond 5.1.1) provide. There are a number of reasons for this. First, the landlord will probably control the form of the insurance and the buyer will have no influence on it. This is frequently the case with any leasehold property, but is particularly so in the case of a flat where a single policy covers the whole block. The landlord generally refuses to alter the sum insured at the behest of a single flat owner, because that involves him in collecting supplementary premiums from all the other flat owners. Secondly, if the landlord is the one to effect the insurance, there is no way in which the buyer can ensure that he keeps the policy on foot. There is neither privity of estate nor privity of contract between a landlord and a contracting buyer of the lease. Thirdly, if a block of flats is destroyed the negotiations involved in rebuilding are likely to be much more complex than for a single property. A buyer would do much better to retire from the transaction if the damage comes between exchange of contracts and completion. The seller may also feel that the complication means he would do better completing and taking the money without involving himself in the building, but he will generally suffer other losses so that he is inevitably involved.

17.3.2 Assignment of NHBC guarantee

The revised NHBC ('buildmark') protection scheme is intended to ensure that it is not necessary for later buyers of flats to give the Council notice of assignment of the benefit of the guarantee. The ten year notice issued by the NHBC clearly states that protection is given to 'the buyer', defined to include both the first buyer and every subsequent buyer. Despite theoretical difficulties of creating contractual obligations benefiting third parties, and the need for assignments of choses in action, it seems unnecessary to take action when a flat is protected by the new scheme introduced in 1988 and the initial protection period has finished. However, during that first two years, notice of assignment should be given to the builder concerned, because it is less easy to be certain that builders will not want to take technical points to fight a serious claim.

Where a flat is covered by one of the NHBC's earlier schemes it is recommended that notice of assignment be given, even though the council has maintained that it is not necessary.

As the conversions and renovations scheme is an insurance, the policy should be assigned, and notice of the assignment given. The benefit of an insurance policy can only be assigned with the consent of the insurer (*Saddlers' Co v Badcock* (1743) 2 Atk 554), but this can be presumed in this case because that is the basis on which the policy is issued.

17.3.3 Warranty that defects reported

A buyer of a flat still under a NHBC guarantee cannot benefit from it in respect of a defect which a predecessor in title should have reported, but did not.

The 1979 edition of the agreement says (cl 7(*b*)):

> The vendor shall not be liable to the purchaser . . . (b) (save when the purchaser is a mortgagee in possession) unless any previous purchaser as soon as practicable gave the vendor notice in writing of any defect or damage complained of.

In respect of claims during the structural guarantee period, the house buyer's insurance policy excludes liability on the part of the NHBC in respect of:

> Any defect or damage of which notice was or should have been given during the initial guarantee period (Special conditions applying to section III, 1).

and

> the council shall not be liable: . . . 4 (Save when the purchaser is a mortgagee in possession) unless any previous purchaser as soon as practicable gave the council written notice of the defect or damage complained of (general exclusions).

A buyer is well advised to require his seller to give a warranty that all known defects or damage have been reported, in writing and as soon as practicable, as both the agreement and the policy require. A seller must consider carefully before giving such a warranty. If it turns out that there was something relevant that he had not reported, and liability under the NHBC guarantee is repudiated as a consequence, he could find himself responsible for the cost of rectifying it. That would be the measure of damages for breach of the warranty.

The printed form of assignment contains an assignor's covenant (although it is intended to be an instrument under hand) 'that he has duly discharged and performed all the obligations imposed on him' by the agreement. The 1979 edition does not impose an obligation. It merely makes liability dependent on giving notice. In that case, the covenant in the printed form of assignment is no longer adequate.

Defects in and damage to the common parts must also be reported. The form of the documentation effectively requires them to be reported by all the flat owners interested in the common parts. Clearly this is not something that the seller will be able to warrant.

17.3.4 Licence to assign

Not many long leases of flats require the flat owner to obtain the landlord's consent before assigning, although some do. In those cases the buyer should insist on the seller obtaining it, because in default the lease will be subject to forfeiture. A licence will frequently be required on the assignment of a short term tenancy.

The Standard Conditions of Sale both require the seller to use all reasonable efforts to obtain a licence (2nd ed, cond 8.3.2(*a*)). They require the consent to be granted at least three working days before the completion date. In default, there is a power of rescission.

Landlords' powers, when considering whether to grant a licence to assign, are limited. A covenant against assignment without the landlord's consent is subject to a proviso that consent is not unreasonably to be withheld (Landlord and Tenant Act 1927, s 19(1)). In respect of a flat, that will usually limit the landlord's discretion to financial considerations, the tenant's ability to pay the rent and service charges. Exceptionally, unneighbourly behaviour elsewhere, reported in the references supplied, could be a good ground for refusal. The landlord cannot normally insist on interviewing the buyer (*Elfer v Beynon-Lewis* (1972) 222 EG 1955). A landlord who is not entitled unreasonably to withhold consent has a statutory duty to give consent if to withhold it would be unreasonable (Landlord and Tenant Act 1988). However, the fact that the seller may have a cause of action against the landlord will not help the buyer.

17.3.5 Offer to surrender

Short term leases of flats sometimes include a tenant's covenant to offer to surrender the lease before applying for consent to assign. This gives the landlord a closer control over who occupies the flat. This provision is valid in short leases (*Bocardo SA v S & M Hotels Ltd* [1980] 1 WLR 17). In a long lease of a flat at a low rent, coming within Part I of the Landlord and Tenant Act 1954 it is not valid, because its effect is to purport to contract out of the right to a statutory tenancy (*Re Hennessey's Agreement* [1975] Ch 252). It seems nevertheless that the offer to surrender must be made, even though its acceptance does not result in a valid contract (*Allnatt London Properties Ltd v Newton* (1982) 45 P & CR 94).

The seller is obliged to demonstrate that he has made the necessary offer, to establish that he is deducing a good title. The contract can conveniently provide expressly for what is to happen.

17.3.6 Service charges

Service charges payable by the tenant under a long lease can cause difficulties on a sale of the lease in two ways. First, there is the question of transferring the benefit of an accumulated balance of a reserve fund. Secondly, there is the need to apportion service charge payments when no accounts have yet been prepared for the period in question.

A buyer will automatically obtain the benefit of the seller's contributions to a reserve fund (Landlord and Tenant Act 1987, s 42(3)(*b*)). One view suggests that the buyer should reimburse the whole amount to the seller, because it will go to reduce the amount the buyer would otherwise have to pay later for services or maintenance. A buyer might argue that saving to replace a boiler or to redecorate the exterior is in effect paying for its gradual deterioration and the seller was simply paying for the use of facilities during his period of ownership. A compromise is for the buyer to reimburse half of the accumulated sum to the seller. The purchase price can be adjusted before contracts are exchanged, or the contract can provide for an addition to be made on completion.

The Standard Conditions of Sale now provide expressly for the apportionment of a service charge of which the amount is not known at completion. They adopt the principle that apportionment should take place as soon as the figure is known, in the same way as it would have done had it been possible to do it on completion (2nd ed, cond 6.3.5). The arrangement is clearly fair, although it does mean that accounts between the seller and the buyer may not be settled for some time. It may be prudent to add a requirement that until the apportionment is finally made, each party must inform the other of any change of address.

An alternative approach is to estimate the current year's service charge by a comparison with the previous year's. This allows the sale to be completed without leaving any loose ends. It might work in this way. If the parties consider that the combined effect of price changes and the amount of work done on the property suggest that the current year's service charge will be say ten per cent greater than in the year before, the contract provides that the service charge is to be apportioned on that assumption.

17.3.7 Tenants' company share

Where the lease requires the flat owner to own a share in a tenants' company, the contract should provide for the share to be sold along with the flat, and for the share certificate and signed transfer to be handed over on completion.

The general terms of a normal conveyancing contract are not appropriate to deal with anything unusual relating to the share. Additional terms should be added if necessary. For example, if the previous flat owner has died and the sale is by executors, the share may still be registered in the deceased's name. The probate should be registered with the company, or the buyer provided with the means of establishing that a transfer signed by the executors is effective to transfer the share to him. A share in a tenants' company will not normally be of any value, and could even be a liability. There may be circumstances in which the buyer would require a warranty from the seller that the share is free from incumbrances.

If there is any doubt whether the directors of the company will register the transfer, the contract can provide that the seller will give the buyer an irrevocable power of attorney to exercise the seller's rights as shareholder.

17.4 Mortgages

17.4.1 Building society requirements

Most building societies have formulated general policy guidelines for lending on the security of flats. Many do not lend on freehold flats. The points most commonly considered in assessing the acceptability of a lease are:

(1) *Length of term*   A term extending anything from fifteen to twenty years beyond the anticipated date for repaying the mortgage loan is required.

(2) *Rent*   If there is an escalating rent, the terms of the lease must not be such that it may become a protected tenancy, so that the price that could be charged on a sale is restricted. Some societies consider that the rent should be more than nominal, while not being great enough materially to prejudice the value of the leasehold interest. A ground rent of £50 a year per flat might be acceptable. They want to ensure that the landlord has a financial interest in the property that will give him an incentive to enforce the tenants' covenants and to see that the block is properly maintained. This necessarily presupposes that the reversion is not owned by a tenants' company. Societies taking this view regard such companies with misgivings.

(3) *Support, repairs, services*   Adequate terms should be included to ensure that not only the flat mortgaged, but also the rest of the block including the common parts, is properly maintained and services are provided. This ensures that the fabric of the flat is secure, and it also prevents the value of the flat being eroded. It is often a requirement that the landlord enters into a positive covenant to do the work required on the default of any other flat owner. Or, less stringently, the landlord may be required to take steps to enforce the covenants in the leases of the other flats.

(4) *Insurance*   Comprehensive insurance is generally a condition of a mortgage offer. Societies now generally accept insurance arrangements set out in leases if the cover is at least as good as they arrange on freehold properties mortgaged to them.

(5) *Other terms*   A proviso to forfeit a lease on the buyer's bankruptcy is generally unacceptable, as prejudicing the lender's security. Some societies will not accept any restriction on the assignment of the lease, except perhaps in the last seven years of the term.

17.4.2 Defective leases

Now that a tenant can apply to the court for an order to vary a lease which is defective in relation to a number of important matters (Landlord and Tenant Act 1987, s 35), it may be that mortgagees will take a stronger line, insisting that prospective borrowers procure variations before mortgaging a flat. However, the likelihood of such moves will be influenced by market considerations, and there is no evidence yet of such demands.

A mortgagee can usually insure against the effects of a defective lease. This cover has a very limited purpose. The policy will grant an indemnity against any loss as a result of the defect incurred by the mortgagee on a realisation. The defect may be the lack of a landlord's covenant to make good any deficiency in service charge contributions caused by one flat owner's bankruptcy. The insurance does not then make good every shortfall. Only if its existence results in a loss to the mortgagee, which it will not if the borrower duly makes his mortgage payments, is there any question of a claim under the policy. If the borrower defaults and the mortgagee exercises his power of sale, the policy is there to make good any deficit, but again if the mortgagee suffers no loss there is no payment by the insurers. Even though only the mortgagee can benefit, the borrower is normally called upon to pay the premium as part of the bargain for the mortgage.

In some circumstances, this type of insurance may be offered to the tenant. This is unusual, and the premium would be far higher than when a policy is effected by a mortgagee.

17.4.3 Share in tenants' company

When the lease requires that the tenant for the time being must own a share in a tenants' company, a mortgagee who exercises his power of sale must be able to vest the share in the buyer. The mortgagee will want to avoid becoming the registered owner of the share.

The simplest method of giving the mortgagee the necessary control, which is often adopted, is to require the borrower to sign a blank share transfer and deposit it, with the share certificate, along with the deeds on completion. On a sale, the mortgagee would complete the transfer in the buyer's name. This is not entirely satisfactory. If there is no further documentation, there is doubt whether the mortgagee has been duly appointed the borrower's agent to complete the transfer. The necessary authority may be implied. However, if the borrower dies, becomes mentally incapable or, perhaps, goes bankrupt, the mortgagee's authority automatically ends even if, unless authority is given by power of attorney, he knew nothing of the circumstances (*Yonge v Toynbee* [1910] 1 KB 215; Power of Attorney Act 1971, s 5(3)).

This difficulty is overcome by the borrower granting a power of attorney to the mortgagee. The power can be incorporated into the mortgage. It gives the mortgagee power to sign a transfer of the share in the borrower's name, transferring it either to the mortgagee or to someone nominated by the mortgagee. As the power is granted 'to secure . . .

the performance of an obligation owed to the donee' and it is expressed
to be irrevocable, it is not revoked by the death, incapacity or bankruptcy
of the borrower (Powers of Attorney Act 1971, s 4(1)).

Part 3
_____

Security of Tenure

Chapter 18

Preliminary

18.1 Summary

Until statute intervened, a lease or tenancy agreement of a flat expired by effluxion of time or when a notice to quit was given, and the tenant could only extend it with the landlord's agreement. There are now a number of statutory rights which apply to particular circumstances and give different benefits.

Tenants of flats let on short or periodic tenancies, who wish to continue to occupy on that basis, have the same rights to security of tenure as tenants of houses, as assured, regulated or secure tenants. Details are not given here, because the rights are not particular to flats; for details, see *Aldridge's Residential Lettings* (Longman).

Long leaseholders of flats now have three possible rights, and may be able to choose between them. They are: first, collective enfranchisement, the right to buy the freehold of the block of flats in collaboration with other leaseholders (Chapter 19); secondly, the right to purchase a new lease, giving a 90-year extension to the current term (Chapter 20); and thirdly, a statutory tenancy, giving the tenant a personal right to continue in occupation at a rack rent. This is another right which applies equally to houses, so the particulars are not given here.

In the public sector, a secure tenant not only has security of tenure as a short term or periodic tenant, but also has a right to buy under which he acquires a long lease (Chapter 21). That lease in turn entitles him to the rights of collective enfranchisement and the purchase of a new lease.

The effect of these rights may be summarised as follows:

	Collective enfranchisement	*Purchased new lease*	*Statutory tenancy*	*Right to buy*
With other leaseholders?	Yes.	No.	No.	No.
Lump sum payment?	Yes.	Yes.	No; maybe payment for initial repairs.	Yes; discounts apply.

141

	Collective enfranchisement	*Purchased new lease*	*Statutory tenancy*	*Right to buy*
Rent?	Ground rent continues.	None.	Fair rent.	£10 pa maximum.
Extension of tenure?	No, but tenants can agree to extend.	Yes, further 90 years.	Yes, indefinite while tenant occupies	Yes.
Need to be resident?	For previous year, or 3 in last 10.	For any 3 years in last 10.	Yes.	Yes.

18.2 Criteria for choice

A tenant of a flat who wants greater security of tenure will need to consider three broad questions in choosing between the statutory rights.

What does he wish to achieve?   Each of these rights extends the period during which the tenant can enjoy the flat. Beyond that, however, there are other considerations. Collective enfranchisement removes the former landlord and substitutes the tenants, collectively, as the people responsible for managing the block. In the other cases, the landlord stays the same. Each of the rights, other than the right to a statutory tenancy, results in the tenant receiving a valuable asset which he can sell (although a former secure tenant who exercised the right to buy may have to repay some discount if he sells within three years).

What can he afford?   Capital payments are required for collective enfranchisement, a purchased new lease or exercising the right to buy. Even the grant of a statutory tenancy may require payment for initial repairs. As far as rent is concerned, the statutory tenancy will be most expensive, because a fair rent can be charged. In the other cases, there may be a ground rent or nothing at all.

Will he have a disposable asset?   The statutory tenancy depends upon continuing personal occupation, so the tenant—who has paid no premium—does not have a disposable asset. In the other cases, he will have.

Does he qualify?   The detailed qualifications for each right differ. They are dealt with in the Chapters devoted to each right below.

Chapter 19

Collective Enfranchisement

19.1 Outline

Collective enfranchisement is a right which the Leasehold Reform, Housing and Urban Development Act 1993 gives long leasehold tenants of flats, which some or all of those in a block may exercise together. The statutory procedure does not create an enforceable right to purchase; it specifies the terms on which the parties are entitled to enter into a binding contract. Once there is a contract, it is enforceable in the usual way.

Tenants who satisfy the conditions which entitle them to join in the purchase are 'qualifying tenants'. They name a 'nominee purchaser' to acquire compulsorily the freehold interest in the block and any intermediate interests. So, after the purchase each becomes the direct tenant of the nominee purchaser. As freeholder, the nominee purchaser will normally have the responsibility of organising services and maintenance and will be able to grant longer leases to the tenants.

On the landlord's side, negotiations are conducted by the 'reversioner' on behalf of all those interested. Any landlord other than the freeholder of the block, ie the owner of an intermediate interest and freeholder of any other land involved, is a 'relevant landlord'. The freeholder is generally the reversioner, but the court has powers to substitute another relevant landlord (Leasehold Reform, Housing and Urban Development Act 1993, Sched 1).

Although tenants who are qualified are given compulsory purchase rights, there are two ways in which the landlord can resist. First, a freeholder who lives in a flat in a converted, not purpose built (as originally constructed: *Barnes v Gorsuch* (1981) 43 P&CR 294), block which contains no more than four flats may refuse to sell. This protection extends to occupation by a beneficiary under a trust of the freehold and an adult member of the family of either the freeholder or such a beneficiary (Leasehold Reform, Housing and Urban Development Act 1993, s 10). Secondly, there are cases in which the landlord, although parting with the freehold, may retain the beneficial ownership of parts of the block by requiring a 999 year leaseback at a peppercorn rent. This applies if the landlord himself occupies a flat as qualifying tenant and to any

143

other part of the building which is not as flat let to a qualifying tenant, eg flats retained by him as investments or commercial units. The landlord has the option whether to require a leaseback in these circumstances, but in the case of some flats let on secure tenancies he is obliged to have one (s 36).

19.2 Qualifications

Tenants qualify to exercise the right of collective enfranchisement if the following conditions are met:

(1) The block contains at least two flats and is self-contained. It must either be structurally detached, or a vertical division of a larger building, capable of independent redevelopment with services which are either separate or which could be separated without significant interruption of supplies to occupiers of other parts (Leasehold Reform, Housing and Urban Development Act 1993, s 3);

(2) No more than ten per cent of the block (measuring internal floor area) is used for something other than residential purposes (which includes ancillary accommodation, eg a garage, storage area) or common parts (s 4);

(3) At least two-thirds of the flats are let to 'qualifying tenants', ie on a long lease (originally granted for more than 21 years) which is not a business tenancy. It must have been granted at a low rent (in its first year no more than two-thirds of: until 1 April 1963, the letting value; 1963–1990, the rateable value; or from 1 April 1990, £1,000 in Greater London or £250 elsewhere) (s 8). Nobody may be a qualifying tenant of more than two flats; if someone would otherwise be, none of them counts as having a qualifying tenant. Joint tenants of a flat count as one qualifying tenant. If a sub-tenant is a qualifying tenant, no superior tenant of that flat qualifies (s 5);

(4) The 'participating tenants' who give notice to exercise the right to enfranchise are at least two-thirds of the qualifying tenants, and are no fewer than half the number of flats in the block. Of those participating tenants at least half must satisfy the 'residence condition', by having occupied the flat as their only or main home for the previous 12 months or periods totalling three years during the last ten years (s 6).

19.2.1 Premises

The block to be enfranchised must satisfy the self-contained test, but the claim can extend further. It can apply to two other categories of property belonging to the freeholder: first, property demised with a flat held by a qualifying tenant, and secondly, common parts which a qualifying tenant's lease entitles him to use. In the latter case, the freeholder can instead of conveying the common parts arrange to grant permanent rights over it or convey the freehold of suitable alternative property (Leasehold Reform, Housing and Urban Development Act 1993, s 1(2)–(4)).

The tenants are not obliged to enfranchise all the property which they could include in their claim (Leasehold Reform, Housing and Urban Development Act 1993, s 1(5)). There can be a number of reasons for this stemming from the rules governing claims, in addition to any practical considerations. The tenants may wish, for example, to exclude some parts used for commercial purposes to bring the proportion below ten per cent, to exclude flats not occupied by qualifying tenants to bring their total up to the two-thirds minimum or to exclude property occupied by tenants who are not participating, the cost of which would have to be borne by the participators. However, the tenants still have to ensure that what is in the claim is self-contained.

The landlord may choose to exclude underlying minerals, as long as proper provision is made for support (Leasehold Reform, Housing and Urban Development Act 1993, s (6)).

19.2.2 Exceptions

Certain exceptions, where there is no right of collective enfranchisement, may be briefly mentioned.

A block does not qualify if it is within the precinct of a cathedral or is heritage property (designated by the Treasury as of outstanding scenic, historic, scientific, architectural or aesthetic interest) (Leasehold Reform, Housing and Urban Development Act 1993, ss 31, 96). Nor can tenants enfranchise if compulsory purchase is pending for any freehold or leasehold interest in the block (s 30).

Enfranchisement does not operate against certain freeholders: the National Trust and charitable housing trusts in respect of flats provided as part of their charitable activity (Leasehold Reform, Housing and Urban Development Act 1993, ss 5, 95). The Crown is also outside the scope of the statutory provisions but, subject to certain exceptions, has agreed to convey on the same terms (s 94). A tenant does not qualify if he has given notice ending his lease or if a possession order has been made against him (Sched 3, paras 1, 3).

19.3 Preliminary agreement

It is prudent for tenants who propose to make a claim for collective enfranchisement to enter into a preliminary agreement between themselves, covering at least the areas considered below. See Precedent A:2, p 169.

19.3.1 Conduct of claim

At the stage of considering whether to join in the claim and of negotiating the preliminary agreement, each tenant would be well advised to take independent legal advice. A solicitor approached at that stage to advise the tenants collectively should suggest that each be advised separately as there is a strong possibility of conflicts of interest arising from the tenants' individual circumstances and aspirations. Once they agree to proceed with the claim, however, joint representation is appropriate and a solicitor could be named by the agreement.

The claiming tenants will also need to be advised by a valuer, whom the Act requires to be named in the initial claim notice. To prevent disagreement, he could be named in the preliminary agreement.

The statutory procedure is conducted on the tenants' behalf by a 'nominee purchaser', to whom the freehold is finally transferred, and the nominee's identity should be agreed in the preliminary agreement. It will generally be most convenient to form a company for this purpose. This avoids the need to replace a nominee who dies or has to be removed from office. The tenants can nominate themselves as nominee purchaser, but that will only be convenient in the smallest cases because the freehold could not be transferred to more than four people. However, where there are only a few flats, trustees could be nominated, with the power of appointment of new trustees vested in the owners for the time being of head leases of the flats.

In establishing a company, care needs to be taken with the shareholding and voting structure. Unless there is a considerable variation in size from one flat to another, the tenants will probably agree that the leaseholder of each flat should exercise one vote, and therefore have one share (service charges could still be allocated in a more sophisticated way).

Many decisions, some more important than others, will be needed during the statutory claim procedure. The directors of the company, or a small steering committee, will be appropriate to take those decisions or to propose to the general body of tenants what should be done. The preliminary agreement can usefully lay down the limits of the directors' power to bind the membership. Matters of particular concern may be: the final price to be paid; the extent of the property to be acquired; what easements should be obtained or granted; taking or defending legal proceedings; changing professional advisers.

The preliminary agreement should provide how decisions are to be taken by the general body of claiming tenants. There could be one vote per flat, or the allocation could vary by the size of the flat or by the financial contribution of each tenant. A simple majority vote could bind all the tenants. Or, a decision could require a weighted majority, eg two-thirds. Also the tenants must agree whether only votes cast are counted or whether the majority is of all those entitled to vote.

Once the claim to enfranchise has been launched a participating tenant cannot individually withdraw, unless he disposes of his flat, although all the claimants may together decide to withdraw at any time before there is a binding purchase contract. This makes it important that each tenant realises the implications of being bound by majority decisions with which he disagrees.

19.3.2 Finance

Every participating tenant should no doubt pay the price of his own flat, so the valuer should be asked to assess each separately. He will also need to pay a share of the total of three other sums: first, the price of any units which are acquired and which are not flats belonging to participating tenants; secondly, the landlords' costs; and thirdly, the tenants' professional costs. Each tenant has to rely on all the others being able to proceed, otherwise the purchase will collapse. So, the preliminary agreement should require each claimant to provide the money to finance his share. Individual tenants may want some limit to that commitment, particularly if they are relying on borrowing and may meet unexpected difficulties with lenders. However, as an individual tenant cannot withdraw while a claim is pending, a limit on one person's commitment is only possible if someone else is prepared to increase his.

Claimants will have preliminary valuation advice and their initial notice must state the proposed purchase price, but this may change during the negotiation for a number of reasons. The landlord may challenge the tenants' valuation, he may claim more than 50 per cent of the marriage value, and he may opt to take leasebacks of some units or may decline to do so.

It is not possible to recommend a single best way to contribute to the cost of the parts of a block not occupied by a purchasing tenant. Taxation will be a major consideration. The tax treatment of any capital gain, and indeed income accruing in the meantime, will be relevant and will be affected by each buyer's particular circumstances. The method of financing will generally determine the ownership structure of these parts of the block once the tenants have acquired the freehold.

The preliminary agreement should prescribe how the burden of costs will be divided between the claimants, although their liability can be made joint and several. Possible formulae include equal shares for each flat or a rateable division according to the tenants' respective shares of service charge or according to the sums provided towards the purchase. The agreement can usefully provide for an advance payment on account of costs.

19.3.3 Ownership structure

The preliminary agreement should set out how the block is to be owned

after the tenants complete the enfranchisement. Clearly, the freehold
will be vested in the nominee purchaser and, until there are any changes,
the leases under which tenants are in possession will continue. There
are, however, possible further variations.

First, the bargain may well be that the contribution of each participating
tenant entitles him to a longer lease of his own flat. The agreement
should provide for the grant of this new lease. There are two other
factors to consider: how the purchase of other parts of the block is
being financed and how the management will be organised.

The price of those other parts of the block may be financed by the
nominee purchaser obtaining loans or subscribed capital. An alternative
is for people, whether or not participating qualifying tenants, to put
up the money to buy specific portions of the property, in return for
the grant of leases of those parts. In the latter case, the owners of those
leases can be treated in the same way as the claiming tenants.

On the other hand, if there is general financial support of the nominee
purchaser the property ownership structure which is appropriate will
depend on how the money is provided. If the participating tenants
contribute rateably, the proportionate share of each remains the same.
A ten per cent subscription, for example, will buy the lease of a flat
which is ten per cent of the flats occupied by participating tenants and
a ten per cent interest in the rest of the block. The valuable reversionary
interests in the parts of the block not occupied by participating tenants
can remain vested in the nominee purchaser. No new interests in the
property need to be created unless it is convenient to do so.

However, if some participating tenants pay more than the price of
their own flats but some do not, or the contributions are not rateable,
a separate investment vehicle will be needed. The nominee purchaser
can grant leases of the relevant parts of the property to that investor,
so that the beneficial ownership is vested in those who contributed the
extra money.

19.3.4 Leases and management

If new leases are to be granted to participating tenants, their terms should
be settled in advance and enshrined in the preliminary agreement. For
this reason, it is useful to make the nominee purchaser a party to the
preliminary agreement. Good estate management will dictate that the
leases should all be in the same form, and this can be scheduled to
the agreement.

The future management arrangement for the block can also be settled
when agreeing the terms of the new leases. If the tenants of all the
flats in the block participate in the purchase the nominee purchaser
can conveniently become the management company.

In other cases, a separate management company would be better. This
can allow all tenants to have a say in the management, whether or not

they joined in buying the freehold. At the same time it overcomes any difficulty which might arise when the nominee purchaser makes a profit by selling a lease of part of the property whose tenant did not participate. Only those who were party to the purchase should share in that profit.

The nominee purchaser can grant a head lease to the management company, and that company would be the immediate landlord of the occupying tenants. The equity value contributed to the purchase of 'non-participating' parts of the block thus remains in the nominee purchaser.

19.3.5 Additional claimants

A tenant who did not join in giving the original claim notice may later ask to participate. In one case he can insist. If a participating tenant assigns his flat, he ceases to qualify, but his successor may join in the claim by giving notice to the nominee purchaser within 14 days (Leasehold Reform, Housing and Urban Development Act 1993, s 14(2), (4)). On the other hand, a tenant who did not qualify or chose not to participate, or his successor, may later qualify and wish to do so. He may only do so if all the participating tenants agree (s 14(3), (4)). The preliminary agreement can usefully make provision for both cases.

Tenants making a claim will normally want any assignee of a flat from one of their number to join in the claim. If he does not, there may be difficulty in financing the purchase. The preliminary agreement could provide that any participating tenant who sells must make it a condition of the sale that the buyer joins in the purchase of the freehold, and agrees to be bound by the preliminary agreement itself. There is some doubt whether this provision would be enforceable, but at least it serves to bring the matter to all parties' attention at an early stage.

As other newcomers can only join in the claim by unanimous agreement, the preliminary agreement need not deal with the matter simply to ensure that unwelcome outsiders are not admitted. On the other hand, a tenant who is not qualified may help with the financing, in return for the grant of a longer lease later and the promise of being admitted to the claim if he manages to qualify. Recording the participating tenants' consent in the preliminary agreement is a way to be sure that the bargain is honoured.

19.4 Terms of enfranchisement

19.4.1 Price

The price which the tenants have to pay to enfranchise is made up of three elements. First, there is the market value of the freehold. This is calculated on assumptions which exclude the value of the tenants' bid, any improvements by a tenant or his predecessor and the 1993 Act statutory rights. To this is added at least half the 'marriage value'.

The value added when a lease is merged in the freehold is what is normally referred to as the marriage value; here, it is any value added when both interests come under a single control. More than half the marriage value is added if the parties agree or a leasehold valuation tribunal determines a buyer would have been paid more in the market. Finally, the landlord can claim compensation for any loss or damage which the enfranchisement causes to other property, including loss of development value, and this is added to the price (Leasehold Reform, Housing and Urban Development Act 1993, Sched 6).

Intermediate leasehold interests are valued in the same way, with two exceptions. In the case of an improved ground rent—giving no more than one month's expectation of possession and a maximum profit rent of £5 a year—the value is calculated according to a mathematical formula. A lease with a negative market value—resulting, eg, from an earlier grant at a premium of a lease reserving a smaller rent than that payable to the superior landlord—is treated as having a nil value. Any deficit is deducted from the value of the next superior interest.

19.4.2 Costs

The nominee purchaser is liable for all the costs of the reversioner and relevant landlords, with certain exceptions (Leasehold Reform, Housing and Urban Development Act 1993, s 33). He does not have to pay costs for which a contract cannot make the buyer of property responsible, and each side bears its own costs of an application to a leasehold valuation tribunal.

19.4.3 Transfer terms

The nominee purchaser takes the freehold free from any existing mortgage. As long as he pays the price to the mortgagee or into court, the security is discharged automatically, although the mortgagor's personal liability will survive if the debt is not fully repaid (Leasehold Reform, Housing and Urban Development Act 1993, s 35).

The transfer may contain easements and restrictive covenants so far as they are necessary to preserve the use of property as it was previously used. There are, however, curbs on the creation of new restrictions, particularly by the landlord (Leasehold Reform, Housing and Urban Development Act 1993, Sched 7, paras 3–5).

A leasehold valuation tribunal settles disputes about the transfer terms.

19.4.4 Leaseback

In those cases in which the nominee purchaser executes a leaseback, it is for a term of 999 years at a peppercorn rent. The landlord (ie the nominee purchaser) is responsible for structural and exterior repairs, to repair other property over which the tenant under the leaseback has rights, to provide services to a reasonable standard, to insure and rebuild and reinstate. The tenant is responsible for interior repairs and decoration, and must contribute to the landlord's expense in repairing, insuring and providing services.

Only in the case of business premises can the leaseback restrict the tenant's right to assign or sublet. In that one case, there is a prohibition against assigning or subletting the whole or part of the property, or changing the use of it, unless the landlord gives prior written consent which is not to be withheld unreasonably. No provision to bring the lease to an end, other than on forfeiture for breach of covenant, is allowed (Leasehold Reform, Housing and Urban Development Act 1993, Sched 9, Pt IV).

19.5 Procedure

19.5.1 Tenants' notice

The formal procedure for collective enfranchisement is started by the participating tenants serving notice on the landlord or the freeholder. There are detailed requirements for what the notice must contain, although there is no prescribed form. In summary, it identifies the tenants and gives details showing that they qualify to exercise the statutory right, it specifies the property to which it applies and the rights the tenants need, it states the price to be paid and names the valuer who has advised the tenants, it also names the nominee purchaser and gives a date by which the reversioner must give a counter-notice (Leasehold Reform, Housing and Urban Development Act 1993, s 13). In advance, the tenants can obtain information they need for their notice (ss 11, 12).

As soon as the tenants have given their notice, they should register it as an estate contract. The notice is not a contract, but special statutory provision allows it to be registered on the land register or as a land charge (Leasehold Reform, Housing and Urban Development Act 1993, s 97). The reason for registering is that it prevents the landlord making a disposal severing his freehold interest (s 19). Enfranchisement is only possible where the freehold in the whole block is owned by the same person (s 3(1)(a)).

Although the tenants may only regard enfranchisement as urgent when their leases are nearing their end, there are two reasons in favour of making an early application. First, the longer the term of the outstanding lease, the lower will be the market value of the freehold reversion. Secondly, the right to defeat enfranchisement on the ground of intended redevelopment only exists if at least two-thirds of the long leases of flats in the block are due to end with five years of the service of the tenants' initial notice (Leasehold Reform, Housing and Urban Development Act 1993, s 23(2)(a)).

19.5.2 Reversioner's counter-notice and redevelopment

The reversioner has to serve a counter-notice to admit or contest the tenants' right to enfranchise. An admission relates only to the principle, it does not necessarily agree to the tenants' terms (Leasehold Reform, Housing and Urban Development Act 1993, s 21).

The counter-notice also provides the reversioner, or indeed any relevant landlord, with the opportunity to contest the enfranchisement because he intends to redevelop. He must have the intention, once the leases have ended, to demolish or reconstruct all or a substantial part of the premises, or to carry out substantial works of construction, which would not be possible without obtaining possession. The landlord in question has to follow up the counter-notice by an application to court within two months (Leasehold Reform, Housing and Urban Development Act 1993, s 23).

19.5.3 Documentation

The objective of the statutory procedure is for the reversioner and the nominee purchaser to enter into a binding contract the sale of the freehold of the block. Once there is a binding contract, it can be enforced as in any other conveyancing transaction.

The terms of acquisition, once agreed by the parties or determined by a tribunal, will need to be set out in the contract. This is prepared by the reversioner and, within 21 days, should be given to the nominee purchaser, who has 14 days to propose amendments (Leasehold Reform (Collective Enfranchisement and Lease Renewal) Regulations 1993, Sched 1, para 6). The contract can provide that the nominee purchaser pay a deposit of £500 or (if more) ten per cent of the premium (para 7).

The transfer has to record the fact that it was made under the statutory provisions, by containing the statement (Land Registration (Leasehold Reform) Rules 1993, r 2):

> This conveyance/transfer is executed for the purposes of Chapter I of Part I of the Leasehold Reform, Housing and Urban Development Act 1993.

19.5.4 Time limits

The statutory procedure bristles with time limits with which the parties have to comply, so that on the one hand the landlord's ability to deal with his property is not suspended for longer than necessary, and on the other hand the tenants' acquisition is not unreasonably delayed.

If the reversioner fails to comply with a time limit, the nominee purchaser may apply to the court or, where the terms of acquisition are in question, to a leasehold valuation tribunal. The sanction for default by the tenants or the nominee purchaser will normally be that the claim is deemed to have been withdrawn.

19.5.5 Withdrawal

Until the nominee purchaser had entered into a binding contract for the acquisition, the tenants may withdraw at any time (Leasehold Reform, Housing and Urban Development Act 1993, s 28). This has two effects. They are jointly and severally liable for the costs incurred by the landlord (s 33). Also, there can be no new application to enfranchisement for 12 months (s 13(9)).

There are certain exceptions to the liability for costs. It does not apply if the landlord establishes an intention to redevelop, if enfranchisement is stopped because of compulsory purchase or if there is an application for an estate management scheme after the tenants' claim.

Chapter 20

Purchased New Lease

20.1 Outline

As an alternative to collective enfranchisement, a qualifying tenant of a flat under a long lease at a low rent has the right to buy a new lease (Leasehold Reform, Housing and Urban Development Act 1993, Pt I, Chapter II). The tenant surrenders his current lease and is granted a new one. This has the effect of extending the current term by 90 years, and is granted at a peppercorn rent.

There are some similarities, but also fundamental differences, between this right and the right of collective enfranchisement. Both rights give the tenant the chance to extend the period of his current lease substantially, and should therefore overcome any marketability problems. Both involve paying the landlord a capital sum, based on market value. It seems likely that acquiring a share in the freehold will be more expensive than buying a new lease, but in many cases the difference may not be great.

On the other hand, there are differences both in outcome and in procedure. Buying a new lease involves no change of landlord, and the management of the block will continue as before. However, the purchase may well prove to be easier than collective enfranchisement because the tenant acts alone and does not have to enlist the co-operation of other tenants in the block.

It should also be noted that the tenant who buys a lease may be faced with the need to give possession to a landlord who wishes to redevelop, although he will be entitled to compensation.

A tenant would not want to apply at the same time both to enfranchise and to buy a new lease. However, while one tenant applies to buy a new lease, others in the block might seek to enfranchise. The enfranchisement application takes priority in the sense that it has the effect of suspending the new lease procedure. So, if the enfranchisement is successful, the tenant buying a new lease does so from the new freeholder.

20.2 Qualifications

On the purchase of a new lease, the only property concerned is the tenant's flat (including ancillary accommodation such as a garden or garage) rather than the block of which it forms part, so that the characteristics of the block are not relevant. Disregarding, therefore, requirements relating to the block, the qualifications to exercise this right closely follow those for collective enfranchisement (para 19.2 above).

There are two variations to note. First, a person may be qualifying a tenant of any number of flats in the block. So, it is only necessary to consider his qualifications for the flat in question. Secondly, there is a residence requirement: he must have occupied the flat as his only or main home for the last three years, or for periods totalling three years in the last ten. This is a more stringent test than for collective enfranchisement, but it still does not require the tenant to be resident when making his claim (Leasehold Reform, Housing and Urban Development Act 1993, s 39).

20.3 Terms of new lease

20.3.1 Landlord

The landlord for the purpose of this procedure is the most immediate landlord who has a sufficient reversion to grant the new lease. He acts for any intermediate landlords (Leasehold Reform, Housing and Urban Development Act 1993, s 40).

20.3.2 Premium, rent and term

The premium which the tenant pays is calculated in much the same way as the price paid on collective enfranchisement (para 19.4.1 above), albeit valuing the leasehold interest acquired rather than a share in the freehold. The tenant pays the aggregate of three sums: the market value of the new lease, at least half of any marriage value and compensation for any loss or damage to other property which the landlord owns (Leasehold Reform, Housing and Urban Development Act 1993, Sched 13).

The lease is granted for a term which adds 90 years to the tenant's current lease, which is surrendered, and reserves a peppercorn rent (Leasehold Reform, Housing and Urban Development Act 1993, s 56(1)). The result is that any ground rent which the tenant pays under his current lease is cancelled for the remainder of the term. The premium payable under the new lease is likely to include, as part of the market value, an element representing the capitalisation of that rent.

20.3.3 Other terms

Taking into account any ways in which the flat has been changed since the current lease was granted, or the omission from the new lease of any property previously demised, the new lease is basically granted on the same terms as then apply under the current lease. There are, however, certain statutory provisions outlined below, although these yield to any agreement between the parties (Leasehold Reform, Housing and Urban Development Act 1993, s 57):

Services and service charge   The tenant may be required to reimburse the landlord for the cost of obligations relating to services, repairs, maintenance or insurance. If a third party, eg a management company, is party to the current lease, he is to join in the new lease, but not so that he is required to discharge any function after the end of the current term.

Renewal or termination   The new lease is not to reproduce provisions in the current lease for renewal or termination, except for termination on breach of covenant.

Sublessees   No sublease, even if a long lease, confers a right as against the landlord to buy a new lease. Nor does a subtenant have other statutory rights of rent control or security of tenure (s 59).

Redevelopment   The landlord's statutory redevelopment rights are reserved.

Landlord's liability   The landlord may limit his personal responsibility to breaches of covenant for which he is responsible.

Statement   The lease must contain a prescribed form of statement (Land Registration (Leasehold Reform) Rules 1993):

> This lease is granted under section 56 of the Leasehold Reform, Housing and Urban Development Act 1993.

20.3.4 Disputes

Disputes about the terms of the new lease are resolved by applying to a leasehold valuation tribunal (Leasehold Reform, Housing and Urban Development Act 1993, s 91).

20.3.5 Redevelopment

Notwithstanding the grant of a new lease, the landlord can obtain possession for the purposes of redevelopment (demolition and reconstruction or substantial works of construction), which he could not otherwise do. He has to apply to the court, and may do so during two periods: within 12 months before the term of the current lease would have expired by effluxion of time and during the five years preceding the end of the new lease term.

A landlord who obtains possession under this provision must pay the tenant the market value of his lease in compensation (Leasehold Reform, Housing and Urban Development Act 1993, s 61).

20.4 Procedure

In this case, unlike collective enfranchisement, the statutory procedure does not end with a binding agreement between the parties, but with the grant of the new lease itself. The tenant's notice has the effect of a contract (Leasehold Reform, Housing and Urban Development Act 1993, s 43), and should be registered as an estate contract (s 97).

20.4.1 Notice and counter-notice

The tenant claims the statutory right to buy a new lease by serving notice on the landlord and any other party to the current lease. There is no prescribed form, although there are detailed provisions about the contents of the notice. It must identify the tenant, the property, and the periods during the last ten years for which he occupied it as his only or main home, specify the terms proposed for the new lease and give a date by which the landlord must serve a counter-notice (Leasehold Reform, Housing and Urban Development Act 1993, s 42).

The landlord's counter-notice admits or contests the tenant's claim in principle, or states that he will claim possession for redevelopment. An admission is conclusive as to the tenant's qualification and satisfying the residence qualification. If the landlord contests the tenant's claim, he must apply to the court (Leasehold Reform, Housing and Urban Development Act 1993, s 45).

20.4.2 Conveyancing

As the tenant's notice has the force of a contract, the detailed procedural terms are laid down by regulations which apply unless the parties choose to vary them (Leasehold Reform (Collective Enfranchisement and Lease Renewal) Regulations 1993, reg 3, Sched 2). The landlord may serve notice requiring the tenant to pay a deposit on account of the premium. This is £250 or, if more, ten per cent of the premium (para 2). The draft lease is prepared by the landlord and must be given to the tenant within 14 days after the terms are agreed or settled. The tenant then has 14 days to propose amendments. The landlord engrosses lease and counterpart (para 7). The matter is completed at the office of the landlord's solicitor or licensed conveyancer (para 8).

20.4.3 Costs

The tenant is responsible for the landlord's costs of the new lease, unless his application is defeated by the landlord's intention to redevelop or because compulsory purchase proceedings are instituted. Each side pays its own costs of any application to a leasehold valuation tribunal (Leasehold Reform, Housing and Urban Development Act 1993, s 60).

Chapter 21

Right to Buy

21.1 Outline of right

A secure tenant—ie a tenant whose landlord is one of a specified list of public authorities (Housing Act 1985, s 80)—has a right to buy a long lease of his flat once he has been a secure tenant of that or other premises for three years. There are exceptions. There is no right to buy if the landlord is himself a leaseholder whose lease has less than fifty years to run, unless every superior interest belongs to a public authority which is subject to the right to buy (Sched 5, para 4; Housing (Extension of Right to Buy) Order 1993). Those with certain types of tenancy— eg some service tenancies and some tenancies intended to be temporary— do not qualify. Similarly some special types of accommodation, eg sheltered housing for the elderly, are excluded. The lease can normally be purchased for the market value of the flat less a discount of between 44 and 70 per cent, depending on the length of the buyer's period as a secure tenant (Housing Act 1980, Pt I, Chapter 1).

The definition of a flat for this purpose (Housing Act 1985, s 183) is important, because the right to buy is a right to acquire the freehold in the case of a house, but a lease in the case of a flat. A flat is not directly defined, but rather is stated to be any dwellinghouse which is not a 'house'. A 'house' is a structure reasonably so-called. Three principles are then to be applied:

(1) Where a building is divided horizontally, the separate units are not houses, eg a normal block of flats;
(2) The units of a building divided vertically may be houses, as in the case of a conventional terrace of houses;
(3) A building not structurally detached is not a house if a material part of it lies above or below the remainder of the structure. This would apply to a mews house where the secure tenancy does not include the garage.

21.2 Terms of lease

In general terms, the lease granted on the exercise of the right to buy may include 'such covenants and conditions as are reasonable in the circumstances' (Housing Act 1985, Sched 6, para 5). A county court has jurisdiction to settle any dispute (s 181(1)). There are some limits with which the terms must comply, and these are set out below.

The lease should state that it is granted under the terms of the Housing Act 1985. The grant of such a lease automatically implies certain repairing obligations, and they apply without being expressly written into the lease. It is therefore important for a full appreciation of the position of the parties—particularly where the lease or the reversion has been assigned, so that those currently interested in the property were not the original parties to the transaction—to know that the statutory duties are to be implied. Conversely, the Act makes some terms void. Again, no-one perusing the lease can know whether a term is invalidated unless he knows that it was granted under the Act.

21.2.1 Term and rent

The lease is normally granted for at least 125 years, or (if shorter) five days less than the landlord's own lease. However, the term can be shorter if the landlord has granted another lease of a flat in the same building for a term of at least that length since 8 August 1980. In that case, the lease can be coterminous with that earlier lease, even if that makes the term of the later one less than 125 years (Housing Act 1985, Sched 6, paras 11, 12).

The rent reserved by the lease is not to be more than £10 a year.

21.2.2 Common parts and facilities

The subsidiary rights that the lease grants to the tenant are governed by the situation before the tenant claims the right to buy. The lease includes the right to use, in common with others, any premises, facilities or services that the tenant enjoyed during the secure tenancy. There are two qualifications. First, the landlord is only obliged to grant rights if it is capable of doing so. Secondly, the landlord and the tenant can agree different arrangements (Housing Act 1985, Sched 6, para 4).

What the tenant is entitled to have granted to him by the lease is what he enjoyed during the secure tenancy, not merely what that secure tenancy granted to him. The lease should therefore include as legal rights what the tenant previously merely enjoyed *de facto*.

To define the rights as enjoyed by the tenant 'during the secure tenancy' is not precise. It could mean: throughout the secure tenancy; or, at some time during the secure tenancy; or, when the secure tenancy ended because the tenant exercised his right to buy. There is as yet no guidance on how the statutory expression is to be interpreted.

21.2.3 Repairs

The Act makes provision for both landlord's and tenant's repairing covenants to be implied into the lease (Housing Act 1985, Sched 6, paras 14–16). The terms will apply, whether or not expressly mentioned, unless excluded, although the landlord does not have a statutory duty to do work which the terms of a superior lease would forbid. The landlord's implied covenants can only be excluded or modified by a county court order. It must be a consent order, and is made if the court thinks it is reasonable to do so. In contrast, the tenant's implied covenants can be excluded by agreement between the parties.

The landlord's repairing obligations are:

(1) To keep the structure and exterior of the flat and the building of which it is part, including drains, gutters and external pipes, in repair, making good any defect affecting the structure. Rebuilding or reinstatement following destruction or damage by fire, tempest, flood 'or any other cause against the risk of which it is normal practice to insure' is included;

(2) To keep in repair any other property over or in respect of which the tenant is granted any rights. This is a considerable departure from the normal general rule that the owner of a servient tenement over which there is a right of way owes no duty to the dominant tenement to keep it in repair (*Newcomen v Coulson* (1877) 5 ChD 133);

(3) To ensure, so far as practicable, that any services provided by the landlord and to which the tenant is entitled either alone or jointly are maintained at a reasonable level, and to keep in repair any installation in connection with providing the services;

(4) To rebuild or reinstate after damage or destruction by fire, tempest, flood or any other risk against which it is normal practice to insure.

Presumably, the landlord's covenant must be construed as a covenant to repair on notice, except where it affects parts of the property of which the landlord is still in possession.

The tenant's implied covenant is to keep the interior of the flat in good repair, including decorative repair.

21.2.4 Charges for repairs and improvements

There is a restriction on the service charge which the lease may require the tenant to pay during the first five years. In the course of the procedure to claim the lease, the landlord must estimate what the tenant will have to pay for repairs and making good structural defects (Housing Act

1985, s 125A(2), (3)). What the tenant has to pay is restricted to the estimated amount plus an inflation allowance (Sched 6, para 16B). The service charge can be index-linked (*Coventry City Council v Cole* [1994] 06 EG 133).

Similar restrictions apply to contributions the lease requires the tenant to make towards initial improvements. Again, the landlord must estimate the amount payable (Housing Act 1985, s 125B), and that, with an inflation allowance, is the most the lease can require the tenant to pay (Sched 6, para 16C).

21.2.5 Void terms

Certain provisions in a lease granted as a result of the exercise of the right to buy, or in a collateral agreement, are made void (Housing Act 1985, Sched 6, paras 17–19). They are those:

(1) To prohibit or restrict the assignment of the lease, or subletting all or part of the flat;

(2) To allow the landlord to recover from the tenant any part of the cost of discharging his implied obligations to repair the flat or other property over which the tenant has rights, or any part of the cost of insuring the liability. This is subject to an exception, which in effect allows a service charge to include the cost of most repairs. What is permitted is a covenant to bear a reasonable part of repairing costs, or insuring against liability for them. The cost of making good a structural defect can only be included if the landlord told the tenant of its existence before granting the lease, or if the landlord does not become aware of it until the lease has been in existence for ten years;

(3) To permit forfeiture or the imposition of any penalty or disability on the tenant if he enforces or relies on any of the statutory provisions concerning the grant or contents of the lease.

Part 4

Precedents

A Sale on Long Lease

Precedent A:1 Contract for Sale of Flat

When a developer sells a flat on a long lease it is convenient to have a preliminary contract. It allows both parties to have the reassurance of a binding obligation before they are ready to grant and take up the lease. Only a short document is needed because all the terms of the lease can be settled by a reference to a draft already agreed, which will presumably be a standard form for all the flats in the block.

This form incorporates the Standard Conditions of Sale (2nd ed).

It assumes that the long term insurance arrangements envisaged in the form of lease will operate between exchange of contracts and completion. If the block is still under construction, the builders will be insuring and this must be reconsidered. In that case it will not be appropriate for either party to agree to insure, but for the buyer's protection what will happen in the event of damage or destruction must be made clear. Presumably, the result will either be a delayed completion— which will be automatic if the date for completion is to be fixed by a notice that the flat is ready for occupation—or the buyer will have an opportunity to rescind. Any lengthy delay in completion can be doubly embarrassing for a buyer. Not only is his occupation of the flat delayed, but any mortgage offer he has may expire.

THIS AGREEMENT is on . . .	Date
between	
'The Seller':	Parties
'The Buyer':	
whereby it is agreed:	
1. ON completion the Seller is to [grant][1] [procure that there is granted][1] to the Buyer who is to accept a lease ('the lease') in the form of the draft annexed of the property ('the property') described in it and	Lease
the Buyer is to pay the Seller the price of £ . . .	Price

---

1   If the lease is to be granted by a tenants' company in whom the developer has already
    vested the freehold, use the second alternative. Otherwise, use the first one.

Title   2. (a) THE Seller is to deduce to the Buyer title to the freehold estate out of which the lease is granted (b) That title [is registered at H M Land Registry with absolute title under Title Number . . .][1] [will start with . . .][1]

---

1   If the Seller's freehold title is registered, delete the second alternative; if it is unregistered, delete the first alternative.

Insurance   3. (a) THROUGHOUT the period between the date of this agreement and completion the Seller is to keep on foot an insurance policy covering the whole of the building[s][1] of which the property forms part and which complies with the landlord's covenants to be contained in the lease. The lease terms relating to information about the policy, proof of payment of premium, and the employment and disposal of proceeds are to apply during that period as if the lease had already been granted [and as if the Seller were the Landlord][2]
(b) On completion the Buyer will, if the Seller requires, pay to the Seller the part of the premium payable on any such insurance policy in respect of that period

---

1   If a separate garage is to be demised, there will be two buildings to insure.
2   Insert if the lease is to be granted by a tenants' company which will insure.

Vacant   4. VACANT possession of the property shall be given
possession   to the Buyer on completion

NHBC   5. The Seller will offer the Buyer the protection set
guarantee   out in the Buildmark booklet on the standard form issued by the National House-Building Council

Share   6.[1] ON completion the Seller is to procure that the Buyer is, without cost to the Buyer, registered as holder of one fully paid ['A'][2] ordinary share in . . . Limited and is to deliver the related share certificate to the Buyer

---

1   This clause is for use when the buyer is to become a member of a tenants' company. It is assumed that the seller will still be administering that company, and will therefore be able to arrange for the share certificate to be prepared in time to hand over on completion.
2   The capital of the company may be divided into two classes if the developer wishes to retain control of the company until he parts with the last flat.

7.[1] Before or forthwith after completion the Seller   Seller's land
is to deposit the land certificate relating to his   certificate
freehold title with H M Land Registry and notify the
Buyer of the deposit number allotted to it[2]

---

1 This clause is only required where the seller's title is registered.
2 An express provision to this effect settles any doubt whether the seller must deposit
   his land certificate: *Strand Securities Ltd v Caswell* [1965] Ch 958.

8. THE completion date is [. . .][1] [fifteen working days   Completion
after the Seller gives the Buyer notice that the
property is ready for occupation and use][1]

---

1 If the flat is complete and a completion date can be fixed when contracts are exchanged,
   delete the second alternative; if the flat is still under construction, delete the first one.

11. THE terms of this agreement include the   General
Standard Conditions of Sale (2nd ed) except   conditions
condition 5.1,[1] so far as they apply to the grant of
a lease and are not inconsistent with the terms of
this agreement which shall, for the purposes of the
Conditions, are special conditions.

---

1 This excludes the terms of the Standard Conditions about insurance.

Precedent A:2   Agreement Between Tenants on Collective Enfranchisement

Tenants under long leases who wish to exercise their statutory right to collective enfranchisement should enter into a preliminary agreement between themselves to regulate the conduct of the claim and, after it has succeeded, the ownership and management of the block.

This form makes a number of assumptions:

(1) Not all the qualifying tenants are joining in the claim, although provision is made for others to participate later. The part of the purchase price not attributable to the flats of the tenants who are party to the claim is being contributed to some, but not all, of the tenants who are buying.

(2) A two-thirds majority of the participating tenants is needed to agree certain important steps, eg litigation or withdrawal of the claim, and a resolution passed by a vote of that size binds the minority.

(3) After the freehold has been acquired, it will be vested in the nominee purchaser, a company owned by the claimants.

(4) The tenants joining in the purchase will surrender their leases after completion and will receive a new long lease, in the form of a draft annexed to the agreement.

(5) Long leases of the other flats, in the same form but in reversion on the existing leases, will be granted to someone nominated by the tenants contributing the price attributable to those flats. That nominee might well be a company formed to exploit the investment made by this syndicate of investing tenants.

(6) The members of the freehold owning company will then be the tenants under the new long leases, with the shares allocated on the basis of the same number per flat.

(7) All costs will be shared between the tenants who join in the purchase in the proportions of their contributions to the price.

THIS AGREEMENT is made on   between   Date

'The original buyers' listed in column 1 of Schedule   Parties
'The Company': . . .

1. IN this agreement, unless the context otherwise   Definitions
requires
1.1 an expression defined for the purposes of any
part of the Leasehold Reform, Housing and Urban

Development Act 1993 bears that meaning
1.2 the following expressions bear these meanings:
'building': the property described in Schedule 2
'buying tenant': as defined in clause 4
'completion date': the date fixed for completion of the purchase of the freehold
'landlord': . . .
'non-participating price': the price payable by the nominee purchaser after deducting sums certified by the surveyor as attributable to participating flats
'participating flat': a flat in the building of which a buying tenant is qualifying tenant
'solicitors': . . .
'surveyor': . . .

Recitals

2. AT the date of this agreement
2.1 the landlord owns the freehold of the building
2.2 each original buyer is qualifying tenant of the participating flat shown in column 3 of Schedule 1 against his or her name
2.3 the original buyers are the shareholders in the Company

Purchase

3. THE original buyers agree to exercise their right to right to collective enfranchisement to acquire the freehold of the building and for that purpose they appoint
3.1 the Company as nominee purchaser
3.2 the solicitors as solicitors for the buying tenants and the Company
3.3 the surveyor as qualified valuer for the purpose of the initial notice and to act for the buying tenants

Buying tenants

4.1 EACH of the following is, for the time being, a buying tenant
4.1.1 an original buyer who is still qualifying tenant of the flat listed against his or her name in column 3 of Schedule 1
4.1.2 the qualifying tenant of a flat in the building which is not listed in Schedule 1 who, with the agreement of every buying tenant, has given the solicitors notice of intention to be bound by this agreement

4.1.3 the tenant as a result of an assignment of the long lease of a flat in the building, under which a former tenant was either an original buyer or a person who gave notice under clause 4.1.2, who has given the solicitors notice of intention to be bound by this agreement

4.2 Whenever the long lease of a participating flat is vested in two or more tenants who together qualify as a buying tenant under clause 4.1, they are treated as a single buying tenant and their liability under this agreement is joint and several

5. WHEN a proposal is put to a vote of the buying tenants   *Votes*

5.1 the buying tenant of each participating flat may cast one vote

5.2 the resolution is passed if at least two-thirds of the possible votes are cast in favour

6.1 EACH buying tenant agrees to contribute towards the price payable by the nominee purchaser   *Price*

6.1.1 the part of the price which the surveyor certifies to be attributable to his participating flat

6.1.2 the percentage (if any) of the non-participating price stated in column 4 of Schedule 1 opposite the number of his flat

6.2 The buying tenant agrees to pay that contribution to the Company

6.2.1 as to ten per cent, within seven days of being notified that the reversioner has required payment of a deposit

6.2.2 as to the remainder (or the whole if no payment was made under clause 6.2.1), seven days before the completion date

7.1 EACH buying tenant agrees to pay his costs proportion (calculated in accordance with Schedule 3) of   *Costs*

7.1.1 the costs incurred by the reversioner and by any other relevant landlord which the nominee purchaser is liable to pay

7.1.2 the cost and expenses incurred by the Company of an incidental to the preparation and implementation of this agreement

7.2 The buying tenant agrees to pay the Company
7.2.1 on signing this agreement, [£500] on account of his liability for costs
7.2.2 on demand, from time to time, such further sums as the Company requests on account of, or in settlement of, his liability for costs

8. A RESOLUTION of the buying tenants is needed, and if passed binds all the buying tenants,

Withdrawal

8.1 before notice of withdrawal is given on behalf of all the buying tenants
8.2 before the Company

Proceedings

8.2.1 commences or defends proceedings before the court or a leasehold valuation tribunal

Price increase

8.2.2 agrees to pay a price for any interest in the building which exceeds, by more than 15 per cent, the proposed purchase price for that interest in the initial notice

Advisers

8.3 to terminate the appointment of the solicitors or the surveyor and to appoint substitutes

Transfer

9. EVERY buying tenant agrees to procure that, following the assignment of his lease, the new owner of it will
9.1 elect to participate in the proposed acquisition of the freehold of the building
9.2 give the solicitors notice of intention to be bound by this agreement
9.3 becomes owner of his shares in the Company

Leases

10. IMMEDIATELY after the Company acquires the freehold
10.1 the buying tenants will surrender their existing long leases of flats in the building to the Company
10.2 the Company will grant leases of the flats in the building as follows
10.2.1 to a tenant who surrendered the lease of a flat under clause 10.1 (jointly if more than one), a lease of that flat
10.2.2 in respect of the other flats, leases in reversion to the existing long leases to a person nominated by those buying tenants who contributed to the non-participating price
10.2.3 each lease will be in the form annexed
10.2.4 the percentages of responsibility for

service charge to be inserted in the respective leases are set out in Schedule 4

10.3 the then members of the Company will procure that its shares are held by the tenants under the new leases of the flats in the building, on the basis that an equal number of shares is attributed to each flat

SCHEDULE 1

1	2	3	4
Participating tenants:		*Flat*	*Percentage*
Name	*Address*	*number*	*of non-par-*
			ticipating
			price

SCHEDULE 2
[Description of the building]

SCHEDULE 3
Costs proportion

The costs proportion of each buying tenant is calculated according to this formula:

$$CP = \frac{P1 + P2}{TP}$$

where:

CP is the costs proportion

P1 is the part of the price attributable to the flat certified under clause 6.1.1

P2 is the amount (if any) payable under clause 6.1.2

TP is the total price

SCHEDULE 4
Service charge percentages

Flat 1:
Flat 2:   etc

Precedent A:3   Long Lease of Flat

This form is primarily intended for the grant of a lease by a landlord—whether a developer or a tenant's company—who proposes to retain the reversion and to manage the block. By adopting the appropriate variations shown, it can also be used on the grant by a developer who proposes to part with his interest to a tenant's company, whether by assignment or by the grant of a reversionary lease. It could be used following collective enfranchisement.

The form assumes that the flat is part of a modern block of purpose built self contained flats. The landlord is made responsible for repairs to the structure, maintenance of the lift and common parts, exterior decorations, provision of hot water and central heating, and for insurance. The cost of all these items is divided between the tenants of the flats as a service charge.

The lease demises a separate lock up garage, one of a block of garages, as well as the flat. If there is no garage, references to it should be omitted from the recitals and from clauses 1, 2(3), 2(4), 3 (introductory paragraph), 4(3), 5(3), Sched 1, Sched 5 para 3 and Sched 6 para 12.

THIS LEASE is made on . . .	Date
'The Landlord': . . .	Parties
['The Developer':]¹ . . .	
'The Tenant': . . .	

---

1   The developer need only be a separate party when the lease is granted at his request, eg, by a tenants' company, as a result of a capital payment to the developer.

(A) The premises which this lease demises form part of a block of 48 residential flats ('the House') and part of a neighbouring block of 48 lock-up garages ('the garage block') which form part of . . . Court at . . . ('the Estate')	Estate
(B) It is intended that a lease of each of the flats and one of the garages be granted in terms identical (*mutatis mutandis*) to this lease so that the tenants under each are able to enforce the restrictions in the other leases	Lease scheme
1. THE [Landlord]¹ [Developer]¹ having received £ . . .² which the Tenant paid, and in exchange for the obligations undertaken by the Tenant, [the Landlord]³ LETS the property first and secondly described in the First Schedule (respectively 'the Flat'	Price
	Demise

175

and 'the Garage', and together 'the demised
premises') to the Tenant WITH the rights set out in
the Second Schedule BUT EXCEPT AND RESERVING
the rights set out in the Third Schedule

Term   FOR Ninety-nine years[4] from [the Twenty-fifth day
of December ....][5] ('the term')

Rent   on the Tenant agreeing to pay a rent of £ . . . a year[6]
and the service charge in accordance with the Fourth
Schedule as further rent[7]

---

1   If the developer is not himself granting the lease, delete the first alternative. If the
developer and the landlord are the same person, delete the second alternative.
2   The acknowledgement of receipt is a sufficient discharge to the tenant who pays (Law
of Property Act 1925, s 67), and it is authority for the tenant to pay the solicitor
or licensed conveyancer producing the lease (s 69).
3   Omit if premium paid to landlord.
4   A ninety-nine year term has become customary for long leases. It is relevant that
the rate of stamp duty doubles if the term exceeds 100 years.
5   The term should be backdated to the quarter day immediately preceding the grant
of the lease of the first flat. All the leases will then end on the same day.
6   The tenant's liability does not commence until the lease is actually granted, even though
the term is backdated (*Earl of Cadogan v Guinness* [1936] Ch 515). If the reversion
is retained by the landlord as an investment, an escalating ground rent may be
appropriate.
7   Reserving the service charge as rent probably gives the landlord power to distrain
for any arrears. Stamp duty is not increased as a result of reserving a separate service
charge as rent.

Tenant's   2. THE Tenant agrees with the Landlord:
covenants

Rent   (1) TO pay the rent on the days and by equal quarterly
instalments in advance on the usual quarter days
(the first payment being a proportionate sum paid
on the grant of this lease) without any deductions
whatsoever and without exercising any right of set
off[1]

---

1   The tenant's right of set off can be negatived by a term of the lease: *Connaught Restaurants
Ltd v Indoor Leisure Ltd* [1993] 2 EGLR 108.

Outgoings   (2) TO pay all taxes and outgoings[1] in respect of
the demised premises including any imposed or
becoming payable after the date of this lease (even
if of a novel nature[2]) but not
     (i) a tax assessed upon the aggregate or a
proportion of the income or the value of the assets
of the Landlord nor

(ii) a tax assessed or payable by reason of the act of the Landlord in granting this lease
to the appropriate authorities respectively responsible for collecting it

---

1 This is a comprehensive obligation, and even covers non recurring items like road charges (*Lowther v Clifford* [1927] 1 KB 130).
2 Novel taxes are not covered unless mentioned (*Mile End Old Town Vestry v Whitby* (1898) 78 LT 80).

(3) NOT to use all or part of the demised premises for any purpose other than as a private dwelling-house and ancillary garage nor to permit anyone else to do so — Use

(4) REGULARLY to inspect the demised premises and other parts of the House and garage block visible from the demised premises and to give the Landlord without delay written particulars of any defect or disrepair which the Landlord is responsible for putting right[1] — Report defects

---

1 The landlord's repairing obligations in respect of the demised premises is a duty to repair on notice. The requirement for written notice provides evidence of compliance. It is a protection for other tenants to require the tenant to initiate the repairing process.

(5) UNLESS subclause (8)(b) applies, not to alter or add to the demised premises or to permit anyone else to do so — Alterations

(6) TO return possession of the demised premises to the Landlord in good repair at the end of the term (however it ends) — Yield up

(7) TO pay all expenses (including legal and surveyors' costs) which the Landlord incurs in preparing and serving — Costs
    (i) a notice under section 146 of the Law of Property Act 1925[1] even if forfeiture is avoided without a court order
    (ii) a schedule of dilapidations recording failure to give up possession of the demised premises in good repair at the end of the term

---

1 This covenant removes the need for leave of the court under the Leasehold Property (Repairs) Act 1938 before suing for these costs (*Middlegate Properties Ltd v Gidlow-Jackson* (1977) 34 P&CR 4).

Notices: (8) (a) AS soon as the Tenant receives a notice
copies   concerning the development of the demised
              premises or neighbouring property, or requiring work
              to be done, to give the Landlord a copy of it, and
              if the Landlord requires to join him in making
              representations about it
requirements (b) If a competent authority acting under a statute
              requires any alteration, addition, modification or
              other work on the demised premises, unless in
              conjunction with any other part of the Estate,[1] to
              do the work promptly and at the Tenant's expense

---

1 Requirements affecting not only the flat or the garage but also other parts of the
   Estate are to be complied with by the landlord, and the cost charged as part of the
   service charge: Sched 6, para 5.

Dealings   (9) NOT to assign, sublet, mortgage, charge or part
              with possession of part only of the demised premises
Give notice   (10) WITHIN one month after every change of
              ownership of this lease, and of every subletting [for
              more than one year],[1] to give notice with full
              particulars to the Landlord or to his solicitors and
              to pay a registration fee of Twenty-five pounds on
              each such occasion

---

1 It may be thought burdensome and unnecessary to have to register even short sublettings.
   They could be excluded by inserting these words.

Permit   (11) (a) TO allow the Landlord and anyone with his
inspection   or his agent's written authority to enter the demised
              premises to view them as or for a prospective
              purchaser, tenant or mortgagee
              (b) During the last year of the term to allow the
              Landlord to fix and display on the demised premises
              a board announcing that they are (with or without
              other property) for sale or to let PROVIDED THAT
              it does not interfere with the Tenant's reasonable
              enjoyment of the demised premises

Tenants'   3. THE Tenant agrees with the Landlord and with
mutual   the tenants of the other flats and garages forming
covenants   part of the Estate:
Repair   (1) TO keep the whole of the demised premises[1] in
              good repair[2] (damage by any insured risk[3] excepted
              unless and to the extent that any act or omission

of the Tenant renders the insurance money irrecoverable)

---

1   The demised premises are so defined as to exclude structural parts (Sched 1). The landlord repairs the structural parts and charges the cost as part of the service charge.
2   The standard of repair required depends on the age and nature of the premises at the start of the lease (*Lurcott v Wakely and Wheeler* [1911] 1 KB 905).
3   This is defined in Sched 6, para 12. The repairing obligation extends to damage caused by insured risks unless it is expressly excluded (*Manchester Bonded Warehouse Co v Carr* (1880) 5 CPD 507, 513).

(2) TO allow the Landlord and any tenant of any other part of the Estate and any person they respectively authorise to enter the demised premises upon reasonable notice (except in emergency) — **Permit entry:**

    (i) to inspect their state of repair and that of adjoining and neighbouring property — **inspection**

    (ii) with or without workmen, to carry out necessary repair or other work to any part of the Estate for which he is responsible, the person exercising the right to make good, promptly and at his own expense, any resulting damage to the demised premises — **to do works**

(3) (a) NOT to use all or part of the demised premises for any dangerous, offensive, noxious, noisome, illegal or immoral activity, or in any manner that may be or become a nuisance or annoyance to the Landlord, to the tenant or occupier of any other part of the Estate or any other neighbouring property, nor to permit anyone else to do so — **Use: objectionable**

(b) Not to do anything on the demised premises, or elsewhere on the Estate, which will or may render any insurance policy covering all or part of the Estate void or voidable or increase the premium payable, nor to permit anyone else to do so — **not to avoid insurance**

(4)[1] DURING the first year of the term to join in promoting, and thereafter to remain a member of, an association of all tenants of parts of the Estate[2] — **Tenants' association**

    (i) which has as its object or among its objects consultation with the Landlord on the expenditure of money on work on the Estate to which the tenants are obliged to contribute and

    (ii) which is recognised as a tenants' association under section 29 of the Landlord and Tenant Act 1985

---

1 This clause will presumably not be needed if the landlord is a tenants' company.
2 For a form of rules for a tenants' association, see Precedent E:2.

Regulations	(5) TO comply with (i) the regulations set out in the Fifth Schedule and (ii) any amendment to them agreed by a resolution of a general meeting of [the said association of tenants or by the tenants of at least sixty per cent of the flats in the House][1] [the Landlord][1] and notified to the Tenant by letter delivered to the Flat and to ensure that all occupiers of any part of the demised premises also do so

---

1 Unless the landlord is a tenants' company, delete the second alternative. If it is, delete the first one.

Landlord's covenants	4. THE Landlord agrees with the Tenant:
Quiet enjoyment	(1) SO long as the Tenant does not contravene any of the terms of this lease, he may possess and use the demised premises without lawful interference by the Landlord or anyone who derives title from, or is trustee for, him.
Service charge items	(2) TO comply with the covenants set out in the Sixth Schedule hereto[1]

---

1 This makes the tenant's right to enforce the landlord's covenant to provide services conditional on prior payment of service charge that is due because payment of service charge is linked to the duty to provide all the services (but see *Yorkbrook Investments Ltd v Batten* [1985] 2 EGLR 100), but the fact that other tenants may not have paid does not prejudice a tenant's right of action (*Marenco v Jacramel Co Ltd* [1964] EGD 349).

Leases of other flats	(3) NOT, during the first sixty-nine years of the term, to grant a lease of any other flat or garage forming part of the Estate unless it is in the same form as this lease (*mutatis mutandis*)
Provisos	5. PROVIDED ALWAYS AND IT IS AGREED AND DECLARED:
Reentry	(1) THE Landlord is entitled to forfeit this lease by entering any part of the demised premises whenever the Tenant:

(i) is twenty-one days late in paying any rent, even if it was not formally demanded

(ii) has not complied with any obligation in this lease

but the forfeiture of this lease does not cancel any outstanding obligation which the Tenant owes to the Landlord

[(2) (a) THIS lease is granted on the condition that the tenant for the time being becomes and remains the registered holder of the one ['A']¹ ordinary share in the capital of [the Landlord]² bearing the same number as the number of the Flat

Company membership

(b) If any tenant fails to apply for registration as shareholder within two months of becoming tenant, or having been so registered does not cease to be registered within two months of ceasing to be tenant, the term shall cease but without cancelling any outstanding claim by either party against the other]³

---

1   The company may have two classes of share to allow the developer to retain control during a break up operation. If it has not, delete 'A'.

2   If the tenant's company does not own the reversion, eg because its purpose is only to hold the common parts, substitute the company's name.

3   This proviso is required where the arrangement is that each tenant is to be a shareholder in the landlord company. It is assumed that the shareholding of each is to be of equal size.

(3) (a) IN any case in which the Flat or the Garage is rendered unusable by damage by any insured risk¹ and it is not possible within three years to enter into a contract for the rebuilding or reinstatement, the insurance moneys and all interest earned shall be [divided between the Landlord and the Tenant in the ratio of the open market values of their respective interests in the Flat or the Garage (as the case may be) immediately prior to the occurrence giving rise to the damage]² [paid to the Tenant]²

Insurance proceeds

(b) If in any case to which paragraph (a) of this subclause applies insurance moneys have been paid under the same policy or policies in respect of more than one flat or garage on the Estate, the parties agree that, unless the extent of the damage to each flat or garage is such as would vary the amount of insurance moneys paid in respect of each, the total sum shall be assumed to be paid in respect of the properties destroyed or damaged [in equal proportions]³ [in the ratio of the proportions of the

expenditure on services for which each is responsible[4] under the respective leases in this form][3]
(c) Any dispute as to the division of such insurance moneys shall be referred to a single arbitrator appointed, in default of agreement between the parties, by the then President of the Royal Institution of Chartered Surveyors[5]

---

1 Defined in Sched 6, para 12.
2 Unless the landlord is a tenant's company, delete the second alternative. If the beneficial interests in the landlord belong to the tenants, delete the first alternative.
3 Where the flats are identical in size or of equal value, adopt the first alternative which is simpler, and delete the second one. Otherwise, delete the first alternative.
4 Ie, the proportion in Sched 4, para 1 (ii).
5 The effectiveness of this arbitration agreement may be subject to the Consumer Arbitrations Agreements Act 1988.

VAT (4) ANY sums payable by the Tenant are exclusive of value added tax and the amount of any such tax payable thereon (whether by the Landlord or by the Tenant) is to be paid by the Tenant to the Landlord

Statutes (5) A REFERENCE to a statute in this lease refers to the statute as amended at the date of this lease and includes (unless the context otherwise requires) any later amendment to or re-enactment of it

Liability after assignment [(6) AS soon as the original [Landlord][1] [Tenant][2] namely . . . Limited has parted with all interest in [the reversion immediately expectant on the termination of][3] the term it shall cease to have any further rights entitlements responsibilities liabilities or obligations under the terms of this lease but without cancelling any outstanding rights of any other party][4]

---

1 A developer granting leases of flats may subsequently assign or grant a reversionary lease to a tenants' company and then wish to have no further responsiblity to the tenants. If this is the intention, delete 'Tenant'. Nevertheless, the landlord's liability will continue until the tenant is given notice of the assignment: Landlord and Tenant Act 1985, s 3(3A).
2 A developer may decide initially to grant the leases to a nominee of his, particularly on a break up operation. In such a case, delete the word 'Landlord'.
3 If it is the original tenant who is to escape further liability, delete these words.
4 This clause, which destroys the continuing benefits of privity of contract between the original parties, is not usual. It will normally only be acceptable in exceptional cases, such as those mentioned in the notes above. In other cases, it should be deleted.

Parties (7) (a) [SUBJECT as aforesaid][1] the expression 'the Landlord' includes the person for the time being

entitled to the reversion immediately expectant on
the termination of the term
(b) [Subject as aforesaid][2] the expression 'the Tenant'
includes the person in whom the demised premises
are vested for the time being
(c) Whenever the demised premises are vested in
more than one person they are jointly and severally
liable to perform every covenant on the part of the
Tenant
(8) (a) Section 196 of the Law of Property Act 1925   Service of
applies to any notice required or authorised by this   Notices
Lease
(b) The Tenant may serve notices (including notices
in proceedings) on the Landlord at the Landlord's
address given above until the Landlord gives the
tenant notice of an alternative address in England
and Wales for that purpose

---

1 Delete unless the previous subclause has been used to cancel the landlord's liability
   after parting with the reversion.
2 Delete unless the previous subclause has been used to cancel the tenant's liability after
   parting with the lease.

6. THE parties certify that this transaction does not   Certificate of
form part of a larger transaction or of a series of   value
transactions in respect of which the amount or value
or the aggregate amount or value of the consideration exceeds £60,000[1]

---

1 The certificate can be given if the price does not exceed £60,000 and the average
   quantifiable rent, excluding anything payable expressly for services, does not exceed
   £600 a year. Stamp duty on the premium is then eliminated.

IN WITNESS etc

The FIRST SCHEDULE   Demised
The Demised Premises   premises
FIRST the residential flat forming part and situate   Flat
on the . . . floor of the House and known as Flat
No . . . as the same is delineated and edged red on
the plan numbered 1 annexed.[1] This demise includes
the ceilings and floors within the flat (but not the
supporting structures) and excludes the roof and
foundations of the House and the boundary walls
of the Flat, whether or not external walls of the House

(except the interior surfaces (including plasterwork), the doors and the glass in the windows)[2]

Garage AND SECONDLY the garage forming part of the garage block and known as Garage No . . . as the same is delineated and edged red on the plan numbered 2 annexed[1] excluding the roof, the foundations and all except the interior surfaces of the walls thereof but including the door

---

1 It is assumed that two plans will be attached to the lease. Number 1 is to show (edged red) the extent of the flat. Number 2 is to show the whole estate, delineating the garage (edged red), and also the drives (coloured yellow) and paths (coloured violet) over which there are rights of way, and the parking and refuse disposal areas (respectively hatched black and coloured blue).

2 It is assumed that the construction of the building is such that none of the internal walls is a structural wall for which the landlord should be responsible.

Appurtenant rights *The SECOND SCHEDULE*
Support *Appurtenant Rights*

1. (a) The right of support for the Flat from other parts of the House as now enjoyed
(b) The right of support for the Garage from other parts of the garage block as now enjoyed

Services 2. The right to the free running of water, waste, sewage, gas and electricity through the pipes, drains, sewers and wires serving the Flat[1] now or at any time during the period of 80 years[2] from the commencement of the term[3] to be laid through or over any other part of the Estate

---

1 It is assumed that the garage has no electricity or other services.

2 The right to lay further services must be restricted to the perpetuity period: *Dunn v Blackdown Properties Ltd* [1961] Ch 433.

3 Assumes that the leases of all the flats start on the same date.

Access 3. (a) The right at all times to use the driveways shown in yellow on the plan numbered 2 with or without vehicles and the pathways shown in violet on foot only for gaining access to and egress from the demised premises
(b) The right at all times to use the hallways, staircases and lift in the House for gaining access to and egress from the flat

Parking 4. The right to use and to permit others visiting the Flat to use the area hatched in black on the plan

numbered 2 for parking private motor vehicles and, in the case of those having business of limited duration in the Flat, trade vehicles

5. The right to use the communal dustbins in the area shown coloured blue on the plan numbered 2 for depositing normal domestic rubbish suitably wrapped in the interests of hygiene and safety

Refuse

6. The right to enter other flats in the House for inspecting the state of repair of the Flat and any pipe, drain, sewer or wire serving it and repairing it, the Tenant promptly making good any damage caused

Entry

7. The benefit of the covenants by the tenants of other parts of the Estate

Benefit of covenants

The THIRD SCHEDULE
Exceptions and Reservations
1. (a) The right of support to other parts of the House as now afforded by the Flat
(b) The right of support to other parts of the garage block as now afforded by the Garage

Rights reserved
Support

2. The right to the free running of water, waste, sewage, gas and electricity through the pipes, drains, sewers and wires now or at any time during the period of 80 years from the commencement of the term to be laid through the Flat for the benefit of any other part of the Estate

Services

3. (a) The right for the tenants of other parts of the House to enter the Flat for inspecting the state of repair of other parts of the House and any pipe, drain, sewer or wire serving them and repairing them, the person exercising such right promptly making good any damage caused
(b) The right for the Landlord to enter the demised premises to comply with any requirement lawfully made of him under the Town and Country Planning Act 1990, notwithstanding that any action reasonably necessary for compliance interferes with the Tenant's enjoyment of the demised premises

Entry

Service charge *The FOURTH SCHEDULE*
Service Charge
1. In this Schedule:
> (i) 'Expenditure on services' means what the Landlord spends in complying with his obligations set out in the Sixth Schedule including interest paid on any money borrowed for that purpose
> (ii) 'Service charge' means one [forty-eighth] part of the expenditure on services
> (iii) 'Interim service charge instalment' means a payment on account of service charge of £100 per quarter until service of the first service charge statement, and thereafter of one-quarter of the service charge shown on the service charge statement last served on the Tenant
> (iv) 'Service charge statement' means an itemised statement of
>> (*a*) the expenditure on services for a year (or on the first occasion a shorter period) ending on the 30th day of June
>> (*b*) the amount of the service charge due in respect thereof (any apportionment necessary at the beginning or end of the term being made on the assumption that expenditure on services is incurred at a constant daily rate) and
>> (*c*) sums to be credited against that service charge, being the interim service charge instalments paid by the Tenant for that year or period, any service charge excess from the previous year or period and an appropriate part of the proceeds of any claim under an insurance policy covering damage to the Estate
> accompanied by a certificate that, in the opinion of the accountant preparing it, the statement is a fair summary of the expenditure on services set out in a way which shows how it is or will be reflected in the service charge and is sufficiently supported by accounts, receipts and other documents that have been produced to him
> (v) 'Service charge deficit' means the amount by which the service charge shown on a service charge statement exceeds any credits shown on it
> (vi) 'Service charge excess' means the amount by which any credits shown on a service charge statement exceed the service charge shown on it

2. The Landlord keeps a detailed account of the expenditure on services and procures that a service charge statement is prepared for every such year or period by an independent member of the Institute of Chartered Accountants in England and Wales, to whom the Landlord furnishes all accounts and vouchers and afford all facilities necessary

3. As soon as the Landlord receives each service charge statement, he serves it on the Tenant by sending him a copy

4. On every quarter day the Tenant pays the Landlord an interim service charge instalment

5. As soon as a service charge statement is served on the Tenant he pays the Landlord any service charge deficit shown

6. As soon as he receives the final service charge statement for the term (however it ends) the Landlord pays the Tenant any service charge excess shown

7. Every service charge statement is conclusive as to the information shown on it

8. Whenever the Landlord is requested under the Landlord and Tenant Act 1985 to supply information about the expenditure on services, or the service charge, compliance with that request fulfils the Landlord's duty under this lease to supply any information or accounts relating to the same period

The FIFTH SCHEDULE   Regulations
Regulations Governing Use and Occupation
1. Nothing is to be done in the flat to cause   Use of flat
inconvenience to other occupiers of the House or to prejudice the character and value of the House as a block of high class residential flats and in particular (but without prejudice to the generality of the foregoing):
(a) No television or radio set, record, disc or tape   Noise
player or other device for the reproduction of recorded sound is to be used in the Flat so as to be audible outside it

Meetings   (b) No political, religious, fund raising or charitable
              gathering is to be held to which the public are invited
              or which is attended by more than five persons

Posters   (c) No poster, advertisement, announcement or
              publicity material is to be displayed so as to be visible
              from outside the Flat, except for no more than two
              periods not exceeding fourteen days in any period
              of twelve months

Washing   (d) No clothes, linen or furnishings are to be hung
              outside the Flat

Curtains   (e) No window (other than a bathroom window) is
              to be left without curtains hanging at it

Floors   (f) No floor (other than the floors of a bathroom and
              a kitchen) is to be left uncovered or covered other
              than with good quality carpet, laid over rubber, felt
              or foam underlay

Pets   (g) No animal for which a licence would be required
              under the Dangerous Wild Animals Act 1976, nor
              any animal or bird about which any other occupier
              of the House justifiably complains that it interferes
              with comfortable enjoyment of a flat and the facilities
              used with it, is to be kept in the flat

Common parts 2. In using the parts of the House used in common
              with others, neither the Tenant nor any member of
              his household is to:

Noise   (a) Make any unnecessary noise

Litter   (b) Leave any litter other than in a receptacle provided
              for the purpose

Obstruction   (c) Leave any furniture, package, bicycles or toys
              where they obstruct the free use of those parts of
              the House by others nor permit anyone else to do
              so

Lift   (d) Use the lift in any manner that contravenes the
              regulations for its use posted in or near it, or notified
              to the Tenant

Use of garage 3. (a) Nothing is to be stored in the Garage other
              than a car parked there and accessories and tools

Petrol   (b) No petrol or other inflammable or explosive
              substance is to be stored in the Garage, other than
              in the petrol tank of a car parked there

Posters   (c) No poster, advertisement, announcement or
              publicity material is to be displayed on the outside
              of the Garage

4. In using the exterior of the Estate, neither the   Exterior
Tenant nor any member of his household is to:
(a) Contravene any reasonable arrangements that   Traffic
the Landlord makes for the regulation and circulation
of vehicular traffic
(b) Make, cause or permit any vehicle to make   Noise
unnecessary noise
(c) Leave any litter, unless in a receptacle provided   Litter
for the purpose
(d) Pick, cut or maim any flowers shrubs or trees   Flowers

The SIXTH SCHEDULE   Service charge
Landlord's Obligations Subject to Reimbursement   items
1. To repair the Estate (except to the extent that   Repair
the Tenant covenants in this lease to make good
any want of repair)

2. To arrange for specialists regularly to inspect and   Boilers
service the boilers, lift and other specialised plant   and lift
and equipment in the House and to repair, modernise
and replace it whenever necessary

3. To repair or (as appropriate) to contribute to the   Party walls
cost of repair of party walls and other facilities used
in common by the occupiers of the Estate and the
owners or occupiers of neighbouring property

4. (a) In every fourth year of the term to paint with   Decorate
two coats at least of good quality paint all parts of   exterior
the exterior of the House and the garage block
previously painted
(b) In every seventh year of the term to paint with   Common
two coats at least of good quality paint and to paper   parts
or cover with good quality wallpaper or wallcovering
and to polish and otherwise treat the hallways,
staircase, lift and all other parts of the interior of
the House used in common by the tenants of more
than one flat previously painted, papered, covered,
polished and otherwise treated

5. To comply with all orders, notices, regulations   Statutory
or requirements of any competent authority under   requirements
any statute which require any alteration, addition,
modification or other work on or to the Estate unless
the property affected is comprised wholly within the

demised premises or the premises demised by a lease in the same form as this lease

Consequential damage
6. Promptly to make good all damage done to the demised premises or to the premises forming part of the Estate demised by a lease in the same form as this lease in the course of fulfilling any of the Landlord's obligations

Hot water and heating
7. To provide to the flat from the communal boilers in the House
(i) an adequate supply of hot water at all times for domestic purposes
(ii) adequate central heating and the hallways and staircase of the House between 7 am and 11 pm between 1 October and 30 April or longer if the Landlord so decides
PROVIDED THAT the Landlord is not liable for the consequences of any failure due to circumstances beyond his control

Clean and light
8. To keep all parts of the Estate used in common by the tenants of more than one flat adequately cleaned and lighted

Gardens
9. To keep the gardens of the Estate neat tidy and adequately stocked with suitable flowers, shrubs and trees

Traffic management
10. To erect or paint on the surface of the driveways and paths such signs as the Landlord from time to time considers expedient for the management direction and safety of vehicles and pedestrians using the Estate and for the regulation of parking

Refuse
11. To provide adequate containers for household refuse in the area coloured blue on the said plan numbered 2 and to provide a reasonable number of litter bins in the hallways of the House and in the gardens of the Estate and to ensure that they are regularly emptied

Insurance
12. (a) To keep the House and the garage block insured at all times to the full cost of reinstatement under a policy which complies with the terms of this paragraph

(b) To produce to the Tenant

(i) on demand (but not more often than once in every year unless either the House or the garage block is destroyed or damaged in circumstances that might give rise to an insurance claim) the insurance policy and the receipt for the last premium paid thereon or (at the option of the Landlord) evidence from the insurers of the full terms of the policy and that the same is still in force

(ii) any endorsement varying the terms of the insurance policy, or a copy or sufficient evidence of the contents of it, as soon as received

(c) An insurance policy complies with the terms of this paragraph if:

(i) it is effected in the name of the Landlord and the interests of the Tenant, and of such other persons interested in any part of the Estate as either the Landlord or the Tenant from time to time requires, are noted on it[1]

(ii) it provides cover against loss or damage by any of the following risks ('insured risks') to the extent that such cover is for the time being available for buildings of the type insured:

fire, lightning, explosion, earthquake, landslip, subsidence, riot, civil commotion, aircraft, aerial devices, storm, flood, impact by vehicles and damage by malicious persons and vandals

Together with such other risks against which the Landlord from time to time reasonably deems it prudent to insure

(iii) it insures an appropriate percentage of the rebuilding cost for professional fees incurred in rebuilding or reinstating any building destroyed or damaged by any insured risk[2]

(iv) it is effected in some insurance office of repute or at Lloyd's

---

1 With 48 separate flats on the same policy, insurance in joint names seems impracticable.
2 There is no reference to loss of rent insurance because, as only a ground rent is reserved, it is not suspended even in the case of total destruction

13. To insure against the Landlord's liability for injury or damage to any person (whether or not a tenant of part of the Estate) entering upon the Estate, on such terms as the Landlord thinks fit   Public liability

Outgoings on   14. To pay to the appropriate authorities respectively
common parts   responsible for collecting the same, all taxes and
                outgoings in respect of any part of the Estate which
                is used in common by the tenants of more than one
                flat, including any imposed or becoming payable after
                the date of this lease, even if of a novel nature

Accounts   15. To keep accounts and records of all sums spent
                in complying with the obligations imposed by this
                Schedule

Employ agents   16. In the management of the Estate and the
and others   performance of the Landlord's obligations to employ
                or retain the services of any employee, agent,
                consultant, contractor, engineer and professional
                adviser that the Landlord reasonably requires

Precedent A:4 Memorandum and Articles of Association of Tenants' Company

A flat development scheme often involves the use of a company of which the members are the flat owners. It is usually the immediate landlord of the flat owners, although it may itself be the tenant of the developer under a head lease. Alternatively, its purpose may be to take a lease of the common parts of the block.

This form of memorandum and articles is for a company of this type, limited by shares. The intention is that each flat owner should be an equal shareholder. Either, the number of shares equals the number of flats, and each owns one or, if the developer wishes to retain control of the company until he has parted with all the flats, there are four times as many shares as flats. They are divided into two classes: one 'A' share is distributed with each flat; the 'B' shares are retained by the developer until all the flats are sold, and then three of them are distributed to each flat owner. This is particularly useful in a break up operation.

In a very small development, every shareholder can automatically be made a director of the company. In other cases, the company needs a board of directors of manageable size to take everyday decisions in the usual way.

This form seeks to guarantee that only flat owners will be shareholders, and that all of them will be, in a number of ways. The memorandum restricts eligibility for membership to flat owners (cl 6). On the assignment of a lease of a flat, the assignor who does not transfer his share loses his vote (art 8) although not his liability to contribute to any shortfall in the company's income (art 13). The assignor is guaranteed registration of the transfer of the share into his name (art 4).

The Companies Act 1985

Company Limited by Shares

Memorandum of Association

of   Limited

1. The name of the company is . . . Limited.
2. The registered office of the company will be situate in England/Wales.
3. The objects for which the company is established are:
(a) To acquire and hold a [freehold]¹ [leasehold]¹ interest in [parts intended to be used in common by or to be held for the joint benefit

of the tenants and occupiers of]² the property known as . . . in the
County of . . . ('the property') and to administer, manage, repair,
decorate, maintain and insure the property and to provide and
arrange for the provision of services to the residents in the property
and for those purposes to employ all workmen, contractors, agents
and professional advisers as may be necessary or desirable, and
to enter into all contracts and execute all deeds as shall be requisite;

---

1 Amend so as to state whether the company's interest will be freehold or leasehold.
2 Unless the company's interest is to be confined to the common parts of the block,
   delete these words.

(b) To sell, let, licence, purchase, take on lease or licence, hire,
exchange or otherwise dispose of or acquire any real or personal
property of any kind which is approriate or convenient for the proper
discharge or conduct of the business of the company;
(c) To borrow or raise money in such manner and in such sums
and on such terms as the company shall deem fit and to give any
form of security therefor and to guarantee and stand surety for
any other company or person to whom money may be lent;
(d) To lend money to any other company or person upon any terms
and to invest the assets of the company in any form of investment,
to place money at interest on any terms, or to use such assets
in the purchase of any property whether or not income bearing;
(e) To effect insurance against any risk to which the company, any
property belonging to the company or any person employed by the
company may be subject and to effect policies of life assurance
in respect of any person in whose life the company has an insurable
interest;
(f) To pay gratuities, pensions, and retirement benefits to persons
formerly employed by the company and their wives, husbands and
dependants, and to pay contributions to any fund established, or
premiums on any insurance policy effected, to provide sickness benefits
for employees and such gratuities pension and retirement benefits.

4. The liability of members is limited.

5. The capital of the company is £[48] divided into [48 shares of
£1 each.]¹ [48 'A' ordinary shares of 25 pence each and 144 'B'
ordinary shares of 25 pence each. The voting rights of the holders
of all ordinary shares shall be the same and all the ordinary shares
shall rank *pari passu* on a winding up.]¹

---

1 Unless the developer is to retain control of the company until he parts with the last
   of the flats, delete the second alternative. If he does wish to keep the control, delete
   the first one.

6. No person (other than a subscriber to this memorandum)[1] shall be a member of the company unless he is a tenant of one of the flats in the property [under a lease to which the interest in reversion is vested in the company].[2] The terms of this clause shall not be altered.[3]

---

1 It is assumed that the subscribers to the memorandum will be nominees of the developer.
2 Omit these words if the company is only to be tenant of the common parts. It is useful to define the interests of the tenants more particularly, to exclude subtenants under short subleases, but this cannot conveniently be done if the company is not the immediate landlord.
3 This precludes the alteration of this clause by a resolution of the members (Companies Act 1985, s 17(2)).

7. The company shall not have power to declare or pay any dividend or bonus or make any distribution of any assets to the members except on a winding up Provided that nothing in this clause shall prevent the payment of proper remuneration or fees to any person employed by or rendering services to the company nor the payment of interest at a rate not exceeding ten per cent a year on money lent by a member to the company.

We, the several persons whose names and addresses are subscribed, are desirous of being formed into a company in pursuance of this memorandum of association, and we respectively agree to take the number of shares in the capital of the company set opposite our respective names:

Names, addresses and descrip-   Number of shares taken by
tions of subscribers   each subscriber

Dated:

The Companies Act 1985

Company limited by shares

Articles of Association

of   Limited

Preliminary

1. In these articles:
'the promoter' means . . .[1]
'the property' means . . . in the County of . . .
'lease' means a lease of a flat (with or without a garage) in the property [to which the interest immediately in reversion is vested in the company][2]
'Table A' means Table A in the schedule to the Companies (Tables A to F) Regulations 1985.

1   The developer.
2   This definition conveniently excludes subleases, but is inappropriate where the company
    merely has a lease of common parts. In that case, the words should be deleted.

2. Save as varied by or inconsistent with these articles, the regulations in Table A apply to the company other than the following: 8–22, 24–26, 28, 30–35, 57, 59, 64–69, 72, 76, 82–84, 87, 94 and 102–110.

Transfer of shares

3. The instrument of transfer of any share shall be executed by or on behalf of the transferor, but need not be executed by the transferee. The transferor shall be deemed to remain a holder of the share until the name of the transferee is entered on the register of members in respect thereof.

4. The directors shall register the transfer of a share to a person who is qualified to be a shareholder.[1] The company shall be entitled to retain any instrument of transfer which is registered.

1   Ie is a tenant of a flat (see clause 6 of the memorandum of association).

'B' Ordinary shares

5.[1] All 'B' ordinary shares shall be alloted to the promoter.[2] Forthwith upon the promoter ceasing to be the registered holder of any 'A' ordinary share,[3] three 'B' ordinary shares shall be transferred to the then registered holder of each 'A' ordinary share.[4] In the event of the promoter not executing an instrument to put into effect that transfer in respect of all or any of the 'B' ordinary shares, the directors may appoint some person as attorney of the promoter for that purpose.

1   This article is not required if there is only one class of share (see clause 5 of the
    memorandum of association).
2   Ie the developer.
3   One 'A' ordinary share goes with each flat, so this would be the moment when the
    developer ceases to own any of the flats.
4   The right to the distribution of 'B' ordinary shares passes to the owners for the time
    being of the 'A' ordinary shares, and hence to the current owners of the flats. If
    the lease of a flat changes hands, the right does not have to be assigned.

Forfeiture of shares

6. If the lease ('former lease') held by a member is forfeited, surrendered or otherwise comes to an end, the directors may at any time thereafter by resolution forfeit all the shares held by that member. Forfeited shares shall be held by at least two directors as trustees. When a new lease is granted demising the same part of the property as the former lease, the shares forfeited from the tenant under the former lease shall be transferred to the tenant under the new lease and the forfeiture cancelled. Until such transfer, the shares shall be held for the benefit of all other members.[1]

---

1 To maintain the scheme of the development, that all the tenants of the flats shall be members of the company, provision has to be made for the possibility that a lease will be forefeited. This article provides for the shares allocated to any flat of which the lease is forfeited to be recovered by the company and effectively held in suspense until the flat is let again.

Votes of members

7. Votes may be given either personally or by proxy both on a show of hands and on a poll.
8. No member shall be entitled to cast a vote, either on a show of hands or on a poll, when not qualified to be a member of the company,[1] nor when any sum demanded from him under article 13 has not been paid to the company, nor as holder of any share while it is forfeited.[2]

---

1 Ie, is not a tenant of a flat (see clause 6 of the memorandum of association).
2 This prevents a director holding a forfeited share as trustee from having a disproportionate share of the votes.

Directors

9. There shall be at least five but not more than nine directors. The first directors shall be . . .
10. Until the promoter ceases to be a member of the company[1] he shall have the power to nominate, remove and replace two directors, to whom the regulations in Table A concerning the retirement of directors by rotation shall not apply.

---

1 Ie, on the operation of article 6, or the sale of his last flat when there is only one class of share.

11. No director shall be entitled to any remuneration from the company. Directors may be reimbursed the amount of necessary expenses incurred in the exercise of their office if authorised by the company in general meeting.
12. A director shall hold at least one share in the company.[1] The

office of director shall be vacated upon the director ceasing to be a member of the company.

___

1   The developer's nominees can each hold one of the developer's shares.

Service charge deficit

13. If the company is not fully reimbursed, by payments received from tenants under the leases, for the cost of performing its obligations in relation to the property, it may require such payments to be made to it by holders of ['A']¹ ordinary shares as are necessary to make good any deficit. Equal sums shall be demanded from the holder of each ['A']¹ ordinary share, but supplementary demands may be made if any shareholder fails to make the payment demanded. On the subsequent recovery by the company of any sum in excess of the costs incurred by it, the surplus shall be applied first in paying or crediting *pro rata* any shareholder who under this provision has paid more than any other shareholder, until such inequality is eliminated.

___

1   Where there are two classes in the company, liability falls on the holders of 'A' shares, as owners of the flats. If there is only one class of share, delete 'A'.

Notices

14. A notice may be given to a member of the company by leaving it addressed to him at the flat demised by the lease held by him at the date of his registration as shareholder.

Precedent A:5 Contract for Sale of First Maisonette

When a pair of maisonettes is sold on the basis that each is to be held on long lease, with the reversioner to each lease being the tenant under the other, both leases should be granted at the same time. The seller cannot conveniently grant the leases in advance of the first sale, because a person cannot grant a lease to himself (*Rye v Rye* [1962] AC 496). Therefore, on completion of the first sale, not only should the lease of one maisonette be granted to the buyer, but the freehold of the other maisonette should be conveyed to him so that he can forthwith grant the long lease of it back to the seller.

This is a form of contract for that transaction. The draft of each of the two leases to be granted is annexed to the contract. They will be in a standard form, eg Precedent A:7. The seller will have to consider how far the buyer should be called upon to bear the additional costs that the unusual complications will generate.

The form assumes that it is the upper maisonette that is being sold. If the lower maisonette is sold first, the references to the two maisonettes and to the forms of lease demising them must be reversed.

THIS AGREEMENT is made on . . .   between   Date
'The Seller': . . .   Parties
'The Buyer': . . .

1. IN this agreement: Definition
(a) 'The property' means the property described in   of property
the Schedule
(b) 'The upper maisonette' means the premises described as to be demised in the annexed form of lease marked 'A' ('the A lease')
(c) 'The lower maisonette' means the premises described as to be demised in the annexed form of lease marked 'B' ('the B lease')

2. ON completion: Sale
(a) The Seller is to sell to the Buyer who is to buy the lower maisonette for an estate in fee simple
(b) The Seller is to grant to the Buyer who is to accept a lease of the upper maisonette in the form of the A lease and

(c) The Buyer is to grant to the Seller who is to accept a lease of the lower maisonette in the form of the B lease

Price

And the Buyer is to pay the Seller the price of £. . .

Title

3. (a) THE Seller is to deduce to the Buyer the title to the freehold estate in the property[1]
(b) The title [is to commence with   ][2] [is registered at H M Land Registry with absolute title under Title Number . . .][2]

---

1 Title is granted to the whole property, not merely to the maisonette being sold, so that the buyer will be in a position to make title to the freehold reversion to the other maisonette when he comes to sell.
2 When the seller's title is unregistered adopt the first alternative and delete the second. When it is registered, adopt the second alternative and delete the first.

Seller's capacity

4. THE Seller sells the lower maisonette as beneficial owner

Insurance

5. FROM this date[1]
(a) The Buyer is to effect and maintain a policy of insurance complying with the terms in the A lease at his own expense
(b) The Seller is to effect and maintain a policy of insurance complying with the terms in the B lease at his own expense
(c) The terms contained in the A lease and the B lease relating to information about the policies, proof of payment of premium, and the employment and disposal of insurance proceeds are to apply immediately as if the lease had already been granted

---

1 As both parties have an interest in the fabric of the building, it is in the mutual interest to make insurance of both maisonettes compulsory.

Vacant possession

6. VACANT possession of the upper maisonette shall be given to the Buyer on completion

Counterpart leases

7. EACH party is to execute and deliver to the other on completion a counterpart of the lease then granted to him

8.[1] BEFORE or immediately after completion, the Seller is to deposit the land certificate relating to his freehold title to the property with H M Land Registry and notify the Buyer of the deposit number allotted to it[2]

Seller's land certificate

---

1   This clause is only required where the seller's title is registered.
2   An express provision to this effect settles any doubt whether the seller must deposit his land certificate: *Strand Securities Ltd v Caswell* [1965] Ch 958.

9. THE completion date is . . .

Completion

10. THE terms of this agreement shall include the Standard Conditions of Sale (2nd ed), so far as they are not inconsistent with the foregoing terms of this agreement which, for the purposes of those Conditions, are special conditions

General conditions

The Schedule above referred to

ALL THAT property[1] known as . . . in the County of . . .

Property

---

1   This is a description of the entire property, comprising both maisonettes.

Precedent A:6   Contract for Sale of Second Maisonette

Once one of a pair of maisonettes has been sold on long lease, and the leases of both have been granted, as contemplated in Precedent A:5, the sale of the second maisonette is merely the sale of the lease of it together with the reversion to the lease of the other maisonette.

This form provides a straightforward contract for this purpose. It can equally be used on subsequent sales of either maisonette.

The form assumes that it is the lower maisonette that is being sold.

THIS AGREEMENT is made on . . . between	Date
'The Seller': . . .	Parties
'The Buyer': . . .	

1. THE Seller is to sell and the Buyer is to buy   Sale
(a) the freehold property known as . . . in the County of . . . [registered at H M Land Registry under Title Number . . .]¹ ('the upper maisonette')
and
(b) the leasehold property known as . . .
aforesaid [registered at H M Land Registry under Title Number . . .]¹ ('the lower maisonette') and demised by and together with the appurtenant rights but subject to the exceptions and reservations set out in a lease² dated . . . and made between . . . and . . .
And the Buyer is to pay the Seller the price of £. . .   Price

---

1   Use only if the title is registered.
2   The lease of the lower maisonette granted under the original sale arrangements.

2. THE upper maisonette is sold subject to the terms   Upper
of a lease¹ dated . . . and made between . . . and . . .   maisonette

---

1   The lease of the upper maisonette granted under the original sale arrangements.

3. (a) THE title to the upper maisonette [is to   Title
commence with . . .]¹ [is registered at H M Land Registry with absolute title under Title Number . . .]¹

(b) The title to the lower maisonette [is to commence with the said lease][1] [is registered at H M Land Registry with absolute title under Title Number . . .][1] No title is to be deduced to the freehold reversion[2]

---

1 Use the first alternative if title is not registered and delete the second. If title is registered, use the second alternative and delete the first.
2 Unless the title to the lease is registered with absolute title, the buyer may reasonably require the reversionary title of the original landlord. It may well be convenient to deduce this before contracts are exchanged.

Seller's capacity

4. THE Seller sells as beneficial owner

Vacant possession

5. VACANT possession of the lower maisonette is to be given on completion

Completion

6. THE completion date is . . .

General conditions

7. THE terms of this agreement shall include the Standard Conditions of Sale (2nd ed), so far as they are not inconsistent with the terms of this agreement which, for the purposes of those Conditions, are special conditions

Precedent A:7 Long Lease of Maisonette

This is a long lease of a maisonette. It is for use when each of two maisonettes is demised simultaneously on the same terms, so that the landlord of the lower maisonette is the tenant of the upper one, and *vice versa*. There is to be complete reciprocity.

The form assumes that the maisonettes are purpose built, each with a front door at ground level. It can readily be adapted for the leases of two halves of a converted house where the common parts are so minimal that their maintenance can be made the responsibility of one party. No plan is referred to, because none may be available and a verbal description is often sufficiently clear. However, an accurate plan is always desirable. There is no reference to any garage or vehicular access. It is assumed that the front garden will be demised with one of the maisonettes and the rear garden with the other.

This is generally not a restrictive form of lease, because of the common interest of the parties. Decorating liabilities are limited to the exterior, because it is only these that are likely to affect the fabric and the value of the other maisonette. There is no restriction on assigning or subletting the maisonette as a whole. No repairing costs are shared, even if they affect the structure. The scheme is to divide the building into halves, making the tenant of each fully responsible for each half. This is less obviously fair than arrangements to share expenses, but it avoids all accounting difficulties.

THIS LEASE is made on . . . between	Date
'The Landlord': . . .	Parties
'The Tenant': . . .	

At the date of this lease:	Recital
The property known as . . . in the County of . . . ('the property') is divided into two self-contained dwelling-houses consisting of	Property
(i) 'the upper maisonette': First the upper storey of the property including the floor and one half in depth of the beams supporting it and the ceiling below Secondly the roof of the property and Thirdly the staircase and hall giving access to the upper storey including the front door and only the decorative internal facing of the exterior walls below first floor level, the wall dividing the staircase and hall from the lower maisonette being a party wall	Upper maisonette

Lower
maisonette

(ii) 'the lower maisonette': First the ground floor of the property including the ceiling and one half in depth of the beams supporting it and the floor above but excluding all parts of the staircase and hall giving access to the upper storey which are included in the upper maisonette, the wall dividing the staircase and hall from the lower maisonette being a party wall and Secondly the foundations of the property

Demise

1. THE Landlord [having received £. . . which the Tenant paid and][1] in exchange for the obligations undertaken by the Tenant, LETS to the Tenant First the [upper][2] [lower][2] maisonette ('the demised premises') And Secondly the [front][3] [rear][3] garden of the property ('the garden') [and the side passage giving access to the garden][4]

Appurtenant
rights

Together with
(1) [a right to place a dustbin in the paved area provided for that purpose and full right of access thereto for the purpose of depositing and disposing of household refuse][5]
(2) [a right of way for the tenant, and all persons whom he expressly or impliedly authorises, over and along the path through the front garden of the property at all times and for all purposes in connection with the use occupation and enjoyment of the demised premises][6]
(3) a right to run maintain and use all pipes cisterns wires drains and gutters for water gas electricity and soil through under and over the [upper][7] [lower][7] maisonette ('the other maisonette') and any part of the property not hereby demised to serve the demised premises as the same now exist or may at any time within eighty years be laid or installed
(4) a right of support as now enjoyed for all and every part of the demised premises from the other maisonette and any part of the property not demised

Term

For the term of ninety nine years from the . . .

Exceptions
and
reservations

Except and reserving to the Landlord for the benefit of the other maisonette
(i) [a right to place a dustbin in the paved area provided for that purpose and full right of access to it for the purpose of depositing and disposing of household refuse][5]

(ii) [a right of way for the tenant of it, and all persons whom he expressly or impliedly authorises, over and along the path through the garden at all times and for all purposes in connection with the use, occupation and enjoyment of the other maisonette][6]
(iii) a right to maintain and use all pipes, cisterns, wires, drains and gutters for water, gas, electricity and soil through, under and over the demised premises and the garden, to serve the other maisonette, as the same now exist or may at any time within eighty years hereafter be laid or installed
(iv) a right of support as now enjoyed by all and every part of the other maisonette from the demised premises and the garden

---

1   Insert only in the lease from the Seller to the Buyer, ie the A lease in the contract precedent A:5.
2   Use the description of the maisonette being demised.
3   Use the description of the garden being demised with the maisonette.
4   It will normally be appropriate to include this in the lease demising the rear garden.
5   In the lease which demises the dustbin area, include the reservation and delete the appurtenant right. In the one which does not include it, include the appurtenant right and exclude the reservation.
6   In the lease which demises the front garden, include the reservation and delete the appurtenant right. In the one that demises the rear garden, include the appurtenant right and exclude the reservation.
7   Use the description of the maisonette which is not being demised.

2. THE Tenant agrees with the Landlord: Tenant's covenants

(1) TO pay all taxes and outgoings in respect of the   Pay rates, demised premises including any imposed or   taxes and becoming payable after the date of this lease (even   outgoings if of a novel nature) to the appropriate authorities
(2) TO keep the whole of the demised premises in   Repair good repair[1] and to return possession of them in good repair to the Landlord at the end of the term (however it ends)

---

1   Damage by insured risks is not excluded because the tenant insures.

(3) (a) TO allow the Landlord to enter the demised   Repair on premises and the garden at any reasonable time on   notice at least seven days' notice (or without notice in an emergency) to inspect the state of repair and on the Landlord giving notice of any want of repair within three months thereafter (or immediately in an

emergency) to start and diligently to proceed to make it good

(b) On any failure to comply with a notice to allow the Landlord to enter the demised premises and the garden, with workmen and others and any necessary scaffolding, machinery and appliances, to do the works to comply with the notice and to pay the cost to the Landlord

Decorate exterior (4) IN every fifth year of the term and in the last year (however it ends) to paint with three coats of good quality paint, creosote or otherwise effectively to make all the wood and metal work on the exterior of the demised premises[1] proof against the weather

---

1 There is no provision to ensure that the whole building is decorated in a single colour, for the reasons discussed above.

Alterations (5) NOT to alter or add to the demised premises nor to build or erect anything in the garden unless (in either case) the landlord consents in writing in advance,[1] nor to permit anyone else to do so

---

1 For improvements, the consent cannot unreasonably be withheld (Landlord and Tenant Act 1927, s 19(2)).

Entry for repair and other work (6) TO permit the Landlord and any occupier of the other maisonette to enter on the demised premises and the garden at any reasonable time on at least seven days' notice (or without notice in an emergency) to inspect, repair, maintain, decorate and clean all or part of the other maisonette unless it can reasonably and conveniently be done without entering upon the demised premises and garden

Maintain garden (7) AT all times to maintain the garden in a neat and tidy condition

Insurance (8) (a) To keep the demised premises insured to the full cost of reinstatement under a policy which complies with the terms of this subclause

(b) To produce to the Landlord on demand (but not more often than once in every year, unless any part or all of the demised premises is destroyed or damaged in circumstances that might give rise to an insurance claim) the insurance policy and the receipt for the last premium paid

(c) An insurance policy complies with the terms of this subclause if:

(i) it is effected in the joint names of the Landlord and the Tenant and in the names of such other persons interested in the demised premises as either the Landlord or the Tenant from time to time reasonably requires

(ii) it provides cover against loss or damage by any of the following risks to the extent that such cover is for the time being available for residential maisonettes:

fire, lightning, explosion, earthquake, landslip, subsidence, riot, civil commotion, aircraft, aerial devices, storm, flood, impact by vehicles and damage by malicious persons and vandals

(iii) it insures an appropriate percentage of the rebuilding costs for professional fees incurred in rebuilding or reinstatement

(iv) it is effected in some insurance office of repute or at Lloyd's

(9) (a) SUBJECT to subclause (b) promptly to apply the proceeds of every insurance policy[1] covering the demised premises in rebuilding or reinstatement
(b) If within one year of the demised premises suffering any insured loss or damage it is not possible to enter into a contract for rebuilding or reinstatement, the insurance moneys and all interest earned thereon are to be paid to the Tenant[2]

Proceeds of insurance

---

1 This applies to a policy even if it did not comply with subclause (8).
2 The landlord's interest is only nominal, so all the proceeds go to the tenant if rebuilding is impossible.

---

(10) NOT to use all or any part of the demised premises otherwise than as a private dwellinghouse in the occupation of a single household, nor to use all or any part of the garden otherwise than as a private garden for the pleasure and recreation of the occupiers of the demised premises nor (in either case) to permit anyone else to do so

Use

(11) NOT to use all or any part of the demised premises or the garden for any dangerous, offensive, noxious, noisome, illegal or immoral activity, or in any manner that may be or become a nuisance or

Objectionable uses

annoyance to the Landlord or to the owner or occupier of the other maisonette or any other neighbouring premises, nor to permit anyone else to do so

Not to prejudice insurance

(12) NOT to do anything in the demised premises or in the garden which will or may render void or voidable any policy of insurance covering the demised premises or the other maisonette or increase the premiums payable thereon, nor to permit anyone else to do so

Not to deal with part

(13) NOT to assign or sublet, for a period exceeding three years, part only of the premises demised by this lease[1]

---

1 Further subdivision of the property is to be discouraged, because of the complication it might cause in the maintenance arrangements.

Notify dealing

(14) WITHIN one month after every change of ownership of this lease, and of every subletting, to give notice with full particulars to the Landlord or to his solicitors and to pay a registration fee of Twenty-five pounds on each such occasion

Landlord's covenants

3. THE Landlord agrees with the Tenant:

Quiet enjoyment

(1) SO long as the Tenant does not contravene any of the terms of this lease, he may possess and use the demised premises without lawful interference by the Landlord or anyone who derives title from, or is trustee for, him

Entry for repair and other work

(2) TO allow the Tenant and any occupier of the demised premises to enter the other maisonette and any other part of the property not hereby demised on at least seven days' notice (or without notice in an emergency) to inspect, repair, maintain, decorate and clean all or any part of the demised premises unless it could reasonably and conveniently be done without so entering

Provisos

4. PROVIDED ALWAYS AND IT IS AGREED AND DECLARED that:

Forfeiture and re-entry

(1) THE Landlord is entitled to forfeit this lease by entering any part of the demised premises or the garden whenever the Tenant has not complied with any obligation in this lease, but the forfeiture does

not cancel any outstanding obligation which the
Tenant owed the Landlord

(2) THIS lease is granted on the condition that the
reversion immediately expectant on the term created
by a lease of the same date which demised the other
maisonette to the Landlord is at all times vested in
the Tenant. On breach of this condition, the term
created by this lease ceases, but without cancelling
any outstanding obligation owed by either party

Link with reversion to other maisonette

(3) NEITHER of the original parties to this lease
has any rights, entitlements, responsibilities or
obligations under its terms after parting with all
interest in the property demised, but without
cancelling any obligation then outstanding[1]

Liability of parties

(4) IN this lease 'The Landlord' and 'The Tenant'
mean respectively the persons for the time being
entitled to the reversion immediately expectant upon
and to the term created by this lease

---

1   A release of the original parties, severing the privity of contract will probably be necessary
to persuade the first purchaser of the first maisonette to grant the lease of the second
maisonette.

---

(5) ANY sums payable by the Tenant are exclusive
of value added tax and the amount of any such tax
payable thereon (whether by the Landlord or by the
Tenant) is to be paid by the Tenant to the Landlord

VAT

(6) ANY dispute between the parties to this lease
is to be referred for decision in accordance with
the Arbitration Act 1950 to a single arbitrator
nominated, in default of agreement between the
parties, by the then President of the Royal Institution
of Chartered Surveyors at the request of either party[1]

Arbitration

---

1   The necessarily close relations between the landlord and the tenant of a maisonette
under this arrangement make it desirable that disputes should be settled as quicky
and as amicably as possible. Arbitration may assist this, but the effectiveness of this
clause may be subject to the Consumer Arbitration Agreements Act 1988.

---

(7)(a) SECTION 196 of the Law of Property Act 1925
is to apply to any notice required or authorised by
this lease

Notices

(b) The Tenant may serve notices (including notices
in proceedings) on the Landlord at the Landlord's
address given above until the Landlord gives the

Tenant notice of an alternative address in England
and Wales for that purpose

[Certificate   5. IT is hereby certified that the transaction hereby
of value   effected does not form part of a larger transaction
                 or of a series of transactions in respect of which
                 the amount or value or the aggregate amount or
                 value of the consideration exceeds £60,000.]¹

---

1 The certificate can be given if the price does not exceed £60,000 and the average
   quantifiable rent, excluding anything payable expressly for services, does not exceed
   £600 a year. Stamp duty on the premium is then eliminated.

B   Sale Freehold

Precedent B:1   Contract for Sale of Freehold Flat

On the sale of freehold flats in a small block, the enforcement of positive covenants can be arranged by the creation of an estate rentcharge vested in a trustee for all the flat owners. This arrangement is suitable where there is only a small number of flats, each flat owner is responsible for the repair and maintenance of his own part of the building and there are no common parts.

Few special provisions are necessary in a contract for such a sale, if a standard form of conveyance or transfer is used and annexed to the contract. This form assumes that a transfer in the form of Precedent B:2 is used. If the property does not have a registered title, consequential amendments will be required.

As the rentcharge is created for the benefit of the buyer, to provide a system for managing the flats, and not for the benefit of the seller, it seems appropriate that the buyer should pay the costs relating to it.

THIS AGREEMENT is made on . . . between	Date
'The Seller': . . .	Parties
'The Buyer': . . .	

1. ON completion the Seller is to sell and the Buyer is to buy the property described in the form of transfer annexed hereto ('standard transfer') and the Buyer	Sale
is to pay to the Seller the price of £. . .	Price

2. THE title is registered at H M Land Registry under title number . . . . The Buyer, having been supplied with an office copy of the entries on the register, is to buy subject to those which affect the property and is not entitled to raise any requisition or objection	Title

Transfer

3. THE transfer to the Buyer is to be in the form of the standard transfer and the property is sold together with the appurtenant rights but subject to the exceptions and reservations set out in the standard transfer

Insurance

4. THE Buyer is immediately to insure the property in accordance with the covenant in the standard transfer and the terms as to proof of payment of premium and employment and disposal of the proceeds of the policy are to apply

Vacant possession

5. VACANT possession of the property is to be given to the Buyer on completion

Duplicate transfer and costs

6. ON completion the Buyer is, at his own expense, to execute and deliver to the Seller on behalf of the trustee named in the standard transfer a duplicate transfer[1] and is to pay the Seller
(a) £. . . costs incurred in connection with the rentcharge
(b) the cost of the stamp duty on the duplicate transfer and
(c) the fee for registering the rentcharge at H M Land Registry

---

1 Necessary for the registration of the rentcharge.

Completion

7. THE completion date is . . .

General conditions

8. THE terms of this agreement shall include the Standard Conditions of Sale (2nd ed), so far as the same are not inconsistent with the foregoing terms of this agreement which, for the purposes of those Conditions, are special conditions

Precedent B:2   Transfer of Freehold Flat

When flats are sold freehold on a scheme reserving estate rentcharges in favour of a trustee, it is essential that a standard form of transfer is used. The trustee should be appointed in advance, and the trust deed can take the form of Precedent B:3.

This form of transfer assumes that the property can satisfactorily be completely divided between the flat owners, and that there will be no residuary common parts. Each flat owner is responsible for the repair of his part of the block. Any garden or other land round the block should be similarly divided.

The rentcharge that this transfer reserves falls into three parts. First there is an annual sum, initially of £10. An estate rentcharge must be limited to 'a nominal amount' (Rentcharges Act 1977, s 2(5)). This initial sum is indexed to allow an increase in later years. The 1977 Act makes no provision for this, but it is assumed that a figure which is originally nominal will remain so if it merely rises to maintain its original value. The proceeds of this part of the rentcharge can provide the trustee with basic remuneration. The other two parts of the rentcharge allow the trustee to recover the costs of enforcing covenants, so far as this is not met by the miscreant, and to supplement the basic rentcharge if necessary to provide a reasonable fee.

H M Land Registry

Transfer of Part (freehold) imposing fresh restrictive covenants and reserving a rentcharge

County and District *or* London Borough:
Title number:
Property:

Dated: . . .   Date

1. IN this transfer: Definitions
'The Seller' is: . . .
and whoever is for the time being owner of all or
any of the land comprised in the above title
'The Trustee' is: . . .
and whoever is for the time being owner of the
rentcharge reserved below and trustees of a deed
dated . . . and made between the Seller and the
Trustee
'The Buyer' is: . . .

215

and whoever is for the time being owner of all or any of the land transferred by this transfer
'The estate' is: all the land now or formerly registered under title number . . .
'The flat' is: the property transferred by this transfer

Price

Transfer

Rentcharge

2. IN consideration of . . . pounds (£. . .) which the Seller has received and of the rentcharge reserved below the Seller as beneficial owner transfers to the Buyer the land at . . . floor level only, shown edged red on the plan, the boundaries of which are defined in the First Schedule, known as Flat Number . . . [Together with the land shown edged brown on the plan][1] being part of the land comprised in the title referred to above TOGETHER WITH the appurtenant rights set out in the Second Schedule but EXCEPTING AND RESERVING to the Seller and the owners for the time being of any part of the estate the rights set out in the Third Schedule AND RESERVING to the Trustee a rentcharge for an estate in fee simple of the aggregate of the sums specified in the Fourth Schedule payable and subject to the covenants and conditions mentioned there

---

1 If any garden or outside area is included, show it by brown edging on the plan and include these words.

Buyer's covenants

3. THE Buyer covenants with the Seller and as a separate covenant with the Trustee to observe and perform the covenants contained in the Fifth Schedule, with the intent to bind all persons in whom any interest in the flat or any part thereof is vested from time to time, to benefit all and every part of the estate and to be enforceable by the Trustee and by the owner for the time being of any part of the estate

Walls, floors and ceilings

4. (a) ALL walls separating the flat from any other part of the estate are party walls maintainable as such
(b) Any beam of which part is owned by the owner of the flat and part is owned by the owner of any other part of the estate[1] shall be repaired maintained

and when necessary replaced at the joint expense
of the owners of it

---

1   See First Schedule.

5. THE Seller covenants with the Buyer to transfer   Standard
all parts of the estate upon the terms contained in   transfers
this transfer *mutatis mutandis*

6. THE parties certify that this transaction does not   Certificate
form part of a larger transaction or of a series of   of value
transactions in respect of which the amount or value
or the aggregate amount or value of the consideration (in addition to the rentcharge) exceeds
£60,000[1]

---

1   Delete certificate if inappropriate.

The First Schedule
Boundaries of Flat

The flat extends to and includes: Definition
(a) The whole of any exterior wall   of
(b) One half divided vertically of any wall dividing   boundaries
the flat from any other building forming part of the
estate
(c) One half divided horizontally of any beam
supporting a floor or a ceiling of the flat and the
ceiling or floor of some other building forming part
of the estate
(d) The boundary wall or fence of any garden ground
included in the flat except and to the extent that
all or part of it belongs to the owner of adjoining
property not forming part of the estate

The Second Schedule
Appurtenant Rights   Appurtenant
                                                       rights
1. The right of support for the flat from all other   Support
parts of the estate

2. The right of free access of light and air over and Light
across all other parts of the estate   and air

Pipes, wires, etc	3. The right to maintain and use the pipes, wires, cisterns, gutters and drains now or at any time within eighty years hereafter laid or running through, under or over the other parts of the estate for the passage of gas, water, electricity and soil to and from the flat
Access	4. The right of way on foot for the Buyer and all persons whom he expressly or impliedly authorises for access to and all purposes in connection with the use
Entry for work on other parts of estate	5. The right to enter the flat at all reasonable times on giving at least seven days' notice (except in an emergency) with or without workmen, scaffolding and appliances for the purpose of inspecting, cleaning, maintaining, repairing, and replacing other parts of the estate, the person exercising such right promptly making good all resulting damage

The Third Schedule

Exceptions and reservations	*Exceptions and reservations*
Support	1. The right of support from the flat for other parts of the estate
Light and air	2. The right of free access of light and air over and across the flat to all other parts of the estate[1]

---

1 This may not be appropriate if no open ground is transferred.

| Pipes, wires, etc | 3. The right to maintain and use the pipes, wires, cisterns, gutters and drains now or at any time within eighty years hereafter laid or running through under or over the flat for the passage of gas, water, electricity and soil to and from other parts of the estate |
| Rights of way | 4. The right of way for the Seller, and the other owners for the time being of any part of the estate and all persons whom they expressly or impliedly authorise, for access to and all purposes in connection with the use, occupation and enjoyment |

of other parts of the estate over and along such part
of the halls, passages and staircases leading to other
parts of the estate as are part of the flat [and over
the land coloured blue on the said plan][1]

---

1   If the access path to the front door of the block is part of the property transferred,
    colour it blue on the plan and include these words. Otherwise, delete these words.

---

5. The right to enter the flat at all reasonable times   Entry for
on giving at least seven days' notice (except in an   work on
emergency) with or without workmen, scaffolding   other parts
and appliances for the purpose of inspecting, clean-   of estate
ing, maintaining, repairing and replacing other parts
of the estate, the person exercising such right
promptly making good all resulting damage

The Fourth Schedule
Rentcharge   Rentcharge

1. The rentcharge shall in any year be the amount   Amount
of the aggregate of:
(a) The sum of Ten pounds PROVIDED THAT in any
year [after 2010][1] the Trustee may require that the
sum shall be the number of pounds nearest to the
sum which is ten pounds increased by the percentage by which the figure of the Index of Retail Prices
published by the Department of Employment (or any
index officially substituted) in December of the previous year exceeds the figure of that Index for
December . . .
(b) One [quarter][2] of the amount of any expenses
incurred by the Trustee, or reasonably estimated as
likely to be so incurred, in enforcing the covenants
in its favour in any transfer of any part of the estate,
credit being given for any sums previously paid in
advance or otherwise received by the Trustee[3]
(c) One [quarter][2] of the amount of any reasonable
fee of the Trustee for its services in connection with
the estate, credit being given for any sums paid under
sub-paragraph (a) of this paragraph

---

1   The figure can remain fixed for an initial period. Delete these words if it is to be
    indexed immediately.

2   This assumes that there are four flats in the block. Alter the fraction to suit the number
    of flats concerned.
3   Eg, costs recovered in an action to enforce the covenants.

When payable	2. The rentcharge is to be paid: (a) As to the sum mentioned in paragraph 1(a), on the Twenty-fourth day of June in every year (b) As to the sums mentioned in paragraph 1(b) and 1(c), within thirty days of a demand being delivered by the Trustee to the flat
Buyer's covenants	3. The Buyer covenants with the Trustee: (a) To pay the rentcharge at the times appointed above for payment (b) To pay on demand any expense incurred by the Trustee in enforcing or requiring compliance with any covenant by the Buyer in this transfer (c) Within four weeks of the date of any transfer of, or the creation of any legal estate in or the devolution of title to, any legal estate in all or any part of the flat to notify the Trustee in writing of the details thereof
Additional enforcement powers	4. In addition to the Trustee's statutory powers as owner of the rentcharge, if and whenever the Buyer fails to observe or perform any of the Buyer's covenants with the Trustee in this transfer the Trustee is entitled (without prejudice to the exercise of any other right or remedy):
Do works	(a) to enter the flat to carry out any works in respect of which the Buyer is in default PROVIDED THAT the Trustee has an absolute discretion as to how the works are done, whether or not the manner chosen is the cheapest or the most economical
Insure	(b) To effect an insurance policy covering the flat in such names and covering such risks and in such sum as the Trustee, in its absolute discretion, deems appropriate
Recover cost	(c) To recover the cost of preparing for or taking any action under this paragraph by action, by distress upon the goods of the Buyer or by taking possession of the flat and letting it until the cost has been repaid from the net income
Forfeiture	(d) To enter the flat or any part of it in the name of the whole and so as to possess and enjoy it in fee simple to the exclusion of the Buyer

The Fifth Schedule   Buyer's
Buyer's Covenants   covenants

1. To keep the whole of the flat in good repair   Repair

2. During the year immediately preceding every fifth   Decorate
anniversary of this transfer to paint with three coats exterior
of good quality paint, creosote or otherwise effectively make all the wood and metal work on the
exterior of the flat proof against the weather

3. Not, unless the then owners of all other parts   Alterations
of the estate[1] give their written consent, to alter or
add to the flat so as to affect the structure of the
building or the external appearance of the flat

---

1 It may be thought that to obtain the consent of all the other flat owners would be
cumbersome, and also involves the difficulty later of establishing that those who gave
consent were indeed then the owners of the other flat. However, some control seems
advisable. The alternative is to require the trustee's consent. The trustee would no
doubt feel obliged to consult the other flat owners, so the time and the expense involved
might be greater.

4. At all times to maintain any garden included in   Maintain
the flat in a neat and tidy condition   garden

5. (a) To keep the flat insured to the full cost of   Insurance
reinstatement under a policy which complies with
the terms of this paragraph
(b) To produce to the Trustee or to the owner of part
of the estate (but not in each case more often than
once in every year, unless part or all of the flat is
destroyed or damaged in circumstances that might
give rise to an insurance claim) the insurance policy
and the receipt for the last premium paid
(c) An insurance policy complies with the terms of
this paragraph if:
(i) it is effected in the joint names of the Buyer
and the Trustee on behalf of the owners of the
other parts of the estate and in the names of such
other persons interested in the flat as the Buyer
reasonably requires
(ii) it provides cover against claims for injury or
damage sustained by users of any accessway hall,
passage or staircase in the flat and against loss
or damage by any of the following risks to the

extent that such cover is for the time being available in respect of property of the nature of the flat:

fire, lightning, explosion, earthquake, landslip, subsidence, riot, civil commotion, aircraft, aerial devices, storm, flood, impact by vehicles and damage by malicious persons and vandals

(iii) it insures an appropriate percentage of the rebuilding costs for professional fees incurred in rebuilding or reinstating the flat

(iv) it is effected in some insurance office of repute or at Lloyd's

Insurance proceeds

6. Promptly to apply the proceeds of every insurance policy covering the flat in the rebuilding or reinstatement unless, within two years of the flat suffering any insured loss or damage, it is not possible to enter into a contract for the rebuilding or reinstatement in which event the insurance moneys and all interest earned thereon shall belong to the Buyer[1]

---

1 As the policy is to be in joint names, it has to be made clear that, if the proceeds cannot be used for rebuilding, the trustee on behalf of the other flat owners has no further claim.

Residential use

7. Not to use all or any part of the flat except as a private dwellinghouse in the occupation of a single household nor to permit anyone else to do so

Objectionable uses

8. Not to use all or any part of the flat for any dangerous, offensive, noxious, noisome, illegal or immoral activity or in any manner that may be or become a nuisance or annoyance to the owner or occupier of any part of the estate or of any other neighbouring premises, nor to permit anyone else to do so

Not to prejudice insurance

9. Not to do anything in any part of the flat that will or may render void or voidable any policy of insurance covering the flat or any other part of the estate or increase the premiums nor to permit anyone else to do so.

Precedent B:3 Deed of Trust for Rentcharges

Where a trustee is to hold the benefit of rentcharges created on the sale of freehold flats, as contemplated in Precedent B:2, the trustee should be appointed in advance of the sale of the flats. It seems likely that a corporate trustee will be considered appropriate but this is by no means essential.

The trustee will have to exercise the all important powers to enforce the covenants entered into by buyers of the flats. If it comes to enforcement action, there will necessarily be a dispute amongst the flat owners, who collectively are the trustee's beneficiaries. It is therefore reasonable that the trustee should be given some protection, both in having a discretion whether or not to take action, and against actions as a result of the decision taken.

This form also deals with the consequences of forfeiture of a flat.

THIS DEED OF TRUST is made on . . . between	Date
'The Developer': . . .	Parties
'The Trustee': . . .	

At the date of this deed:	Recitals
(1) The Developer owns the property known as . . . in the County of . . . shown edged red on the plan annexed[1] ('the estate'), of which the freehold title is registered at H M Land Registry under title number . . . and which comprises [four] residential flats	Property

---

1   An accurate definition of the extent of the estate is important to avoid later difficulties in defining who qualifies to be a beneficiary.

(2) The Developer wishes to sell the separate flats to purchasers for estates in fee simple and has been advised that the future owners of the flats will be able properly to maintain and use the estate if on each sale he reserves a rentcharge in favour of a trustee for the owners for the time being of the estate	Sales of flats

(3) The Trustee has agreed at the request of the Developer to enter into transfers on the sale of the flats in the form annexed hereto ('standard transfer')[1] in order to hold the rentcharges reserved ('original	Agreement on trust

223

rentcharges') and to enforce the covenants in the transfers

---

1   It is assumed that the transfer is in the form of Precedent B:2.

Trust
1. THE Trustee is to hold the original rentcharges in trust for the owners for the time being of the estates in fee simple in the said flats comprising the estate ('beneficiaries')

Register
2. THE Trustee is to keep a register of all notifications made to it under paragraph 3(c) of the Fourth Schedule to the standard transfer and is to register the names of the current beneficiaries and these registers are to be made available on demand for inspection by any beneficiary or by any person authorised in writing by a beneficiary

Enforcement of covenants
3. THE Trustee is to exercise its powers to enforce the observance and performance of the covenants in the transfers in such cases, in such manner and to such extent as it shall in its absolute discretion consider to be in the best interests of the beneficiaries, taking particular account of the need to maintain the safety, stability, good repair and value of the estate and the individual flats. In no case is the Trustee to be liable for any loss suffered by all or any of the beneficiaries as a result of any enforcement action taken or any decision not to take or to defer taking action

Forfeiture
4. (a) IF the Trustee exercises power to forfeit a flat the Trustee shall as soon as practicable take steps to sell it on such terms as it considers reasonable[1] and on any such sale the transfer shall be in the form of the standard transfer *mutatis mutandis*
(b) The Trustee is to deduct from the proceeds of sale:
(i) expenses of enforcing the obligations of the owner from whom the flat was forfeited ('former owner')
(ii) expenses of the sale
(iii) expenses incurred in works on or in insuring the flat before the sale
(iv) arrears of the original rentcharge and
(v) the sum that would have been payable as part of the original rentcharge between the date of

forfeiture and the date of completion of the sale had
there been no forfeiture

(c) The Trustee is to hold the net proceeds of sale
in trust for the former owner

(d) The Trustee is not to be liable for any loss suffered
by the former owner or any beneficiary as a result
of a sale

(e) After a sale the rentcharge reserved by the
transfer is to be treated for the purposes of this deed
as an original rentcharge

---

1   The trustee is bound to obtain a reasonable price, not the very best price, so the
sale cannot be impugned on the ground that the price was not the best.

5. THE Trustee is entitled to charge a reasonable
fee for all work done by it and is entitled to retain
the part of the original rentcharge defined in paragraph 1(a) of the Fourth Schedule to the standard
transfer on account

Trustee's remuneration

6. ALL the beneficiaries acting jointly[1] have the
power to remove a trustee of this deed from office
and to appoint new trustees

Removal of trustee and appointment of new trustees

---

1   It is reasonable that the power should be vested in the flat owners as the trust is
solely for their benefit. It is to be exercised by all of them, which prevents a trustee
who declined to take action against one flat owner being removed by the others and
replaced by a more compliant one.

C Shared Ownership

Precedent C:1 Clauses for Shared Ownership Lease Granted by Housing Association

Some housing associations can grant shared ownership leases. These leases can be in the ordinary form for a long lease, with additions to deal with the payment of a partial rack rent until the tenant exercises his purchase option.

This form merely consists of the additions that are needed. It offers the possibility of the tenant progressively increasing his stake in the flat. That is not essential if it will make the administration too complicated for the landlord. The landlord may require additional restrictions on dealings by the tenant until ownership ceases to be shared.

Under this form the terms of eventual purchase are not settled, in cash terms, at the date the lease is granted. Both the proportionate rack rent and the final purchase price follow current property values. The rack rent is what would be payable under an assured tenancy and is subject to review.

A stamp duty concession is available if a special statement is included in the lease. A clause for this purpose is set out in this form.

Reservation of rent

Two amendments are required to the reservation of the rent in the reddendum. The normal ground rent should be defined as 'the ground rent'. There should also be added:

AND YIELDING AND PAYING the shared ownership
rent as hereinafter defined

Shared ownership clause

(a) In this lease: Definitions
(i) 'The shared ownership rent' means the appropriate percentage of the open market rent for the demised premises from time to time, reduced by an appropriate percentage of the ground rent
(ii) 'The open market rent for the demised premises' is the rent which could be expected to be paid by a willing tenant to a willing landlord if the demised

227

premises were let on an assured tenancy, as determined by an independent fellow of the Royal Institution of Chartered Surveyors. That determination may be made at the demand and cost of either party at any time, but not less than twelve months after the date of this lease nor less than twelve months after the last such determination

(iii) 'The outstanding capital value' means the appropriate percentage of the open market value for the time being of the term hereby granted (disregarding any effect on value of this clause and any reference in this lease to the shared ownership rent), as assessed when required by an independent fellow of the Royal Institution of Chartered Surveyors appointed for the purpose by the Landlord.

(iv) 'The appropriate percentage' means . . . per cent[1] [or, after any reduction in the shared ownership rent pursuant to the terms of this clause, that percentage reduced by the proportion or the total of the proportions by which that rent has been reduced][2]

---

1   This is the initial percentage of the ownership retained by the landlord.
2   These words are required if the tenant has the option to buy ownership by instalments, otherwise delete.

Tenant's option   (b) The Tenant may at any time [and from time to time][1] opt, by at least two months' written notice to the Landlord, to cancel the shared ownership rent [or to reduce it by a proportion specified in the notice][1]

---

1   These words are required if the tenant has the option to buy ownership by instalments, otherwise delete.

Effect of assignment   (c)[1] On an assignment[2] of this lease the Tenant shall be deemed to have served a notice, opting to cancel the shared ownership rent, to expire two months after the date of the assignment or transfer

---

1   This subclause confines the advantages of shared ownership to the original tenant and his estate. It is not essential to the scheme and can be deleted if not required.
2   'Assignment' is normally interpreted to mean a voluntary assignment, not including, eg, involuntary assignments on death or bankruptcy. It does not include subletting.

Price of cancellation [or reduction][1]   (d) On the expiry of the Tenant's notice the shared ownership rent shall be cancelled [or reduced by the proportion specified in the notice][1] and the Tenant shall pay to the Landlord the amount of the outstanding capital value at that date [, or the proportion thereof by which the shared ownership rent is to be reduced,]¹ and any fee incurred by the Landlord on the assessment of the outstanding capital value

---

1   These words are required if the tenant has the option to buy ownership by instalments, otherwise delete.

(e) If all or any part of the sum due from the Tenant to the Landlord is not paid on the expiry of the notice it shall bear interest at the rate from time to time prescribed under section 32 of the Land Compensation Act 1961 (with yearly rests). The Tenant equitably charges the term granted by this lease with the payment thereof and of the interest thereon

Interest on and charge for unpaid price

(f) When the Tenant has paid the full sum due following service of [any]¹ notice served under this clause, a memorandum shall be annexed to this lease and to the counterpart thereof recording the facts

Memorandum

---

1   This word is required if the tenant has the option to buy ownership by instalments, otherwise delete.

(g) As soon as the shared ownership rent has been cancelled this clause and any reference in this lease to the shared ownership rent shall cease to have effect, but without cancelling any claim by the Landlord for any arrears of shared ownership rent or for any payment due under this clause

Result of final payment

Stamp duty statement

For the purpose of the stamp duty payable on this lease the parties declare:

(a) That they intend that it shall be charged in accordance with section 108 of the Finance Act 1981 for which purpose the minimum annual rent is £...¹ and the premium obtainable on the open market for the grant of a lease containing the same terms as this lease, but with the substitution of the minimum rent for the rent hereby reserved, is £...²

Minimum rent and deemed premium

---

1   The rent which will be payable under the lease when the tenant completes his purchase of the ownership. Duty is charged under the head 'Lease or tack' as if the lease reserved this rent from the outset.

2   The open market value from what the tenant pays initially is calculated. Duty is charged under the head 'Conveyance on sale' on this figure.

Certificate
of value

(b) That this transaction does not form part of a larger transaction or of a series of transactions in respect of which the amount or value or the aggregate amount or value of the consideration exceeds £60,000[1]

---

1   The sum is to relate to the market value inserted at the end of the previous subclause, not to the tenant's actual initial payment. Delete certificate if it is inapplicable.

D   Short Term Letting

Precedent D:1   Tenancy Agreement of Flat (Assured Tenancy)

This form of tenancy agreement is suitable for most short lettings of a flat. Options allow its use for either furnished or unfurnished tenancies, and for either fixed term or periodic tenancies. There is no provision for the grant of appurtenant rights, on the assumption that the tenant will be able to rely on s 62 of the Law of Property Act 1925.

The form provides for the indexation of rent after the end of the first years of the tenancy, linking it to the Index of Retail Prices. Adjustment is to be automatic, by multiplying a fixed sum by the previous month's Index figure. That fixed sum should be the opening monthly rent divided by the then current Index figure. If this continuous adjustment is considered too burdensome, the form could be amended to provide for, eg, annual changes. There is a general provision to cope with changes to the compilation of the Index (see *Cumshaw Ltd v Bowen* [1987] 1 EGLR 30).

A landlord who proposes to rely on one of the mandatory grounds for possession can use this form. There is a clause at the end of the form giving the notice required by some of the grounds; this will suffice if the agreement is concluded before the tenancy starts.

Assured shorthold tenancies

This form is also suitable for use in granting an assured shorthold tenancy. In this case there must be a term certain of at least six months. In addition, the landlord must serve a prescribed form of preliminary notice.

THIS TENANCY AGREEMENT is made on . . .   Date
between
'The Landlord':   Parties
'The Tenant':

1. THE Landlord lets the flat on the . . . floor of the   Flat
property known as . . . in the County of . . . to the
Tenant excepting and reserving to the Landlord the

231

rights to the free running of water, gas, electricity and soil through pipes, wires and drains now in the flat and serving other parts of the building [together with the furniture, furnishings, linen, bedding, utensils, equipment and other chattels in the flat listed on the annexed inventory ('contents')]¹

---

1   Include if the flat is let furnished, otherwise delete.

Length
of tenancy

2. THE tenancy commences on . . . and continues [until . . .]¹ [and then from month to month]² [as a monthly tenancy]³

---

1   This is used if the tenancy is for a fixed term, whether or not it is then to run until notice is given. A fixed term must be granted if certain of the mandatory grounds for possession are to be relied on. An assured shorthold tenancy must be granted for a term certain of at least six months.
2   For use if the tenancy is to be for a fixed period and then monthly, otherwise delete.
3   For use if monthly.

Rent

3. (a) DURING the first year of the tenancy the Tenant is to pay the Landlord, in advance on the First day in each month, rent at the rate of £ . . . per month
(b) During the remainder of the tenancy the Tenant is to pay the Landlord, in advance on the First day in each month, rent equal to £ . . .¹ multiplied by the last officially published figure for the Index of Retail Prices. If the basis of computation of that Index is changed the calculation of rent shall be adjusted to give a result as closely comparable as possible to the calculation based on the previous method of computation.

---

1   This should be the initial rent divided by the Index of Retail Prices figure when the tenancy is granted.

Deposit

4. ON signing this agreement, the Tenant is to deposit the sum of £ . . . with the Landlord. The Landlord is to repay the deposit without interest when the tenancy ends after deducting any sum then due in respect of rent, damage to the flat [, damage to or loss of any of the contents]¹ or in compensation for the breach of any other terms of this agreement

---

1   Include if the flat is let furnished, otherwise delete.

5. THE Tenant is to pay promptly to the appropriate   Outgoings
authorities all taxes and outgoings of an annual or
recurring nature and is to pay all charges for the
supply of water, gas, electricity and telephone
services to the flat

6. THE Tenant is to keep the interior of the flat in   Repair
good repair and well decorated throughout the
tenancy, fair wear and tear excepted[1]

---

1   It is a matter of bargain whether or not fair wear and tear is to be excepted. If it
    is, the tenant is not thereby exempted from treating the property properly and carrying
    out minor running repairs.

7. THE Tenant is to inspect the flat regularly for   Report
defects and wants of repair which are the Landlord's   defects
responsibility and is to give the Landlord written
notice promptly of any work required to be done

8. THE Tenant may not make or permit any   Alterations
alterations or additions to the flat

9.[1] THE Tenant is not to damage or remove any of   Contents
the contents and is responsible for replacing any
items not in good condition at the end of the tenancy

---

1   Use this clause if the flat is let furnished, otherwise delete.

10. THE Tenant may not use the flat except as a   Use
single private dwellinghouse in the occupation of
one household

11. THE Tenant is not to use the flat for any   Prohibited
dangerous, offensive, noxious, noisome, illegal or   uses
immoral activity, or in any manner that may be or
become a nuisance or annoyance to the Landlord
or to the owner or occupier of any neighbouring
premises, or in any manner that may make any
insurance on the premises void or voidable or
increase the premium payable, nor permit anyone
else to do so

12. THE Tenant is not to keep any animal or bird   Pets
in the flat

Transfer   13. THE Tenant may not assign sublet mortgage
                  charge part with possession of or share all or any
                  part of the flat

Notices   14. THE Tenant is immediately to forward to the
                  Landlord any official notice that he receives relating
                  to the flat, its use or value, or relating to the
                  development of neighbouring property

Costs   15.[1] THE Tenant is to pay all costs (including legal
                  and surveyors' fees) which the Landlord incurs in
                  connection with the preparation and service of a
                  notice under section 146 of the Law of Property Act
                  1925, even if forfeiture is avoided without a court
                  order

---

1 This clause is not needed in a periodic tenancy, where notice to quit can be served
   instead of forfeiting.

Right of   16. THE Landlord and anyone he authorises may,
entry   at any time during the hours of daylight, enter the
                  flat to inspect its state and condition, [inspect and
                  make inventories of the contents,][1] show it to
                  prospective purchasers and tenants, carry out any
                  repairs and decorations to the flat (whether or not
                  the Landlord has a duty under this agreement to
                  carry them out) or carry out repairs to adjoining
                  property

---

1 Use if the flat is let furnished, otherwise delete

Landlord's   17. THE Landlord is responsible for all repairs
repairs   covered by section 11 of the Landlord and Tenant
                  Act 1985[1]

---

1 This section will apply automatically, so this clause is in the nature of a memorandum.

Forfeiture   18. THE Landlord is entitled to forfeit this tenancy
                  by entering any part of the flat whenever the Tenant:
                  (a) has not complied with any obligation in this
                  agreement
                  (b) has not resided in the flat for a consecutive period
                  of more than 21 days

(c) is adjudicated bankrupt, or an interim receiver of his property is appointed.
The forfeiture of the tenancy does not cancel any outstanding obligation which the Tenant owes the Landlord

19. [THE Landlord gives the Tenant notice that possession of the flat may be recovered under Ground . . . in Schedule 2 to the Housing Act 1988][1] — **Recovery of possession**

---

1   This clause is to be included where the Landlord wishes to have the opportunity to rely upon one of the mandatory grounds for possession. Notice must be given not later than they beginning of the tenancy (Grounds 1, 3–5), so if the notice is to be given in the tenancy agreement, it is essential that completion of the agreement is not delayed until after the tenancy starts.

20. THE parties certify that there is no agreement to which this lease gives effect.[1] — **No prior agreement**

---

1   This certificate is required for stamp duty purposes (Finance Act 1994). Delete it if there was a prior agreement to grant the tenancy.

Precedent D:2   Agreement for Holiday Letting

A tenancy created for holiday purposes is not an assured tenancy (Housing Act 1988, Sched 1, para 9). A flat for holiday purposes will generally be fully furnished.

This form is primarily for use by professional agents managing holiday flats. It assumes that the tenant will pay a booking deposit, which will be held to cover liability for breakages and damage. The rent is to be paid in full in advance in addition to the deposit. The form is to be completed in duplicate by the tenant, after which one copy is endorsed with an acceptance by the landlord's agents.

To: Landlord's
                                                                     agents

I . . .   Tenant
of . . .
apply for a tenancy of Flat No . . . in the building   Flat
known as . . .
for holiday purposes for the period of [two] weeks   Period
from Saturday . . . 19 . . . to Saturday . . . 19 . . .

1. I ENCLOSE a deposit of £ . . . to reserve the flat,   Deposit
on the understanding that it will be repaid to me
within fourteen days after the final day of the
tenancy, subject only to any deductions for sums
due for losses breakages and damage

2. I WILL pay you the total rent of £ . . . (inclusive   Rent
of value added tax at [17.5] per cent: any change
in the rate before payment will cause a proportionate
change in the rent)[1] not later than [four weeks] before
the letting starts. I understand that in default you
are entitled to cancel my booking and forfeit my
tenancy and deposit without notifying me

---

1 If the landlord, not merely his agent, is registered for VAT purposes, the rent will be subject to tax at the standard rate: Value Added Tax Act 1983, Sched 6, Gp 1, item 1(a).

3. THE landlord will provide:
(a) Complete furniture, furnishings, bedding, linen,   Contents
glassware, crockery, cutlery, kitchen utensils and

cleaning equipment for the convenient use of [six] people living in the flat

Fuel

(b) Gas and/or electricity as required for heating lighting and cooking in the flat

4. I AGREE to the following terms:

Entry

(a) I shall take possession of the flat between 3.30 pm and 5.00 pm on the first day of the tenancy,

Inventory
of contents

when I shall check over the inventory of the contents with your representative and sign two copies (one for you to keep and one for me to keep)

Cleaning;
damage

(b) Throughout the tenancy I shall keep the flat and the contents clean, and I shall not cause any deliberate or avoidable damage to the flat or its decorations

Number
in party

(c) I shall not permit more than [six] people to live in the flat during the tenancy

Leaving

(d) On the final day of the tenancy I shall vacate the flat by 10.00 am[1]

---

1   It would be more satisfactory to ensure that the inventory was rechecked on the tenant's departure, but, at least from some holiday areas, holidaymakers often like to depart very early in the morning.

Tenant's
responsibility

(e) I shall be fully responsible for the acts and omissions of members of the party I invite to occupy the flat and any other persons permitted to enter the flat during my tenancy[1]

---

1   This is intended to ensure that the tenant cannot escape responsibility for loss or damage by blaming someone else.

Loss of or
damage to
contents

(f) I shall pay the replacement value of any items on the inventory lost, damaged or destroyed during the tenancy

Regulations

(g) The following regulations for the protection of the flat and its contents, and for the benefit of those occupying the other flats in the building, will be observed by me and by every other person in the flat during the tenancy:

(i) No animal or bird is to be brought into or kept in the flat or the building

(ii) No parcels, luggage, clothing, footwear, toys, sporting or leisure equipment is to be left in the passages, hall or lift or on the stairs of the building

(iii) No clothes, towels or bed linen are to be hung out of the windows or on the balcony

(iv) No musical instrument, television, radio, recording machine or record or disc player is to be played before 10.00 am or after 10.00 pm in such a manner that it is audible outside the flat

(v) No car is to be parked in the drive or forecourt of the building, except in the marked parking bays

(vi) All rubbish is to be placed in the receptacles provided.

5. IN the event that fire or some other insured risk renders the flat unusable for all or part of the period of my tenancy:

Fire damage

(a) If the damage occurs before the tenancy begins you will forthwith return my deposit and the rent (if then paid). My tenancy will then be cancelled and I shall have no further claim

(b) If the damage occurs during my tenancy I shall vacate the flat and you will forthwith return my deposit and a proportionate part of the rent. The remainder of my tenancy will be cancelled and I shall have no further claim

(c) In no case will the landlord or his agents have any responsibility for any loss or damage to any of my belongings or those of any of my party, nor for any loss to me or any member of my party as a result of the cancellation of all or part of my tenancy under this clause[1]

---

1 This exclusion clause may not be fully effective as a result of the Unfair Contract Terms Act 1977.

6. I AGREE that any breach on my part, or on the part of any of my party, of any of the terms of the tenancy will entitle you to end it forthwith and to re-enter the flat[1]

Consequence of breach of terms

---

1 This proviso for re-entry, albeit in simplified form, may not really be practical for a tenancy as short as most holiday lettings are likely to be, but it may be useful for the landlord to hold over the tenant *in terrorem*.

Signed: . . .
Date: . . .

WE . . .

as agents for the landlord . . .

agree to grant you a tenancy on the above terms,
acknowledge receipt of the deposit stated and
confirm that the accommodation has been reserved
for you.

Signed: . . .

Date: . . .

Precedent D:3   Agreement for Sharing Flat

A licence to share a flat with other licensees is a method by which an owner may be able to avoid granting an assured tenancy. Its legal effectiveness cannot, however, be guaranteed.

The essential elements are that the grant should be a licence and not a tenancy, that the possibility of the occupier sharing with someone nominated by the landlord should be a realistic possibility, the licensee should not have exclusive possession of any part of the flat, the various agreements should not be able to be read together as a joint tenancy and the preliminary negotiations should not mislead the prospective occupier as to the nature of the arrangement. Accurate drafting cannot, by itself, overcome all these hurdles.

This form seeks to make the occupier's position quite clear, and assumes that an explanation has been offered to him in advance. There is no joint responsibility on the part of the various occupiers, and this has disadvantages for the property owner. If one of the sharing agreements comes to an end, he loses that part of his income until a new agreement is entered into. The remaining occupiers have no responsibility for the balance of what in other circumstances might have been a joint rent. Also, there may be practical difficulties in proving which of several occupiers is responsible for any damage. The effectiveness of the occupier's obligations must be judged in the light of this.

The form seeks to avoid the terminology of tenancy agreements, to reinforce the claim that document grants a licence and not a tenancy.

Date: . . .   Definitions
Parties: . . .
1. The Owner: . . .
2. The Occupier: . . .
Property: Flat No . . .
Furniture and effects: The contents of the property listed in the inventory attached to this agreement and any items substituted for those listed by or with the consent of the Owner
Period: From . . . to . . . [and thereafter until one party gives the other at least one month's written notice expiring at any time]
Monthly payment: £ . . . payable in advance on the . . . day of every month during the period. The first payment is to be made on the signing of this agreement
Deposit: £ . . .

242   PRECEDENTS

Exclusion of statutory rights	1. THIS agreement does not create a tenancy in favour of the Occupier and is not intended to confer on the occupier any of the rights of an assured tenant. The Owner explained to the Occupier before this agreement was signed the significance of the fact that the Occupier is a licensee sharing the property with others
Non-exclusive licence	2. THE Owner grants to the Occupier a licence during the period to occupy and use all parts of the property and the furniture and effects, together with the necessary means of access to the property, in common with all such other persons from time to time given the right by the Owner. The Owner reserves the right to himself his authorised agent and any workmen to enter the property at any time for the purposes of inspection repair or showing it to any other person
Monthly payments	3. THE Occupier agrees to make monthly payments to the Owner throughout the period without deduction
Occupier's obligations	4. THE Occupier agrees to observe and perform the obligations set out in the Schedule to this agreement throughout the period
Agreement not transferable	5. THE benefit of this agreement is personal to the Occupier and may not be transferred assigned or shared
Deposit	6. THE Occupier has paid the deposit to the Owner as security against the Occupier breaking any of the terms of this agreement. The Owner will return the deposit to the Occupier without interest when this agreement ends, deducting any sum necessary to compensate the Owner for breaches in the terms of this agreement
Termination	7. IN any of the following cases the Owner may end this agreement forthwith by written notice to the Occupier:[1] (a) If any monthly payment is not paid in full within seven days after it becomes due (b) If the Occupier does not comply with any of the obligations in the Schedule to this agreement

(c) If destruction or damage renders the property not
reasonably habitable as a residence[2]
(d) If (without the prior written consent of the Owner)
the Occupier ceases to occupy the property for at
least fourteen days[3]

---

1 As no tenancy is created, s 146 of the Law of Property Act 1925, relating to forfeiture,
   does not apply.
2 The Owner is well advised to insure, and to make provision for consequential loss
   of income after destruction or damage.
3 When premises are let furnished, the owner often wishes to ensure that they remain
   occupied, for their better protection. Continuous occupation can be more important
   in this case, so that it is always apparent that the flat is shared by more than one
   occupier.

8. THE Owner agrees with the Occupier: Owner's
(a) To pay the charge for water supplied to the   obligations
property
(b) While the Occupier complies with the terms of
this agreement, not to interfere with the occupation
of the property by the Occupier
(c) Not to charge (or as the case may be to return)
any monthly payment or a proportionate part for any
period during which the property is rendered
uninhabitable by fire[1]
(d) To observe repairing obligations equivalent to
those cast on a landlord by the Landlord and Tenant
Act 1985 section 11[2]

---

1 The risks causing the damage could be extended to others included in the owner's
   insurance policy.
2 The implied covenants do not themselves apply to a licence.

9. A NOTICE under this agreement may be given   Notices
by sending it by first class ordinary letter post or
by leaving it
(a) addressed to the Occupier at the Property
(b) addressed to the Owner at the address given at
the head of this agreement or such other address
in Great Britain notified to the Occupier

THE SCHEDULE
Occupier's obligations

1. To use and treat the property the fixtures and   Care of
fittings and the furniture and effects in a careful property

and responsible manner and in particular (without prejudice to that general obligation):

(a) to take steps to preserve them from damage or deterioration doing any necessary minor repairs

(b) promptly to report to the Owner the need for any repairs which are the responsibility of the Owner

(c) to keep the interior of the property, the fixtures and fittings and the furniture and effects clean and in good condition and repair (damage by accidental fire only excepted) and immediately to replace all broken glass

(d) not to alter the property in any way nor alter add to or modify the electrical gas and plumbing systems

(e) not to throw dirt, rubbish, rags or refuse or any deleterious substance into the sinks, baths, basins, lavatories, cisterns or waste or soil pipes, or out of the windows

(f) not to remove any of the furniture or effects

(g) regularly to launder or appropriately clean all bed linen used by the Occupier

Use of property

2. In occupying and using the property, to behave responsibly and considerately to others, and in particular (without prejudice to that general obligation):

(a) to use the property only as a private residence of the Occupier (in common with others when the Owner authorises)

(b) not to do anything in or in the vicinity of the property which may be or become a nuisance, damage or annoyance to other authorised occupiers of the property, or to the Owner, or to the owners and occupiers of adjoining or neighbouring properties

(c) not to use or play any musical instrument, radio, television set or apparatus for reproducing recorded sound so that it is audible outside the property

(d) to ensure that all electrical apparatus used in the property is fitted with an effective suppressor, to prevent interference with radio or television reception

(e) not to hang or shake any clothes linen or bedding out of any window

(f) to place all rubbish in the dustbin provided, which is to be left in the place designated for it

(g) not to keep any animal or bird on the property unless the Owner gives written consent in advance (consent may be withdrawn at any time)
(h) not to exhibit any advertisement, poster, name plate or announcement so that it is visible from outside the property
(i) not to hold any public meeting, public entertainment or sale by auction on the property
(j) not to use the property for any illegal or immoral purpose
(k) not to do anything which may vitiate the insurance of the property against fire or increase the rate of premium payable for such insurance

3. To use the means of access to the property with due consideration for others, and in particular (without prejudice to that general obligation): **Means of access**
(a) to keep the main entrance door, to the building of which the property forms part, closed
(b) not to leave any property goods, parcels or refuse in any entrance hall, staircase or passage in the building
(c) not to loiter, obstruct or play in any entrance hall staircase or passage in the building

4. To ensure that any visitor invited to the property, or permitted to be there by the Occupier, complies with the terms of this Schedule **Visitors**

E   Miscellaneous

Precedent E:1   Contract for Sale of Leasehold Flat by Original or Subsequent Purchaser

The sale of a leasehold flat, after it has originally been sold off by the developer, is a routine conveyancing transaction. There are, however, some special features which may need to be considered.

This form contains clauses relating to a share in a tenant's company held by the seller, and apportionments of service charges and the balance on a reserve fund.

THIS AGREEMENT is made on . . . between	Date
'The Seller': . . .	Parties
'The Buyer': . . .	
1. THE Seller is to sell the property known as Flat No . . . at . . . in the County of . . . ('the property'), described in a lease ('the lease') made on . . . 19 . . . between . . . (1) and . . . (2) to the Buyer for the residue of the term created by the lease for which the Buyer is to pay the Seller £ . . .	Sale
	Price
2. THE title to the property [is registered at H M Land Registry with absolute title under title number . . .]¹ [commences with the lease]¹ [and continues with . . .]²	Title

---

1   If the title is registered, use the first alternative and delete the second. Otherwise, use the second alternative and delete the first.
2   To be used only if the title is unregistered and a full fifteen year title can be deduced from a root of the title later than the lease.

3. THE Seller sells as beneficial owner	Seller's capacity
4. VACANT possession of the property is to be given to the Buyer on completion	Vacant possession

Company
share

5.[1] (a) ON completion the Seller shall deliver to the Buyer the share certificate and signed transfer in his favour in respect of one ordinary share of £1 in . . . Limited ('the company') [with any evidence the directors of the company may reasonably require that the Seller is entitled validly to transfer the share][2]

(b) the Seller warrants that the share will on completion be free from any incumbrance, lien or other third party claim

(c) The Buyer is to present the transfer to the directors of the company for registration promptly after completion

(d) If the Buyer requires, and at his cost, the Seller is to appoint the Buyer as his attorney[3] to exercise at any time after completion on his behalf all his powers as a member of the company. In any event the Seller is not to exercise any of those powers after completion without the Buyer's consent

---

1   This clause is only needed if the ownership of a share in a tenants' company is linked to the ownership of the lease.
2   Include these words if the seller if not the registered holder of the share.
3   The appointment as attorney must be by deed: Powers of Attorney Act 1971, s 1.

Furniture
and
furnishings

6. THE Seller is to sell the items of furniture and furnishings in the property listed in the annexed inventory to the Buyer [for £ . . .][1] [and they are included in the price of the property].[1] They are to be handed over to the Buyer on completion

---

1   If a separate price is to be charged for the chattels use the first alternative and delete the second. Otherwise, delete the first alternative and use the second.

Service
charge

7. WHAT the Buyer pays the Seller on completion is to be calculated on the basis that

(a) the Seller gives the Buyer credit for one half[1] of the balance which the Landlord[2] states is in the reserve fund, accumulated under clause . . .[3] of the lease, in respect of the property

(b) the service charge for the current year is provisionally apportioned on the assumption that [twenty per cent more than the][4] [the same][4] sum is paid in respect of the previous year[5]

(c) until the final apportionment[5] is made each party shall notify the other of any change of address

---

1 This implements the compromise about the credit to be given for the balance of the reserve fund suggested above.
2 Unless the landlord is under an obligation to state the amount of the balance of the fund, it may not be possible to implement this.
3 This reference is to the provision in the lease as to the reserve fund.
4 If an interim apportionment of the current service charge is to be made, before the accounts are available, some assumption about the level of the charge must be made. The alternatives given are suggestions.
5 The final apportionment will be made when the accounts are available. See: Standard Conditions of Sale (2nd ed), cond 6.3.5.

8. THE completion date is . . .   Completion

9. THE terms of this agreement shall include the   General
Standard Conditions of Sale (2nd ed), so far as the   conditions
same are not inconsistent with the foregoing terms
of this agreement which, for the purposes of those
Conditions, are special conditions

Precedent E:2 Rules of Tenants' Association

Tenants of flats in a block often wish to form an association to represent their interests, even where there is no tenants' company with an interest in the property. In that case, the formalities and expense of incorporation may be considered unnecessary.

This form gives the rules for an unincorporated association of tenants of a particular block of flats. Membership is open to all tenants, although some may not take it up. Provision is made for subletting, and for the position of company tenants, to allow the actual occupiers of the flats to be the active members of the association.

As no regulations have yet been made specifying the matters to be taken into account in giving a certificate to make an association a recognised tenants' association for the purposes of the statutory control of service charges (Landlord and Tenant Act 1985, s 29(5)), it is not possible to be sure that an association formed with these rules would be recognised.

Rules of . . . Court Tenants' Association

1. IN these rules: Definitions
(a) 'The Association' means the . . . Court Tenants Association
(b) 'The block' means . . . Court
(c) 'A flat' means one of the [24] flats that together comprise the block
(d) 'A tenant' means a tenant for the time being under a head lease of a flat or, when a head lease is vested in more than one tenant, all the tenants
(e) 'The Committee' means the committee established under rule 8
(f) 'The Chairman', 'the Treasurer' and 'the Secretary' means the officers for the time being of the Association elected under rule 9.

2. THE Association is established   Objects
(a) To maintain and improve the amenities and facilities provided for residents of the block
(b) To represent the views of members to the freehold owner of the block, local and other authorities, the owners and occupiers of neighbouring property and the suppliers of any services to the block or to the occupants of it
(c) To employ such staff and professional advisers

251

as the Committee may deem necessary satisfactorily to carry out the functions of the Association.

Membership

3. (a) A MEMBER of the Association may be a full member, an associate member or a representative member

(b) A tenant[1] is eligible for full membership of the Association, and becomes a full member upon applying in writing to the Secretary[2]

(c) A full member who sublets his flat may nominate his subtenant as an associate member[3] and the subtenant becomes an associate member on sending to the Secretary a written nomination and his written consent

(d) A corporation which is a full member may from time to time, by written notice to the Secretary, nominate a person resident in the block to be a representative member and may withdraw that nomination

(e) A person ceases to be a member:

(i) On delivering his written resignation to the Secretary

(ii) In the case of a full member: on ceasing to be a tenant; in the case of an associate member: on ceasing to be subtenant of a flat, or on the full member who nominated him ceasing to be a member; in the case of a representative member: on ceasing to be resident in the block, on the full member who nominated him ceasing to be a member, or on the full member who nominated him withdrawing that nomination

(iii) On failing to pay all or part of any sum due to the Association within 28 days after it becomes due, or any longer time permitted by the Committee.

1 Where there are joint tenants, 'tenant' includes them all (rule 1(d)), so there is a single full membership for each flat.
2 The Committee has no discretion to refuse an application for membership from an eligible tenant.
3 Only a full member's direct subtenant can become an associate member, not a derivative subtenant.

Register of members

4. THE Secretary is to maintain and keep up to date a register of members showing in the case of each full member the flat of which he is tenant and the

names of any associate member or representative member nominated by him.

5. (a) ALL members (other than full members who have nominated a representative member) are entitled to attend general meetings of the Association
(b) There is to be an annual general meeting of the Association in the month of [March] in every year
(c) The Committee is to call the annual general meetings and may call other general meetings of the Association
(d) Full members who together are tenants of at least [six] flats may, by notice in writing to the Secretary, require the Committee to call a general meeting within twenty-eight days to consider one or more resolutions set out in their notice. If the Committee does not call a meeting within that time limit, any member who gave notice to the Secretary may do so
(e) The Chairman shall, if present, preside at general meetings of the Association. Otherwise, the members present shall elect one of their number to preside at that meeting
(f) Full members who are tenants of [six] flats constitute a quorum at a general meeting of the Association.

Meetings

6. (a) A GENERAL meeting of the Association is to be called by at least fourteen days' notice to all those entitled to attend
(b) A notice of a meeting is to be
(i) in writing and incorporate an agenda
(ii) posted or left addressed to the member at the flat in which he resides or of which he is tenant, unless he requests the Secretary in writing to send notices to a different address
(iii) deemed, when sent by post, to be served on the day on which they would have been delivered in the normal course of post, whether or not in fact delivered
(c) A meeting is validly called notwithstanding the accidental omission to give notice of it to any member.

Notice of meetings

Votes

7. (a) AT a general meeting of the Association, each tenant who is a full member may cast one vote. Where more than one person is tenant of a flat, the vote may be cast by the member who, of those present, is first named in the register of members
(b) A full member may appoint a proxy to attend and vote at a general meeting of the Association on his behalf. The instrument of proxy must be in writing and delivered to the Secretary at least one clear day before the meeting. A proxy need not be a member of the Association
(c) A representative member may cast the vote of the full member who nominated him
(d) A full member may surrender his vote in favour of an associate member nominated by him if he so notifies the Secretary in writing.

Committee

8. (a) THE Committee is to consist of at least [six] and not more than [ten] members elected at each annual general meeting of the Association, and its members are to resign at the next following annual general meeting
(b) Associate members are eligible for election to two seats on the Committee, but otherwise members of the Committee are to be full members or representative members
(c) The members of the Committee are entitled to co-opt members to fill any casual vacancy
(d) The Committee is responsible for the discharge of all the functions of the Association, subject to the directions of any general meeting of the Association
(e) [Four] members of the Committee constitute a quorum
(f) No member of the Committee may be employed, retained or otherwise remunerated by the Association, except with the prior approval of a general meeting of the Association.

Officers

9. (a) THE Officers of the Association are: the Chairman, the Secretary and the Treasurer
(b) The Committee elects the officers from amongst their number immediately after the annual general meeting, and fills any vacancies during the year.

10. (a) THE Treasurer is to keep accounts of the **Accounts**
income and expenditure of the Association and
produce a statement thereof for each calendar year
(b) The accounts are to be audited by an auditor who
may be a member of the Association, but not a
member of the Committee, nor tenant of the same
flat as the Treasurer
(c) The audited accounts for the preceding year are
to be presented to each annual general meeting and
a copy of them is to be sent to each member
(d) Cheques drawn on any bank account of the
Association must be signed by at least two members
of the Committee.

11. (a) MEMBERS are to pay an annual subscription **Sub-**
for each calendar year to cover the routine **scriptions**
expenditure of the Association. The subscription is
payable on 1 January or, by a member who joins
during the year, on joining
(b) The rate of subscription for the time being is fixed
by the Committee. Different rates of subscription may
be fixed for different classes of members and
different circumstances.
(c) In addition to the annual subscription, the
Committee may require payment of special
subscriptions, at such time and at such rates as they
may from time to time decide, for purposes approved
by a general meeting of the Association
(d) No part of any subscription paid or payable by
a member is refunded or cancelled on his ceasing
to be a member.

Index

257

Purchased new lease—*contd*
  landlord, position of, 155
  Leasehold Reform, Housing and Urban
    Development Act 1993, 5–6
  notice and counter-notice, 157
  outline, 154
  premium, 155
  procedure, 157–8
  qualifications, 154–5
  redevelopment, 156–7
  rent, 155
  terms, 155–6

Quiet enjoyment—
  interference with, 68

Rebuilding—
  extent of right of, 54–5
  insurance and, 79–80
Recognised tenants' association—
  nature of, 27
Redevelopment—
  collective enfranchisement, 152
  purchased new lease, 156–7
Reform—
  commonhold, 6
  generally, 5
  Leasehold Reform, Housing and Urban
    Development Act 1993, 5–6
Registration—
  rentcharge, of, 104–5
Regulated tenancy—
  dispositions, 82–3
  service charge, 35
Rent—
  book, provision by landlord, 87
  precontract enquiries, 131
  purchased new lease, 155
  rent free letting, 127–8
  right to buy lease, 160
Rentcharge—
  deed of trust for, 223–5
  estate, 60–2
  expenses on creating, 103
  registration of, 104–5
Repairs—
  alternative accommodation, 52
  Buildmark scheme—
    common parts, 53–4
    conversions, 54
    cover provided, 52–3
    generally, 52
    other flats, 53
  common parts—
    generally, 47
    lift, 48
    means of access, 47–8
    roof, 48

Repairs—*contd*
  enforcement of obligations—
    manager, appointment of, 48–9
    secure tenant of local authority, 50
    traditional remedies, 49–50
  entry, right of, 51–2
  fitness for human habitation—
    landlord's consent, 44
    public health, 44–5
  implied covenant—
    right to buy lease, 43
    short lease, 41–3
  inspection and repair, right of entry for,
    51–2
  landlord—
    responsibility for flat, 40–1
    right to buy lease, implied covenant
      and, 43
    short lease, implied covenant and,
      41–3
    view of scheme, 38–9
  maisonette, 105
  other flat owners, by, 45–6
  owner's responsibility as tenant, 40
  rebuilding, 54–5
  right to buy lease, 161–2
  scheme—
    generally, 38
    landlord's view, 38–9
    tenant's view of, 39–40
  tenant—
    flat owner's responsibility as, 40
    view of scheme, 39–40
Reserve fund—
  generally, 32
  other safeguards, 33–4
  trust, held in, 32–3
Resident landlord, 124
Residential use of flat, 65–6, 70
Restrictive covenant—
  building flats, 71–2
  enforcement of, 58–60
Reversion—
  reversioner's counter-notice, 152
  tenants' company, vesting in, 98–9
Right to buy lease—
  common parts and facilities, 160–1
  dispositions, 83
  improvements, 161–2
  landlord's implied covenant, 43
  outline of right, 159
  rent, 160
  repairs, 161–2
  service charge, amount of, 30
  terms of, 160–2
  void terms, 162
Roof—
  repairs, 48